Work Experience and Psychological Development Through the Life Span

AAAS Selected Symposia Series

Published by Westview Press, Inc.
5500 Central Avenue, Boulder, Colorado

for the

American Association for the Advancement of Science
1333 H Street, N.W., Washington, D.C.

Work Experience and Psychological Development Through the Life Span

*Edited by Jeylan T. Mortimer
and Kathryn M. Borman*

AAAS Selected Symposium **107**

AAAS Selected Symposia Series

Chapter 4, "Continuity of Learning-Generalization: The Effect of Job on Men's
Intellective Process in the United States and Poland," by Joanne Miller, Kazimierz
M. Slomczynski, and Melvin L. Kohn, is reprinted with permission from the *American
Journal of Sociology,* Volume 91, Number 3, November 1985, pages 593-615.

This Westview softcover edition is printed on acid-free paper and bound in softcovers
that carry the highest rating of the National Association of State Textbook Administrators, in consultation with the Association of American Publishers and the Book
Manufacturers' Institute.

Published in 1988 in the United States of America by Westview Press, Inc.; Frederick
A. Praeger, Publisher; 5500 Central Avenue, Boulder, Colorado 80301

Library of Congress Cataloging-in-Publication Data
Work experience and psychological development through
   the life span.
   (AAAS selected symposium; 107)
   1. Work--Psychological aspects. 2. Developmental
psychology. I. Mortimer, Jeylan T., 1943-   .
II. Borman, Kathryn M. III. Series.
BF481.W67 1988   158.7   87-28190
ISBN 0-8133-7467-7

Printed and bound in the United States of America

The paper used in this publication meets the requirements
of the American National Standard for Permanence of Paper
for Printed Library Materials Z39.48-1984.

6   5   4   3   2   1

About the Series

The AAAS Selected Symposia Series was begun in 1977
to provide a means for more permanently recording and
more widely disseminating some of the valuable material
which is discussed at the AAAS Annual National Meetings.
The volumes in this Series are based on symposia held at
the Meetings which address topics of current and
continuing significance, both within and among the
sciences, and in the areas in which science and
technology have an impact on public policy. The Series
format is designed to provide for rapid dissemination of
information, so papers are reproduced directly from
camera-ready copy. The papers are organized and edited
by the symposium arrangers who then become the editors of
the various volumes. Most papers published in the Series
are original contributions which have not been previously
published, although in some cases additional papers from
other sources have been added by an editor to provide a
more comprehensive view of a particular topic. Symposia
may be reports of new research or reviews of established
work, particularly work of an interdisciplinary nature,
since the AAAS Annual Meetings typically embrace the full
range of the sciences and their societal implications.

ARTHUR HERSCHMAN
Head, Meetings
and Publications
American Association
for the Advancement
of Science

Contents

1. Introduction

Throughout the modern era, scholars have shown a continuing concern with the extent to which position in the occupational structure affects psychological development. Social scientists now view this issue as a key question in the study of social structure and personality (House 1981). There is widespread recognition that work can be a liberating force, contributing to the development of human potential and individual expression. However, there is disagreement as to whether work in modern industrial (and post-industrial) societies fulfills this promise. Many years ago, Emile Durkheim argued that the complex division of labor in modern societies encourages more autonomous, individuated personalities: "..far from being trammelled by the progress of specialization, individual personality develops with the division of labor...individual natures, while specializing, become more complex" (Durkheim 1964:403-404). Others, led by Karl Marx, declared to the contrary that the industrial revolution contributed to the fragmentation and simplification of work tasks and a vast reduction in the worker's control over the productive process and the uses of labor. To Marx, these changes were alienating and dehumanizing: the worker "does not fulfil himself in his work, but denies himself, has a feeling of misery, not of well-being...is physically exhausted and morally debased" (Marx 1964:169).

Contemporary scholars have continued this line of inquiry, affirming the negative consequences of highly routinized and fragmented jobs (Walker and Guest 1952; Blauner 1964; Seeman 1967), and the pervasive

psychological benefits to be drawn from more complex,
self-directed work activities (Kohn and Schooler 1983;
Mortimer et al. 1986). There is growing consensus upon a
"generalization model" of adult socialization at work,
that attitudes, values, and ways of thinking are learned
and generalized from basic modes of adaptation to
problems encountered in the workplace (Kohn 1977;
Mortimer and Simmons 1978). People observe their actions
at work and the consequences of those actions, and form
judgments about themselves, other people, and
orientations toward life in general in accord with these
processes of learning, generalization, and attribution
(Bem 1972; Kohn 1981:290; Rosenberg 1981).

But while it is often assumed that occupations
"mold" the personality (Park et al. 1925; Hughes 1958;
Kanter 1977), empirical relationships between dimensions
of the job and measures of psychological development at
any single point in time could as well be due to
processes of occupational selection. That is, persons may
choose their jobs, or be selected for them by employers,
according to their previously existing psychological
dispositions (Rosenberg 1957; Davis 1965; Holland 1976).
Studying the same persons through time is necessary to
demonstrate that work experiences do engender change in
psychological attributes. However, the occupational
selection and socialization hypotheses should not be
considered mutually exclusive or contradictory; persons
might choose or attempt to alter their jobs (with varying
success), while at the same time being subject to the
influence of work experiences.

In fact, a rapidly accumulating body of empirical
research indicates a continuous reciprocal relationship
between the person and the job environment, as workers
influence the character of their experiences on the job,
and occupational conditions, in turn, affect the further
course of their psychological development. In studying a
large, nationally representative sample of men in 1964,
and then re-surveying them ten years later, Melvin Kohn,
Carmi Schooler, and their colleagues (1983) demonstrated
that the psychological differences between persons with
varying conditions of work cannot be fully explained by
processes of selection to the job. Thus, the most
plausible rival explanation for the relationships of work
and personality has been effectively refuted.

Analyses of other data sets have similarly shown
that work experiences influence psychological
development, as well as being affected by prior

psychological characteristics. Thus, work autonomy was found to have positive effects on occupational values (Mortimer and Lorence 1979a), the sense of self-competence (Mortimer and Lorence 1979b), and work commitment (Lorence and Mortimer 1981) in a panel of highly educated young men ten years out of college (Mortimer et al. 1986). Similarly, autonomy at work fostered self-esteem in a national panel of recent high school graduates (Mortimer and Finch 1986a). Finally, in a representative panel of the U.S. labor force, this same dimension of work experience contributed significantly to job involvement (Lorence and Mortimer 1985) and job satisfaction (Chapter 5, this volume). This clarification of the causal linkage between work and psychological functioning enhances our understanding of the connections between social structure and personality.

The evidence is therefore quite compelling that work experiences--especially those indicative of autonomy and self-direction--have pervasive psychological consequences. Only very recently, however, have researchers begun to investigate whether occupational experiences have the same or different implications for psychological development in various phases of the work life. In addressing this intriguing question, this book joins the concerns of sociologists interested in the life course and life span developmental psychologists. For each of these areas of scholarly work, understanding the extent to which individual psychological attributes remain the same or change through the course of life, and understanding the environmental (e.g., work) conditions which influence the magnitude and direction of such change, are of central importance. Moreover, the questions addressed in each chapter have relevance for the more applied concerns of educators, counsellors, personnel workers, and administrators whose efforts are directed toward guiding the person through the career or toward designing developmentally optimal work environments.

This book examines whether work experiences and age (often considered as a proxy for stage in the work career) interact such that the effects of occupational conditions on the person change in different phases of the life cycle. That is, do the effects of work on psychological development vary as workers move through their careers? When do the processes by which work affect the personality begin? Do they taper off, continue with the same strength indefinitely, or increase with longer exposure to the job environment? Do work-related attitudes stabilize with age, or is psychological development in response to work a life-long process? Do jobs have psychological effects of the same kind throughout the worklife, or might work conditions that are deleterious in one phase have more salutary consequences in another? Very few empirical studies have been directed toward understanding whether there is differential responsiveness, depending on age, to the varying conditions and rewards of work.

Further, it is now well recognized that workers do not just passively absorb their work experiences; they actively choose and alter their jobs. Selection of work and/or molding the job in accord with prior attitudes and orientations would support a conceptualization of the person as actively determining the course of development, influencing the work role which may importantly affect further processes of personal change. In considering occupational choice or selection, it is common to focus on the youngest workers, those initially entering the labor force. For they may be most consciously trying to match their values, abilities, and needs with the rewards that are potentially available in the work sphere (Blau et al. 1956; Mortimer and Lorence 1979a). As workers "settle in" to their jobs, psychological orientations may be seemingly less consequential, unless they substantially influence the worker's level of performance and resulting promotion opportunities. As workers reach their career ceilings, occupational experiences and rewards may further stabilize, being determined more by structural factors, such as organizational policies regarding seniority, than by psychological orientations. These observations would indicate a declining influence of psychological orientations on work experiences as workers move through their work lives. However, other considerations suggest that the person may continue to actively affect the character of his or her work environment thoughout the career. For example, as the young worker moves beyond the initial entry position, increases in seniority as well as informal power could heighten the potential to change or mold one's job in line with personal wishes. And the worker's personality characteristics could lead to different reactions to both successes and setbacks on the job, which might occur at any time in the career.

However, we have just begun to address the issue of process and change in these reciprocal interrelations of work and personality. How do the processes by which occupational experiences influence the personality, and how do the processes by which the person selects and molds the job in accord with prior values, self-concepts, needs, and other dispositions, change as the individual moves through the work career?

Most prior studies in the area of work and personality have not been designed to investigate whether occupational conditions have distinct implications for personal development in different phases of life, or in various stages of the work career. While it is possible to compare the relationships between work conditions and psychological constructs in different age groups with survey data collected at a single time, a cross-sectional design is not optimal for addressing issues of psychological change. An explicit focus on process is needed. A better understanding of change over time can be derived from studying workers of different ages over a period of time. In the absence of a longitudinal study, an interview or questionnaire schedule could be designed to elicit retrospective accounts of transitions and changes at earlier points in the career. Alternatively, an investigator could examine processes of adjustment contemporaneously in relation to particular problems and transitions in distinct phases of the worklife. The chapters in this book pursue all of these strategies.

The first section of this volume assesses young people's initial encounters with the work world, considering adolescent part-time workers who hold jobs while they are still in school and young adults who have recently left high school. These studies are very pertinent to the question as to when work begins to influence psychological development. It is sometimes said that because of the marginal and transitory character of employment among students, it has relatively little psychological impact upon them. If work experience and the worker identity in this early stage of life have little "salience" (Rosenberg 1981), employment may have negligible implications for personal development. Another line of reasoning, however, supports the view that for young people, employment is a highly influential experience. There is evidence that people are most responsive to the impacts of environmental forces shortly after the acquisition of new social roles (Van Maanen and Schein 1979; Hall 1971; Nicholson 1984). Employed adolescents have taken on a new role which consumes many of their waking hours.

Moreover, it is widely assumed that adolescence is a critical period for the formation of personality (Erikson 1959), and that personal attributes developed in this phase of life are likely to persist through the life course. If this is the case, the personalities of young people, including adolescent part-time workers as well as those who have recently left high school, may be even more malleable in response to work than those of older persons (Sears 1981; Glenn 1980).

Greenberger, in her chapter on work in adolescence, points out that part-time work is an increasingly prevalent phenomenon, extending across class groups. The developmental implications of this experience, however, are not well understood. While many commentators have been quite optimistic that work experience in youth will build character, promote positive work values, and integrate the young into adult society, empirical research has indicated both negative and positive developmental consequences. From her study of part-time workers in four California high schools, it would appear that working long hours is not particularly beneficial for adolescents' psychosocial development, nor is it conducive to achievement and involvement in school. Her utilization of follow-up data collected on a subset of her sample helps to clarify the causal processes through which early part-time work while in high school influences adolescents' personal development.

Greenberger is particularly interested in the effect of work on individual autonomy--"personal attributes that should help individuals to function effectively and maintain themselves independently in society"--and social integration. She reports some evidence that self-reliance increases among girls, but not boys, in response to work. Adolescent girls are more likely than boys to view working as an expression of their independence and initiative. Her study also suggests that the ability to work with persistence and to obtain satisfaction from completing tasks are fostered by adolescent employment. But because of the age-segregated character of most jobs available to the young, for most youngsters working promotes greater integration into the adolescent, and sometimes deviant, peer society of fellow workers than the more conventional and work-oriented adult society.

Moreover, given the nature of "youthwork," she argues that employment on the part of young people is less likely than in earlier eras to provide effective

socialization to future occupational roles. Most young
people do simple work that requires little training or
skill, and has minimal potential for advancement.
Further, since most youth now work to enhance their own
immediate consumption potential and style of life--not to
help their families-- their employment does not imply the
assumption of social responsibility, as was the case for
youngsters in earlier eras, for example, during the Great
Depression. Elder's (1974) study of that cohort of
adolescents as they moved into adulthood demonstrates
that for them, work had very positive developmental
consequences.   The findings of Greenberger's study,
along with other recent work (Mortimer and Finch 1986b;
Finch and Mortimer 1985), challenge the popular wisdom
that adolescent part-time work while in school
facilitates the transition to adulthood or fosters other
positive developmental outcomes.

Borman intensively studied 25 adolescents who had
recently left high school to obtain regular full-time
jobs, using systematic observation and interviewing
techniques. She followed these young people over a
one-year period, documenting their initial attempts to
locate jobs and to successfullly adjust to the world of
work. The lack of higher educational credentials and
work experience on the part of these young job-seekers
made their entry to the work world an especially
problematic period in their careers. They faced pressing
issues: locating a job, learning to manage their time and
other resources, balancing their work and nonwork
interests, developing personal habits that met with the
expectations of their employers, integrating themselves
into the work setting, and maintaining their employment
through time when the work they performed was, for the
most part, routine, uninteresting, low-paying, lacking in
advancement opportunity, and dissatisfying. She
describes the formal and informal methods the respondents
used to locate jobs, and reports that the young males in
her study were more effective than young females in
utilizing informal contact networks in job search.

Borman's study draws attention to important nonwork
experiences that foster the development of an
occupational identity and commitment to work. Having a
supervisor who acted as mentor was especially conducive
to the emergence of positive work orientations and to the
integration of the novice into the work setting.
However, relatively few employers or supervisors were
willing to invest their time and energy in developing

such a relationship, since they tended to view the young worker as transient and as lacking the capacity to assume major responsibility. The availability of emotional support, as well as more tangible resources from the family of origin, was a further dimension of these youths' life experiences that eased their transition to work.

The two chapters in the first section of this book offer important insights with regard to the timing of occupational influence on the person. They support the position that the processes by which work affects psychological development begin in the very initial stages of the work career. Greenberger indicates both beneficial outcomes--e.g., increases in self-reliance and the ability to work with persistence--and what might generally be considered more deleterious consequences--such as diminishing interest, involvement, and achievement in school. Borman describes the formation of an initial occupational identity and commitment among young workers who are just entering the labor force after leaving school.

In Section II of this volume, differences in the psychological consequences of work in adulthood, depending on age and gender, are explicitly addressed. The issue of timing and magnitude of occupational influence in different phases of life is pursued in Chapters 4 and 5. Both Miller et al. and Mortimer et al. show that occupational experiences have significant effects on intellective process and job satisfaction among workers of all ages.

Using longitudinal survey data from U.S. male workers and cross-sectional data from a comparable group of male workers in Poland, Miller, Slomczynski, and Kohn investigate whether the impacts of occupational self-direction on intellective process are conditional on age. Their analysis demonstrates that the effects of occuptional self-direction on intellectual flexibility and authoritarian conservatism are quite similar for young, middle-aged, and older workers in the United States and Poland. Job conditions indicative of occupational self-direction had significant effects on the ideational flexibility and authoritarian conservatism of workers in each age group. Notwithstanding one prominent cross-national difference--closeness of supervision was a more important determinant of authoritarian conservatism in Poland than in the United States--the evidence is clear that the experience of self-direction at work fosters more flexible thought processes and less authoritarian attitudes in both countries.

Most important from the perspective of this volume, there was no indication that the psychological effects of self-direction diminish in strength in later phases of the worklife. Moreover, there was evidence that prior intellectual flexibility continued to have positive effects on self-directed work throughout the career. The reciprocal paths from earlier intellective process to the substantive complexity of work and closeness of supervision were, in fact, larger in magnitude for older U.S. men than for younger U.S. men. Their research supports the position that the learning-generalization processes through which job conditions affect the adult personality occur in similar fashion in all age groups, in diverse cohorts, and across national boundaries.

Mortimer, Finch, and Maruyama address the same basic question: Do work conditions have the same magnitude of effect on the psychological attributes of workers of different age? But their focus is upon job satisfaction, the overall evaluative reaction to the job, not the basic intellective processes of concern to Miller et al. Furthermore, they include both women and men in their analysis. Data from the 1972-3 to 1977 Quality of Employment Survey Panel are used to examine the interrelations of work experiences and job satisfaction in six groups of workers defined by gender and age.

Comparison of the six causal models provides support for the "aging stability hypothesis" that individual attitudes become more stable as workers grow older. There was evidence that the increasing stability of job satisfaction is related both to environmental conditions (the tendency for work environments to become more stable as workers move into the middle and later phases of their careers) and to a tendency for persons to become less psychologically responsive (at least with respect to this psychological construct) to differences in their work environments as they age. Both men and women manifested increases with age in the stabilities of work autonomy and job satisfaction over the four-year period of study. Moreover, work autonomy had stronger effects on job satisfaction in the younger age groups, though the decline in the impact of autonomy with age is patterned somewhat differently among men and women. The varying patterns of causation across gender and age groups support the "fit hypothesis," prominent in the job

satisfaction literature, that workers' responses to their
jobs are importantly affected by their personal
characteristics.

The different patterns of findings reported by
Miller and Mortimer and their colleagues are certainly
intriguing. While Miller et al. find basically
equivalent effects of self-directed job conditions on
intellective functioning in three age groups, Mortimer et
al., whose age groupings are defined almost identically,
find that work autonomy has the strongest positive impact
on job satisfaction in male workers who are younger than
30, and on female workers below the age of 45.
Furthermore, using the same data set, Lorence and
Mortimer (1985) report corresponding processes of "aging
stability" when a very similar causal model is applied to
job involvement. It is not clear why intellectual
flexibility should show a different pattern of
determination, with respect to work conditions and age,
than the psychological constructs of job satisfaction and
commitment. The juxtaposition of these two studies
indicates the need for further research, encompassing
other psychological dimensions, so as to identify the
domain of individual attributes that are most responsive
to work experience in the early phases of the work
career, and those that work continues to influence, with
the same magnitude of effect, throughout the work life.

Whereas the literature on women's dual roles is
vast, it does not explicitly focus on age, but instead
addresses the question as to whether the work role, when
added to women's traditional domestic responsibilities
--defined by marital status, stage in the family life
cycle, or number of children--promotes well-being and
health, or alternatively, leads to debilitating strain
and disease. Because there is substantial evidence that
women usually continue to bear the major responsibility
for housework and childcare, even when they are employed
full-time, many believe that the dual role commitments of
adult women increase their risk of illness. Employed
women with children are thought to be particularly
vulnerable to stress-related disease. However, the
scientific evidence on the relationship between work and
health does not uniformly support this point of view.
Sorensen and Mortimer's chapter identifies four plausible
hypothetical models, examines the major arguments
supporting each, and assesses the relevant empirical
evidence.

According to the first "stress model," work

experiences threaten workers' health because of the demands and pressures work poses. A second "health benefits model" emphasizes the advantages of employment for health, pointing to the fact that work experiences may provide opportunities for autonomy, job satisfaction, and social support, all of which enhance health. Rather than examining job characteristics, as the first two models do, a third "role expansion model" focuses on the number of roles a person occupies, such as worker, spouse, and parent. It suggests that multiple roles offer increased opportunities for building self-esteem and satisfaction from alternative sources, thus benefiting health. Finally, according to a fourth "person-environment fit model," health outcomes are predicated on the match or "fit" between work characteristics and job demands rather than on job experiences alone.

Sorensen and Mortimer attempt to synthesize the wide-ranging and often contradictory literature by juxtaposing these four models and by drawing out their implications for an understanding of work and health as a woman proceeds through her life span. While there is empirical evidence supporting each model, the question remains as to whether these explanatory frameworks are differentially applicable to women in the various phases of their lives. For example, to what extent are the stress-promoting and health-benefiting dimensions of work, as well as family roles, unevenly distributed across age groups? Since family demands tend to be greatest when young children are at home, adding to the workload and pressures associated with employment, the "stress model" appears to provide important insights to an understanding of the interrelations of work and health among women in early adulthood. Moreover, there is evidence that the health-promoting features of work are the least prevalent among very young workers.

Because the number of roles a woman occupies typically expands in early adulthood and then contracts in middle age, when children leave home, or in the event of divorce, separation, or widowhood, the "role expansion" model is clearly applicable to a life course perspective. One might ask whether the occupancy of multiple roles has the same beneficial outcomes for women of different age. Women may be increasingly able to reap the health benefits of their employment and family roles as they acquire greater tenure in the labor force and experience in juggling conflicting work and family demands. Finally, the degree of "fit" between worker and job may be largely a function of age, career phase, or other indicators of position in the life course.

The chapters in the final section of this volume review the special problems of workers who are in mid-career or later phases of the worklife. Clark and Corcoran, drawing on their research in a large multiversity as well as a synthesis of extant research findings, consider whether "vitality" (what might also be referred to as enthusiasm and commitment to work, and the resulting level of effectiveness and productivity) diminishes mid-way through the career, long before any physiological or cognitive decline would decrease the ability to effectively carry out job tasks or diminish productivity. They review the literature on the relationship between aging and productivity, and identify broad macro-conditions (e.g., cultural, economic, technological, and organizational) which give rise to issues of vitality, obsolescence, and productivity among midcareer and older professional workers.

Taking a more social psychological perspective, the authors also examine middle-aged and older workers' feelings about their jobs in a youth-oriented society, the special meaning of obsolescence in professional fields, and the problems of career "peaking" and "stuckness" as reported by a substantial minority of the professors and scientists whom they interviewed. Following the early phases of their careers, university faculty members are often faced with powerful expectations that they will be less vital and productive than younger workers. There is a constant threat of knowledge obsolescence which can only be averted through continuous acquisition of new information and/or skills.

While the chapter by Miller et al. attests to the psychological advantages of complex work, the findings of Clark and Corcoran suggest that under conditions of rapid knowledge growth and technological change, the level of complexity with which the worker must cope can outstrip individual capacities, generating feelings of obsolescence and declining morale. They illuminate the potentials of institutional practices, administrative leadership, and colleagues, as well as the orientation and initiatives of the affected workers themselves, for alleviating these negative feelings and improving performance in this phase of the worklife. In doing so, they indicate effective corporate strategies for enhancing vitality, reducing obsolescence, and stimulating productivity among middle-aged and older employees.

Whereas injuries, accidents, and other job-related disabilities can occur during any phase of the career, they become more prevalent among older workers as they approach the time of retirement. They also involve especially difficult processes of adjustment and resocialization on the part of mid-career and older workers, whose recuperative capacities may be diminished and whose employment opportunities may be more severely restricted than is the case for younger workers. The self-concept, including the sense of personal efficacy, self-worth, and dimensions of identity, is both profoundly affected by such disability and importantly implicated in the prospects for rehabilitation and recovery. Schwalbe and Gecas examine the manner in which job-related disabilities affect workers' self-concepts and other psychological states (such as depression and anxiety). They also indicate how the individual's attempts to restore a sense of self-efficacy, self-worth, and self-coherence (a sense of meaning), in turn, influence the course of recovery.

In interpreting the relationships between job-related disabilities and psychological states, Schwalbe and Gecas draw on social psychological theories of self-concept maintenance and individual functioning in adulthood. As in Clark and Corcoran's preceding chapter on vitality, however, they also take the institutional and organizational context into account. It is evident from their analysis that an occupation's location in the stratification structure determines the nature and frequency of risk to workers, the worker's access to resources which affect the capacity to cope with disabilities, and the disabled worker's exposure to self-enhancing experiences. Moreover, the phenomenon of worker disability extends to wider contexts, external to the job situation. There are disruptions in the family, as well as involvement with workers' compensation programs, rehabilitation agencies, the legal and medical professions, and various government agencies. The features of these institutions can importantly influence the process of recovery, enhancing efficacy and valued identities, or reinforcing dependency and passivity while fostering a "disabled" self-image. In the concluding section of their chapter, Schwalbe and Gecas indicate the diverse ramifications of the literature they review for social policy.

In summary, this volume examines the interrelations of work experience and psychological development throughout the career, from late adolescence to pre-retirement age, presenting insights, conceptual frameworks, and findings from a variety of social science perspectives. Substantively, the contributors investigate a wide range of issues surrounding the life span implications of work: the broad impacts of part-time work while in school on adolescent development; the processes by which the work role is learned by young adults just out of high school; the effects of occupational self-direction on cognitive functioning for young, middle-aged, and older workers; the varying implications of occupational experiences for job satisfaction depending on age and gender; the health risks and benefits associated with adult women's dual roles in the home and in the workplace; the special problems, variously referred to as "loss of vitality," "stuckness," or as having reached a "career plateau" confronting midcareer and older workers; and the reciprocal interrelations of self-concept and job-related disabilities among injured workers.

On the basis of these studies, it must be concluded that while work has important consequences for the individual irrespective of age, the character and magnitude of its influence on at least some psychological orientations differs, depending on the worker's stage in the work career or in the life course. They demonstrate the pervasive importance of work autonomy and complexity for psychological development throughout the worklife. In investigating the reactions of people to their work experiences in different phases of life, these studies also address important theoretical issues regarding the malleability of the person over time.

Furthermore, these studies illustrate the active stance of the person in all phases of the work career--in seeking the work role initially, in influencing the character of the job in subsequent phases of the career, and in determining the character of reactions to given work experiences. Borman describes the job-seeking strategies of young people, and indicates that they have varying levels of ability to find jobs and to maintain their employment over time. Miller et al. demonstrate that prior intellective flexibility influences the substantive complexity of the job at subsequent times. Clark and Corcoran find that mid-career faculty react differently to the threat of obsolescence, some taking an

active, problem-solving approach, and others manifesting
a less resourceful and ineffective stance. As Schwalbe
and Gecas point out, even work-related injuries and
disabilities do not have uniform effects on the
individual, but their impacts vary depending on the
self-efficacy and other psychological attributes of the
person.

Finally, the contents of this volume, as noted in
Borman's concluding chapter, have considerable practical
importance. Understanding the interrelations of work
experiences and psychological development through the
life span can inform efforts to improve the quality of
working life for persons of all ages.

16

REFERENCES

Bem, Darryl J. 1972. "Self-Perception Theory." Pp. 1-62
in L. Berkowitz (ed.), Advances in Experimental Social
Psychology, Vol. 6. New York: Academic Press.
Blau, Peter M., John W. Gustad, Richard Jessor, and Richard
C. Wilcox. 1956. "Occupational Choice: A Conceptual
Framework." Industrial and Labor Relations Review 9
(July):531-543.
Blauner, Robert. 1964. Alienation and Freedom: The
Factory Worker and His Industry. Chicago: University of
Chicago Press.
Davis, James A. 1965. Undergraduate Career Decisions:
Correlates of Occupational Choice. Chicago: Aldine.
Durkheim, Emile. 1964 (first published, 1893). The
Division of Labor in Society. Translated by George
Simpson. New York: Free Press.
Elder, Glen H., Jr. 1974. Children of the Great
Depression. Chicago: University of Chicago Press.
Erikson, Erik H. 1959. "The Problem of Ego Identity."
Psychological Issues 1:101-164.
Finch, Michael D., and Jeylan T. Mortimer. 1985.
"Adolescent Work Hours and the Process of Achievement."
In Alan C. Kerckhoff (ed.), Research in Sociology of
Education and Socialization 5:171-196.
Glenn, Norval D. 1980. "Values, Attitudes, and Beliefs."
Pp. 596-640 in Orville G. Brim and Jerome Kagan (eds.),
Constancy and Change in Human Development. Cambridge,
Mass.: Harvard University Press.
Hall, Douglas T. 1971. "A Theoretical Model of Career
Subidentity Development in Organizational Settings."
Organizational Behavior and Human Performance 6
(January):50-76.
Holland, John L. 1976. "Vocational Preferences." Pp.
521-570 in Marvin D. Dunnette (ed.), Handbook of
Industrial and Organizational Psychology. Chicago: Rand
McNally.
House, James S. 1981. "Social Structure and Personality."
Pp. 525-561 in Morris Rosenberg and Ralph H. Turner
(eds.), Social Psychology: Sociological Perspectives.
New York: Basic Books.
Hughes, Everett C. 1958. Men and Their Work. Glencoe,
Ill.: Free Press.
Kanter, Rosabeth M. 1977. Men and Women of the
Corporation. New York: Basic Books.
Kohn, Melvin L. 1977. Class and Conformity: A Study in

Values (Second edition). Chicago: University of Chicago
Press.

Kohn, Melvin L. 1981. "Personality, Occupation, and
Social Stratification: A Frame of Reference." Pp.
267-297 in Donald J. Treiman and Robert V. Robinson
(eds.), Research in Social Stratification and Mobility,
Vol. 1. Greenwich, Conn.: JAI Press.

Kohn, Melvin L., and Carmi Schooler, with the collaboration
of Joanne Miller, Karen A. Miller, Carrie Schoenbach, and
Ronald Schoenberg. 1983. Work and Personality: An
Inquiry into the Impact of Social Stratification.
Norwood, N.J.: Ablex Publishing Corporation.

Lorence, Jon, and Jeylan T. Mortimer. 1981. "Work
Experience and Work Involvement." Sociology of Work and
Occupations 8 (August):297-326.

Lorence, Jon, and Jeylan T. Mortimer. 1985. "Work
Involvement Through the Life Course: A Panel Study of
Three Age Groups." American Sociological Review
50(October):618-638.

Marx, Karl. 1964. Karl Marx. Selected Writings in
Sociology and Social Philosophy. Translated by Tom B.
Bottomore. New York: McGraw-Hill.

Mortimer, Jeylan T., and Michael D. Finch. 1986a. "The
Development of Self-Esteem in the Early Work Career. Work
and Occupations. 13 (May):217-239.

Mortimer, Jeylan T., and Michael D. Finch. 1986b. "The
Effects of Part-time Work on Self-Concept and
Achievement." Pp. 66-89 in Kathryn Borman and Jane
Reisman (eds.), Becoming a Worker. Norwood, N.J.: Ablex
Publishing Corporation.

Mortimer, Jeylan T., and Jon Lorence. 1979a. "Work
Experience and Occupational Value Socialization: A
Longitudinal Study." American Journal of Sociology 84
(May):1361-1385.

Mortimer, Jeylan T., and Jon Lorence. 1979b. "Occupational
Experience and the Self-Concept: A Longitudinal Study."
Social Psychology Quarterly 42 (December):307-323.

Mortimer, Jeylan T., Jon Lorence, and Donald Kumka. 1986.
Work, Family, and Personality: Transition to Adulthood.
Norwood, N.J.: Ablex Publishing Corporation.

Mortimer, Jeylan T., and Roberta Simmons. 1978. "Adult
Socialization." Annual Review of Sociology 4:421-454.

Nicholson, Nigel. 1984. "A Theory of Work Role
Transitions." Administrative Science Quarterly
29:172-191.

Park, Robert E., Ernest W. Burgess, and Roderick D.
McKenzie. 1925. The City. Chicago: University of

Chicago Press.

Rosenberg, Morris. 1957. Occupations and Values. Glencoe, Ill.: Free Press.

Rosenberg, Morris. 1981. "The Sociology of the Self-Concept." In Morris Rosenberg and Ralph Turner (eds.), Social Psychology: Sociological Perspectives. New York: Basic Books.

Sears, David O. 1981. "Life Stage Effects on Attitude Change, Especially Among the Elderly." Pp. 183-204 in Sara B. Kiesler, James N. Morgan, and Valerie K. Oppenheimer (eds.), Aging: Social Change. New York: Academic Press.

Seeman, Melvin. 1967. "On the Personal Consequences of Alienation in Work." American Sociological Review 32 (April):273-285.

Van Maanen, John, and Edgar H. Schein. 1979. "Toward a Theory of Organizational Socialization." In B. M. Staw (ed.), Research in Organizational Behavior 1:209-274. Greenwich, Conn.: JAI Press.

Walker, Charles, and Robert Guest. 1952. The Man on the Assembly Line. Cambridge, Mass.: Harvard University Press.

Part 1

Work and Psychological Development in Youth

2. Working in Teenage America

In the 1930s, when abuses of child labor were still commonplace, the authors of a book entitled <u>Child Workers in America</u> wrote:

> They go...to work with no plan and no training, their jobs usually anything they can get, having nothing to do with their interests and their capabilities, only with business demand...

These same writers, lamenting the fate of these children of the poor, asked, "What would the average middle-class parent say to such an 'educational' program for his adolescent boys and girls?" (Lumpkin and Douglas 1937). The answer, in the 1980s, is that the teenage children of the middle class are a visible presence in the part-time labor force, and that they are there with the blessing of their parents. Belief in the moral and developmental benefits of work leads many adults to sanction and support this "educational program" for youth--even when youngsters must juggle commitments to their job with commitments to school.

My purpose in this chapter is to raise questions about the value of intensive labor force participation during the school year. This critique of teenage employment is not a critique of working per se. Rather, my arguments focus on the costs, and debatable benefits, of working long hours at the kinds of jobs that are typically available to youth today, for the reasons that motivate many youngsters to seek employment.[1]

21

HIGH SCHOOL STUDENTS IN THE WORKPLACE: TRENDS

From shortly after the end of World War II until the
present time, the proportion of school-going youngsters who
work has risen dramatically, especially among youngsters 16
and older. Between 1947 and 1980, for example, there was a
65% increase in the labor force participation of school-
enrolled 16- and 17-year-old boys, and a 240% increase among
girls of the same age. Because of legal constraints on the
work of children younger than 16, smaller increases were
recorded for school-going 14- to 15-year-olds: virtually no
change among boys, but a 57% increase in the rate of
employment among girls, very likely in response to changing
conceptions of gender roles (Greenberger and Steinberg
1986).

At the present time, it is projected that 80% of youth
will have held paid employment at some time before
graduating from high school. Forty-two percent of high-
school sophomores and 63% of seniors are employed at any
given point in the school year (Lewin-Epstein 1981). Still
more recent data on high school seniors suggest that these
figures are now higher: e.g., 72% of seniors worked in any
given week of the school year (Bachman, Johnston, and
O'Malley, in press). Many youngsters, moreover, work
substantial numbers of hours per week. For job-holding
sophomores (mostly 15- and 16-year-olds), the average
school-year work schedule in 1981 was 15 hours per week for
boys, 11 for girls; for seniors, the comparable figures were
21 and 18 hours per week. The extent of teenagers'
involvement in work emerges more vividly when one considers
the proportion who work the equivalent of a half-time or
full-time job: One in four sophomores, and two in five
seniors, hold what amounts to a half-time job; and fully one
in ten seniors work 35 hours or more while also attending
school (Lewin-Epstein 1981).

Perhaps the most noteworthy dimension of change in the
labor force behavior of school-enrolled youth concerns their
social origins. In the early decades of this century,
adolescents from poor families often had to forego a high
school education in order to work. School-going was
incompatible with employment. Over time, however,
increasing mechanization of the workplace created a labor
surplus that rendered children's labor unnecessary, and
simultaneously created a need for workers with more advanced

cognitive skills. For these and other reasons, laws were enacted that mandated school attendance until well into the teen years (currently, age 16 in nearly all states). Consequently, children from virtually all socio-economic strata now obtain some secondary education, and most obtain a high school diploma.

One might suppose that it is the inclusion of the lower socio-economic classes in the high-school-going population that has prompted the observed increase in working during the teenage years. This is not the case, however. In the 1980s, teenage employment is a cross-class phenomenon that bears the special stamp of the middle classes: Youngsters from homes with comfortable incomes are more likely to be employed than those from less affluent families, whites are more likely to find employment than Blacks or Latinos, and youngsters from the suburbs are more likely to work than youngsters from the cities.

Changes in the proportion of school-going youth who work and in the social origins of these young workers were prompted by a host of interlocking economic and social factors. Perhaps most important was the expansion of opportunities for part-time work and the creation of jobs that required only a modest level of skill. The extraordinary growth of the retail and service sectors of the economy created just such opportunities: more than 15 million new jobs between 1950 and 1976, located chiefly in the suburbs (Ginzberg 1977). Most adolescent workers today serve or sell to customers in stores and restaurants; concommitantly, the proportion of youngsters employed in the crafts, in factories, and on farms--once the major arenas for youthwork--has declined sharply. Today's jobs, paid at or close to the minimum wage and usually requiring part-time hours, often at night or on weekends, are ideally suited to teenagers, whose "regular" work hours already are committed to school attendance and whose wage requirements are low, because they enjoy parental support for the most costly expenses of living.

Social changes, too, have led youth into the workplace. The diminished value of education as a goal in its own right, and lowered demands for time-consuming homework, have made school-year employment more feasible. And the increased consumer spending of teenagers, including their consumption of luxury goods, has made employment, in this restricted sense, a necessity (Yovovich 1982). Part-time employment fills teenagers' time and pockets.

These economic and social changes in turn have changed the functions of children's work. Youngsters' paid employment, once motivated primarily by their families' financial need, now serves chiefly their own ends. The great majority of youngsters spend most of their earnings on their own needs and activities, not on contributions to family subsistence (Johnston, Bachman and O'Malley 1982). Youngsters' jobs, once a stepping stone to adult employment, are now usually discontinuous with adult employment: Relatively few adolescents aspire to, or continue in, jobs similar to the ones they held in high school. And the workplace, once a meeting ground for young people and their more stable, experienced elders, is now substantially segregated by age: Most youth work in the company of, or serving, others close to them in age, their supervisors often their senior by only a scant year or two.

CONSEQUENCES OF ADOLESCENT WORK

An abundant literature has demonstrated that employment has substantial impacts on adults' social relations, personality development, and mental and physical health (Dooley and Catalano 1980; Cobb and Kasl 1977; Durkheim 1951; Elder 1974; Kohn and Schooler 1973; Kohn and Schooler 1978; Mortimer and Lorence 1979; Special Task Force 1973). Very little research, however, has addressed the possible impacts of employment on adolescents, perhaps precisely for the reasons noted above: the absence of its roots in economic necessity and of long-term commitment by adolescents to their jobs. In the following sections, I overview studies of work that investigate the role of work in youngsters' psychosocial development, education, and employment prospects.

Work and Psychosocial Development

In order to assess the costs and benefits of working to adolescents' psychosocial development, it is important to identify a standard of healthy development against which the outcomes of working can be judged. Greenberger (1984), based on an earlier formulation by Greenberger and Sørensen

(1974), has proposed an interdisciplinary model of
psychosocial development that emphasizes the importance of
growth in the directions of autonomy and social
integration. Psychological research, it should be noted,
has tended to emphasize the former and neglect the latter.
In my view, the two dispositions are equally important. As
I use the constructs "autonomy" and "social integration,"
they connote sets of attributes that contribute to both the
optimum psychological development of the individual and the
smooth functioning of society.

Autonomy. Research on adolescent employment has
addressed several issues relevant to autonomy, defined
broadly to include personal attributes that should help
individuals to function effectively and maintain themselves
independently in society. Thus, studies have provided data
about the relations between working and self-reliance;
constructive work habits; knowledge of business and money
concepts; and experience in financial decision-making. Many
of these studies originate from Greenberger and Steinberg's
Adolescent Work Project, which examined correlates and
consequences of working in a sample of high school
sophomores and juniors drawn from diverse family backgrounds
in four Orange County, California, high schools.[2]

Longitudinal data from this project showed that scores
on a self-report measure of self-reliance from Greenberger's
Psychosocial Maturity Inventory (Greenberger et al. 1975;
Greenberger and Bond 1976) increased slightly but
significantly over a one-year period among girls who worked,
but did not increase among working boys. More specifically,
gains in self-reliance were a positive function of time
spent in the workplace, with girls who had had more total
hours of job experience showing greater gains (Steinberg et
al. 1982).[3] Attempting to explain the sex difference in
effects of working on self-reliance, Steinberg et al.
discounted differences in opportunities of boys and girls to
exercise autonomy on the job--there were none, according to
youngsters' self-reports--and focused on possible
differences in the meaning of the work to the two sexes.
Because employment is strongly expected of men, but less
consistent with social expectations of women, the authors
suggested, girls may be more disposed to see entry into the
labor force as an act of independence and to draw from
ongoing participation in the workplace an increased sense of
initiative and self-direction (cf. Bronfenbrenner 1961;
Elder 1974).

Several findings from the same study suggest that working also may have a number of positive effects on work habits. First, youngsters themselves claim that working has taught them to be more dependable and punctual. Indeed, if they do not have these traits in sufficient measure, or do not acquire them quickly, they may lose their jobs: The existence of a large supply of potential youngsters who can replace them no doubt serves as a vivid reminder of the importance of these basic "workers' virtues." Second, working youngsters showed small but significant gains in scores on the work orientation scale of the Psychosocial Maturity Inventory. This self-report scale measures the ability to work with persistence and to obtain satisfaction from completing tasks competently. As before, gains were positively associated with youngsters' time commitment to working. However, having traits that would enable one to work well, if motivated to do so, and actual performance on the job are potentially different matters. From all indications, working does not transform youngsters into paragons of the Protestant ethic. Although half of a subsample of youngsters who were interviewed indicated that they performed assigned tasks conscientiously, half reported neglecting duties or "goofing off." Often, the same youngsters described themselves as both conscientious and neglectful. Hardly any youngsters spontaneously described incidents of going beyond the call of duty on the job (Greenberger and Steinberg 1981).

Knowledge of economic and business concepts (e.g., the meaning of "overhead," "interest"), skill in consumer arithmetic, and awareness of informed consumer practices also should help young people to function adequately on their own. In cross-sectional analyses of workers' and nonworkers' scores on a timed test of practical knowledge, with controls for grade-point average and social class background, working adolescents scored higher than their nonworking peers. However, longitudinal analyses left considerable doubt as to whether the observed difference was actually caused by working, or was attributable to factors related to self-selection of youngsters with more practical knowledge into the labor force (Steinberg et al. 1982).

Thus far, I have considered only the relationship of employment status (working vs. not working) and intensity of employment (weekly hours of work) to autonomy, thus treating all jobs as being alike in their potential effects on

youngsters' development. Indeed, most researchers of
adolescent employment implicitly have adopted the position
that for teenagers, "a job is a job is a job" (Greenberger,
Steinberg, and Ruggiero 1982). Yet researchers who study
the implications of work for adults have produced compelling
evidence that jobs with different characteristics differ in
their effects on adults' personality development, value
orientations, and psychological well-being (Kohn 1969;
Miller et al. 1986; Mortimer and Lorence 1979). A
characteristic of jobs that has received particular
attention in these studies is the extent to which employees
have opportunities for self-direction, as indexed by the
closeness and restrictiveness of supervision; the degree to
which their tasks at work vary in content and sequence; and
the extent to which their work is complex, or involves
working with people and ideas. The extent to which men
encounter opportunities for occupational self-direction has
been shown to increase the importance men place on jobs that
allow self-expression--i.e., the exercise of one's ability,
interests, and creativity (Mortimer and Lorence 1979); the
importance they attach to their children's capacity for
self-direction (Kohn 1969; Kohn et al. 1986); and men's own
intellectual flexibility (Kohn and Schooler 1978).

In our study of high school students, we assessed two
indicators of opportunities for self-direction--closeness
and style of supervision and degree of routinization--using
both self-report measures and behavioral observations of
adolescents while at work. We did not attempt to measure
substantive complexity of work. (In general, most
youngsters' jobs would rate low on this dimension, with
youngsters in the retail sector perhaps involved in somewhat
more complex work than others.) Contrary to expectations,
individual differences in job routinization and
restrictiveness of supervision were not associated with
differences in such areas of potential impact as self-
reliance, positive work habits, or valuing autonomy in one's
future occupation (Greenberger and Steinberg, unpublished
data). However, it is important to note that these findings
were based on cross-sectional data, and that the average
youngster had been on the job for only six months. It is
possible that with a longer-term study, using a longitudinal
design, a different picture might emerge.

The most dramatic way that working promotes young
people's autonomy, however, is not through the general

experience of working, nor through features of their jobs that are directly autonomy-enhancing, but through the financial consequences of working. In 1981, the average high school sophomore who held a job earned $143 per month; the average senior, $272 (based on Lewin-Epstein 1981). Adolescents who work report more freedom (less parental control) in deciding how to spend their money than do nonworkers who receive only an allowance from their parents. In those sectors of society from which adolescent workers are drawn today, parents, for the most part, do not need the earnings of their children, and treat their earnings as their youngsters' private property. That this was not always the case is well known. Less well-known, perhaps, is the fact that parents still have legal rights in their minor children's earnings, although they seldom exercise them.

In any case, adolescents who work are less financially dependent on their parents. They assume responsibility for buying for themselves some of the things that their parents previously had provided (e.g., items of clothing), not only in response to parental demands but as a matter of choice. They also buy luxury items that they did not own before, and that their parents could or would not provide for them (e.g., an automobile). The privacy and freedom of choice that youngsters gain when they become wage-earners probably explain to a considerable degree why three out of four adolescents said they would rather work than simply receive the same amount of money from their parents (Greenberger and Steinberg 1986). Although youngsters' net gain from working, in dollars, is somewhat less than it seems at first glance, since they give up a measure of parental support, it appears that the gain in autonomy they experience more than balances the psychological ledgers.

The greater financial independence of teenagers may be short-lived, however. Over 80% of a national sample of high school seniors saved "none" or only "a little" of their earnings for either their post-high school education or other, long-range purposes (Johnston, Bachman, and O'Malley 1982). One wonders how many youngsters who bought themselves expensive stereo equipment or designer clothes while in high school must turn to their parents for financial help in the ensuing years.

Social Integration. Scholars since Durkheim have expounded upon the socially integrative functions of work: Work gives our lives structure and significance by linking us to the productive sector of society, reduces feelings of isolation and alienation, and lessens the probability that we will engage in deviant or self-destructive behavior (Durkheim 1951; Cloward and Ohlin 1960; Special Task Force 1973). Critics of the American high school, in reports published in the 1970s, implicitly argued this same brief in behalf of youthwork. Apparently unaware of the influx of school-going youth into the part-time labor force, they proposed that earlier integration into the world of work would help youngsters establish ties to adult society.[4] Too little participation in the productive work of society, and too much time in an age-segregated adolescent enclave, they claimed, encouraged the formation of an irresponsible youth culture (Coleman 1972; National Panel on High School and Adolescent Education 1976; President's Science Advisory Committee 1973). Research from several quarters has explored the impacts of working on adolescents' social integration, defined broadly to include a sense of participation in the larger society, ties to generations other than their own, and commitment to the norms of adult society.

The evidence concerning effects of work on feelings of social participation is mixed: not altogether positive, but hopeful. In our Orange County, California, study, the great majority of employed youngsters--over 80%--felt that their work produced goods or services of value to others (Greenberger and Steinberg 1986). A nationally representative sample of high-school boys seemed less sanguine, however. Fifty-eight percent thought the work they were assigned to on the job "almost always" or "often" was meaningful (Mortimer and Finch 1986). The different outcomes of these two survey studies may be due in part to differences in the thrust of the questions asked. Respondents in the Orange County study perhaps pondered the overall, or summative, effects of their work, whereas respondents in the second study considered the more micro-level, individual tasks they performed on the job.

Even if youngsters see themselves as performing productive work, it is not necessarily the case that they believe they are a uniquely valuable part of the productive enterprise itself. Interviews with 103 workers in our study

suggested that only one in four youth perceive themselves to
be an integral, or indispensable, part of the work force--no
doubt a realistic view, in light of the low skill-
requirements of their jobs and large pool of replacement
labor. Nearly one in five youngsters felt that their
participation at work was only marginally important:

>Interviewer: What would happen...if you didn't come
>   in one day?
>Manual Laborer: They'd just call someone else to work
>   for me.

There is little support for the expectation that
youngsters who work will develop extensive ties to the older
generation. The evidence from our Orange County,
California, study suggests that adolescents who work do not
typically encounter mentors who impart valuable skills or
knowledge, nor confidants to whom they can turn for advice
and comfort (Greenberger and Steinberg 1981; Greenberger,
Steinberg, and Ruggiero 1982). The major reasons, we
believe, have to do with the nature of adolescents' jobs and
the settings in which they work. Most youth-work requires
little training: Youngsters already know a good deal about
washing cars, mopping floors, and wrapping sandwiches before
they come to work. Most youngsters do not stay on the job
for long, by adult standards, thus limiting the rewards to
adults of investing in their training or of taking a
compassionate interest in their personal lives. And the
workplace itself, as noted earlier, is considerably peer-
saturated, if not age-segregated. Youngsters often work
largely in the company of their peers, supervised by persons
only a few years their senior. In support of these
statements, consider the following data from our study.

Behavioral observations of youngsters employed in the
six most common types of job revealed that training and
instruction were infrequent: an average of .43 incidents
per hour, for example, among food service workers, and just
under two incidents per hour among retail clerks.
Questionnaire data revealed that only 5% of youngsters work
on joint tasks with an adult, with the term "adult"
conservatively defined as a person at least two years older
than the respondent. (In view of the age-distribution of
our study sample, "adult" thus defined implies a person 18
to 19 years old, or older.) Most interaction with adults in
the workplace was task-oriented, according to our
observations, and only 9% reported that they would
definitely discuss a personal problem with an adult at

work. Moreover, only a minority of youngsters reported interacting outside the workplace with either a co-worker (21%) or supervisor (11%) who was two or more years their senior.

Studies that address commitment to the goals and values of the larger culture have focused largely on the relations between working and deviance (Gottfredson 1985; Ruggiero 1984; Ruggiero, Greenberger, and Steinberg 1982; Shannon 1982). However, Gottfredson also assessed youngsters' attachment to the social order, using measures of belief in conformity to rules, involvement with peers who get into trouble (a negative indicator), and aspirations for further education and prestigious (i.e., conventionally desirable) jobs. In this study of seventh through twelfth graders, drawn from schools at risk for high rates of juvenile delinquency, working did not increase youngsters' degree of attachment to mainstream culture. Similarly, Greenberger and Steinberg (unpublished data) detected no effects of working on youngsters' educational or occupational aspirations and expectations in their Orange County, California, study. As we shall soon see, however, heavy involvement in work actually may reduce youngsters' educational and occupational attainments.

The Gottfredson study also demonstrated that working does not reduce workers' pre-employment level of delinquency, as indexed by measures of interpersonal aggression, property damage, and frequency of using alcohol, marijuana, and other drugs. In this study, the employment variable was simply work status (working or not working); no data were collected on the number of hours youngsters worked. Studies by Ruggiero (1984) and Ruggiero, Greenberger, and Steinberg (1982) confirm Gottfredson's finding that employment--and indeed, intensity of employment--bears no relationship to rates of interpersonal aggression or property damage. However, Ruggiero found that in the more affluent Orange County sample, working actually led to increased deviance of certain types: more school-related deviance (copying other students' homework, disrupting classes), more deviance involving money (selling drugs, buying false ID cards), and more use of alcohol and marijuana. In general, deviant behaviors were more strongly associated with intensity of employment than with work status (employed vs. non employed) per se. Based on her analyses of the cross-sectional and longitudinal study

samples, Ruggiero found "considerable support for the
conclusion that involvement in drug-, money-, and school-
related deviance is a consequence of work experience rather
than an antecedent condition affecting selection into the
work force" (Ruggiero 1984:362).

Ruggiero also demonstrated that working opens doors to
an entirely new arena for deviance, one to which only youth
who work have access. This new arena is the workplace
itself. According to Ruggiero's (1984) study, reported
earlier in Ruggiero, Greenberger, and Steinberg (1982), 62%
of adolescents reported committing one of nine illegal or
unethical acts while holding their first part-time job. The
most common forms of occupational deviance were, in
declining order, calling in sick when not to excuse a job
absence; giving away goods or services for nothing, or for
less than their assigned value; stealing money or goods from
the workplace; working while intoxicated or "high" on drugs;
and putting extra hours on one's time card.

In a series of related studies, investigators in the
Orange County, California, study proposed three mutually
compatible explanations of the relations between working and
increased deviance (Greenberger and Steinberg 1986;
Greenberger, Steinberg, and Vaux 1981; Ruggiero 1984;
Ruggiero, Greenberger, and Steinberg 1982; Vaux 1981).
These explanations center on money, job stress, and the
nature of the peer culture. Thus, for example, they showed
that amount of income is associated with money-related
deviance and substance use (Greenberger, Steinberg, and Vaux
1981; Ruggiero 1984). On the other hand, they showed that
working under more stressful conditions makes a significant
contribution to the prediction of substance use, even after
the amount of income is statistically controlled (Ruggiero
1984; Vaux 1981). As well, they argued that the increase
among workers in behaviors such as buying and using alcohol
and marijuana, including use of these substances on the job,
reflects the influence of the peer culture. Let us consider
the issues of job stress and conformity to the peer culture
in more detail.

Following Kasl's discussion of sources of job stress
among adults (1974), we had youngsters rate the degree of
routinization and restrictiveness of supervision they
experienced on the job (conceptualized earlier as dimensions
of opportunity for self-direction); and measured perceived

meaninglessness of work (the extent to which work was judged
boring, likely to produce little of value, and low in level
of education required); poor environmental conditions (the
frequency of working under time pressure, in heat or fumes,
and doing heavy or dirty tasks--a category similar to Kohn
and Schooler's [1973] "job pressures"); impersonal
organization (the extent to which the social atmosphere at
work was remote and unsupportive); low wage structure (low
hourly wages and poor prospects for pay raises); and role
conflict (the degree to which working or the hours of work
interfere with other activities and obligations). Ruggiero
(1984) found that these characteristics of jobs generally
were associated with higher rates of deviance both in and
outside the work setting (see also Greenberger and Steinberg
1986; and Ruggiero, Greenberger, and Steinberg 1982).[5]
These findings are consistent with a stress-reduction
perspective, according to which deviant behavior is viewed
as an outlet for anger and strain.[6] It should be noted,
however, that these studies did not control for level of
deviance prior to employment, which leaves open the
possibility that more deviant youth get lower-quality jobs,
or find more to complain about in jobs of the same quality
that less deviant youth also hold.

One characteristic of jobs merits special attention
because of its different relations to deviance in the
workplace and in other environments. It was anticipated
that a negative social atmosphere at work would be
associated with higher scores on the various measures of
deviance. Although the expected association was observed
for money-related and school-related deviance, the opposite
direction of effects was observed for occupational
deviance: Youngsters who worked in a more positive social
atmosphere committed more deviance on the job. This
apparently anomalous finding can be interpreted in light of
special characteristics of the adolescent workplace and the
peer culture.

The workplace in which many youth are employed has, in
several respects, a distinctly adolescent flavor: a high
concentration of young workers and young supervisors; a
relative absence of serious economic motivation for work;
and little long-range commitment of employees to their
jobs. Against this backdrop, close ties among co-workers
may provide the instigation and support for workplace
shenanigans. Even the form that occupational deviance

takes, moreover, reflects the fact that young workers bring
the peer culture with them into the workplace. Activities
such as giving away clothing or food for nothing or less
than the ticket price are ways in which youngsters maintain
and strengthen ties to their friends, who are the chief
beneficiaries of these giveaways. Violations of adult
notions of responsible behavior, such as working while
"high" or "buzzed," also may enhance youngsters' status in
certain peer groups; and in view of the sizable peer
presence in the workplace, may draw an interested and
admiring audience.' The ties of young workers to the peer
culture are further suggested by the finding that working,
and intensity of employment, both are positively associated
with a measure of peer orientation (Ruggiero 1984).

Taken together, our findings raise serious questions
about the "larger society" into which young workers are
becoming integrated. Are they building bridges to the adult
world, or are they strengthening their ties to the peer
culture?

Work and Schooling

The social and political unrest of the 1960s prompted
serious concern about the condition of youth--especially,
the sources of their restive mood and alienation from
mainstream culture. A number of blue-ribbon reports that
were commissioned over the ensuing years suggested, to
borrow Coleman's (1972) phrase, that the children had
outgrown the schools. They argued that more options for
combining school and work not only would bring youth into
closer touch with the adult culture, as noted earlier, but
would create new opportunities for learning (President's
Science Advisory Committee 1973; National Panel on High
School Education 1976). In the workplace, they claimed,
youngsters could practice school-taught skills in a real-
life setting; as well, they would learn skills and
information not likely to be encountered in the classroom.
As Greenberger and Steinberg (1986) observed, the unstated
assumption behind such advocacy of youthwork was that "work
experience can reinforce and expand the curriculum of the
school without detracting from learning in that setting."
It is important to develop an empirical base for testing
both parts of this proposition: Does working provide

expanded opportunities for learning? And does it do so at
no cost to schooling?

Learning at Work. It is appealing to think that young
workers are deploying school-taught cognitive skills in an
arena where performance may have real consequences for them
and for others. The employee who can't make accurate change
in a timely manner, or who misreads instructions, surely
will not win favor with the boss. However, in an era when
cash registers compute the change and symbols on the
register associate the hamburger with its price, far less
arithmetic and reading are required than was once the
case. Our observations of youngsters at work indicate, as
one would expect, that the amount of time youngsters are
engaged in the 3 Rs varies significantly with the type of
work they do. Food service workers, manual laborers, and
youngsters who work as cleaners or janitors spend an average
of 2% or less of their time using those skills; retail sales
clerks, 11%; clerical workers, and operatives and skilled
laborers taken together, about 30% and 15%, respectively.
In general, the jobs in which the greatest number of youth
are employed are those that offer the least opportunity for
practicing basic cognitive skills (Greenberger and Steinberg
1986; Greenberger, Steinberg, and Ruggiero 1982).

The expectation that youngsters will learn new skills
and information in the workplace also comes up against some
disappointing facts. As indicated earlier, most
adolescents' jobs appear to require little training; and, in
any case, little training is in evidence after the first few
months on the job. Once again, the jobs in which fewest
youth nationwide actually find employment--jobs as clerical
workers, or as operatives and skilled laborers--appear to be
those in which training and instruction are greatest. These
jobs, furthermore, offer the best prospects for adult
careers. Whether exposure to the business world, and
earning and spending a substantial amount of money, lead to
increased knowledge of business and consumer issues is not
known. Research findings discussed earlier are ambiguous on
this point. The possibility that working increases young
people's practical knowledge in these domains deserves to be
studied further.

Some of the most important lessons a young person
learns at work are far subtler, however, and far more
difficult to assess. For example, youngsters who work may

experience first-hand a number of role relationships that are new to them, and may grow, consequently, in their level of social maturity. Working with people whose level of motivation and work-style are different from one's own; working for supervisors whose values and expectations must be factored into one's own behavior; and dealing with customers whose preferences and demands must be accommodated, could do much to expand youngsters' understanding of others and increase their adeptness in social situations. Our interviews with working youngsters led us to suggest that advances in social understanding were most likely in jobs that offer greater opportunities for self direction: that is, jobs in which youngsters deal frequently with people, play different roles (e.g., experience both supervising others and "working for" a supervisor), and have the leeway to make decisions about how to conduct important transactions with others at work (Greenberger and Steinberg 1986; Steinberg et al. 1981). Jobs of this kind oblige young persons to take the perspective of others, and thus place their own social insight and competence at a premium. Our interview data suggest that sales clerks in general are most likely to gain in social understanding, and that adolescents whose interactions with others are either scant (the night-time janitor) or highly routinized (the fast food worker) are less likely to benefit in this way from work experience. Although work of some kinds may enhance youngsters' social understanding, it does not follow, of course, that the absence of work experience results in impaired social understanding. We did not interview nonworkers, and we did not seek to learn whether extensive participation in family activities, in the peer group, and in activities centered in the school also might increase youngsters' ability to understand and "manage" social situations.

Effects of Working on Schooling. We have considered, thus far, some of the ways that working might supplement classroom learning. We consider next whether holding a job during the academic year has any impact on what is learned in the classroom.

The most obvious, though not altogether satisfactory, way to judge the effects of work on classroom learning is to look at the bottom line: youngsters' grade point average (GPA). Before addressing the possible effects of working on school performance, however, we should consider whether students with lower GPAs are more likely to select into the school-year labor force. There is little, if any, evidence to support this notion (Greenberger and Steinberg 1986; Lewin-Epstein 1981; Mortimer and Finch 1986). There is more evidence, however, that academic performance is a factor that influences youngsters' decisions about how _intensively_ to work: Poorer students, it seems, are more likely to work longer hours (Greenberger and Steinberg 1986).

Selection effects do not rule out the possibility that working long hours also causes further harm to students' grades. Several studies--but not all--suggest that this is the case. In none of these studies, however, is the effect of working on GPA of large magnitude. Finch and Mortimer (1985), for example, examined the relations between intensity of employment and students' grades in a nationwide sample of male high-school students. They found that weekly hours of work in the sophomore year bore a negative relationship to the GPA earned in the junior year, whereas hours worked in the junior year had no effect on grades earned in the senior year. In this analysis, students' GPAs in the preceding years of school were controlled statistically. Similarly, among boys who had begun working earlier (in grade 10), those who had more extensive work experience (i.e., those who worked during more years of high school) had lower cumulative GPAs in their senior year than those who had worked fewer years (Mortimer and Finch 1986). Both sets of findings suggest that younger students may be the most vulnerable to the negative academic impacts of intensive employment.

Several lines of evidence suggest that adolescent employment exerts its adverse effects on grades and other aspects of school performance by diminishing youngsters' interest in school. The relevant studies focus on the amount of time youngsters spend doing homework, their degree of involvement in various facets of school life, and ways in which youngsters may balance the demands of work with the demands of school.

In most, but not all, studies, intensive employment is associated with fewer hours spent on homework. D'Amico (1984) showed that as the percentage of weeks in which youngsters worked very long hours (more than 20) rose, study time declined among whites, and showed a nonsignificant trend in the same direction among minority youth. This

relationship prevailed even after differences in future
educational plans, educational attainment of the head of
household, and grade level had been controlled. Because the
measurement of intensity of employment and time spent on
homework was concurrent, however, the usual problem of
disentangling selection factors from causal relations
arises. Our own research suggests that both forces may be
at work. In the Orange County study, youngsters who were
seeking, but had not yet obtained, their first job were
already spending significantly less time on homework than
their peers who were not interested in getting jobs. On the
other hand, taking a job reduced further the amount of time
youngsters invested in homework. In the latter analysis,
based on longitudinal data, we controlled for the amount of
time youngsters had spent on homework in the year preceding
employment (Steinberg et al. 1982).

McNeil (1984) presents a more far-reaching proposal.
Based on a study of students and teachers, she suggests that
employment not only causes students to disengage from
learning, but teachers to reduce their investment in
teaching. Many students reported that they compensated for
demanding work schedules by taking fewer and easier
courses. Sixty percent of working students said that
working interfered with completing class assignments and
staying alert in class. Frustrated by students' persistent
failure to meet their expectations, McNeil asserts, many
teachers accommodate by assigning less homework, making
assignments less challenging, and simplifying their
classroom lessons. If this practice is widespread, the
impacts of adolescent employment on schooling and learning
are profound indeed (Greenberger and Steinberg 1986).

Taken together, the studies reviewed in this section
cast doubt on claims that work expands the curriculum of the
school at no cost to youngsters' formal education. At the
least, the likely educational benefits of working have been
exaggerated: The workplace is not a hotbed of learning. At
worst, intensive commitment to the job interferes with
attainments in school. Although effects of working on GPA
and on amount of time devoted to homework are not large (nor
regularly detected), two facts are worth noting: No studies
point to positive effects of working on school performance
or time spent on studies. Moreover, change in school
performance, as measured by change in GPA, is an imperfect
measure of the impact of working, because students may

adjust the level of difficulty of the courses they take in response to the demands of employment.[8] The possibility that the educational system has accommodated to the emergence of massive numbers of student-workers by lowering its standards is a social impact of broad consequence (Greenberger and Steinberg 1986).

WORK AND FUTURE PROSPECTS FOR EMPLOYMENT

The high rate of unemployment among young adults is a widely acknowledged social problem in this country (Freeman and Wise 1982). Over the past twenty years, furthermore, the labor market position of young people in the 18-25 cohort--especially nonwhites--has worsened relative to that of older adults. Efforts to explain this phenomenon center on changes in the supply of labor (e.g., increased labor force participation of women, the distribution of literacy and job skills in the older and younger generations) and in employment demand (e.g., a shrinking proportion of low-skill jobs in the economy). On the grounds that previous work experience might make young adults more competitive for the jobs that are available, it is reasonable to study the impacts of employment during the high school years on subsequent labor force success. The relevant questions are whether school-year work pays off in higher rates of employment or wage rates during the early adult years, and whether this advantage persists over time.

Employment in Early Adulthood. A number of studies demonstrate that youngsters who were employed more intensively during high school fare better over the next four or five years (Finch and Mortimer 1985; Freeman and Wise 1979; Mortimer and Finch 1986). Unfortunately, however, the findings of these studies do not suggest that a solution to the problem of youth unemployment is on the horizon. Although intensity of high school employment significantly reduces the number of weeks that young adults are unemployed, the size of this effect is very small. In contrast, intensive work experience during high school has a substantial, positive effect on hourly wages.

One might anticipate that the positive effect of high-school work on wages in the ensuing years is restricted to youth who do not pursue further education. Their employment opportunities after high school would likely be more similar to the ones they had as students; thus their work skills and contacts would be relevant to jobs that do not require post-secondary education. In contrast, students who went on to college would likely be entering positions for which their early work skills were insufficient. Surprisingly, the positive effect on wages of more intensive employment during the high school years holds for both groups of young people, those who did and those who did not receive post-secondary education (Mortimer and Finch 1986).

Economists and other social scientists have emphasized that high school employment may not be directly responsible for the greater labor force success of young adults. Unmeasured variables, such as achievement motivation and social skills, may account for differences in both the intensiveness of young people's employment during high school and the extent of their success in the labor market during the next several years. As Freeman and Wise (1979) note, the two explanations are not incompatible: It is possible that youth with certain motivational and social assets invest more time in the workplace as high-school students, and then have experiences in the workplace that enhance those characteristics, making them more valuable to potential employers.[9] However, even after differences in motives, educational attainment, and the like are accounted for, amount of experience in the labor force (seniority) contributes significantly to wage rates.

The most explicit type of seniority would accrue, of course, to youngsters who continue in their high school job after graduation. Indeed, a direct linkage of this kind between high school work and "better" adult employment would warm the hearts of youthwork advocates concerned with easing young people's transition to adulthood. Few youngsters, however, enjoy a direct path from their high-school job to an adult occupation. For example, only about one-third of high-school seniors who are employed as food service workers or retail sales clerk indicated that they were continuing in their job after completing school, yet these are the two types of jobs in which nearly 40% of seniors are employed (Lewin-Epstein 1981). At the opposite end of the spectrum, between one-half and two-thirds of those youth working in the skilled trades and in factories said they expected to continue in their present job. The bad news is that only 10% of high school seniors nationwide are employed in jobs of this type, which generally offer better wages and

prospects for advancement than other forms of youthwork.
Even for youngsters who switch jobs, however, a more
extensive work history pays off in higher wages during the
early adult years.

   The Longer Perspective. Increased earning power in the
first few years after high-school graduation is an
attractive outcome of intensive high-school employment. It
would seem less attractive, however, if it were accompanied
by offsetting losses in longer-range occupational
attainments. The major way that the early labor-force
advantage of intensive high-school workers might be
dissipated is by limiting their education. In general,
people with more years of schooling enjoy greater long-range
labor force success, measured in terms of earnings, job
prestige, and job satisfaction (Sewell, Hauser, and
Featherman 1976).

   Research suggests that intensive work experience
increases the probability of dropping out of high school for
some youth. Thus, D'Amico (1984) found that as the
percentage of weeks in which they had worked more than 20
hours rose, certain age-sex-race subgroups showed increased
rates of school-leaving. Another study found that males
with more extensive high-school work experience reported, as
seniors, weaker commitment to obtaining further education;
and, five years after graduation, in fact, had achieved
fewer years of post-secondary schooling (Mortimer and Finch
1986). Still other studies indicate that the wage advantage
of youth with extensive high school labor force experience
does not persist indefinitely. A national, longitudinal
study of the high-school class of 1972 revealed that from
age 21 on, the wages of college-educated adults have a
faster growth rate than that of their less-educated peers.
By 21, the wage rates of women who obtained post-secondary
education already were higher than those of women with less
education. For men, the cross-over point comes later, and
more-educated men still have not caught up with their less-
educated peers by age 25 (National Center for Education
Statistics 1982). These differences in the cross-over point
are obviously due, in part, to the lower pay ceiling and
narrower range of variation in pay that women encounter in
the world of work. In any case, it is important to note
that the economic benefits of higher education, although not

reaped immediately, increase <u>as individuals acquire greater
job experience</u> (Sewell, Hauser, and Featherman 1976).

Taken together, data on the effects of high school
employment on schooling and learning, and data on high
school employment and future occupational success, point in
this direction: Although greater work involvement during
high school is clearly beneficial to youngsters' wage
prospects in early adulthood, intensive employment also
carries risks. Insofar as it may lower youngsters'
investment in education, it undermines their long run
chances for occupational and economic success.

SUMMARY AND IMPLICATIONS

In this chapter, I have overviewed youthwork in America
and summarized some of its causes, correlates, and
consequences. It is my conviction that enthusiasm for the
integration of schooling and work needs to be tempered by an
appreciation of the realities of the naturally occurring
workplace. The jobs that most youth find in the private
sector have serious limitations with respect to their
developmental potential. This is hardly surprising, since
employers hire young workers to increase profit margins, not
to invest in futures.

On the positive side of the ledger, youthwork seems to
improve young people's work habits; and, under certain
conditions, may enhance their ability to interpret and
manage social situations. Working gives some, but not all,
youngsters a sense of participating in socially useful
work. Intensive employment during high school leads to
higher wages in the first few years after graduation. On
the negative side of the ledger, there is little evidence to
suggest that working paves a solid path to adulthood.
Adolescent employment instead seems to be an integral part
of the peer culture, an experience shared by youngsters from
virtually all social and economic backgrounds. The greater
financial autonomy of adolescents who work is translated
into a high level of consumer spending, some of it on
essentials, but much of it on luxury goods that are likely
to enhance one's status in the peer group. Working does not
strengthen youngsters' ties to the older generation, nor
foster deeper attachment to the norms and values of
mainstream society. And youthwork typically does not offer

opportunities for discovering adult jobs that will be satisfying. Perhaps most important, intensive commitment to a job during the school year is likely to exact costs. These costs materialize in areas such as increased drug and alcohol use, due in part to the stresses associated with long hours of work; reduced commitment to education; and, as a result of lower educational attainment, less favorable occupational prospects for the adult life course.

The dangers of overcommitment to work--in the context of the developmentally limited jobs available to youth today--are discussed in detail by Greenberger and Steinberg (1986). We suggest that youngsters who devote too much time to earning a paycheck end up shortchanging themselves. Too much time at a dull job that is not motivated by economic necessity, nor tied to hopes for an adult career, leaves other forms of work undone. These forms of work include the unpaid, but important, "identity work" of adolescence, which requires time and energy for experimentation and introspection; and involvement in activities in the school, the community, and settings where one's work is volunteered, that have been shown to yield positive consequences for young people's development.

The study of people's work lives used to begin with their formal school-leaving, and typically, their entry into the full-time labor force. This practice once may have reflected the small proportion of youth who actually combined school-going with substantial labor force participation. Today, with extensive labor force activity during the school years so widespread, and with evidence that early work experiences are consequential for young people's lives, a new time perspective is in order: The study of work over the life course must begin far earlier, perhaps with children's introduction to work in the household (Goldstein and Oldham 1979). Among the studies that are most needed are those that explore the impacts of intensive school-year employment in greater breadth and detail; longer-term studies of the effects of specific job characteristics on youngsters' well-being and development; and studies that trace the effects of extensive youthwork on the quality of teaching and learning in the nation's high schools.

NOTES

1. This chapter is based on my joint research with Laurence Steinberg and on our book, When Teenagers Work: The Psychological and Social Costs of Adolescent Employment. Readers interested in a fuller treatment of issues raised in this chapter, including recommendations for policy and practice, should consult that source (Greenberger and Steinberg 1986).

2. Two hundred twelve youngsters holding their first part-time job were studied, along with 319 comparable, nonworking students. All youth were employed during the school year in the naturally occurring workplace (i.e., they were not employed in deliberately designed programs for youth). Youngsters employed in family enterprises also were excluded. The project had both a cross-sectional design and a longitudinal component, in which nonworkers at Time 1 were re-surveyed one year later, when a substantial number had become workers. The research methods included self-report questionnaires, behavioral observations of adolescents in the workplace, and interviews with working teenagers and their parents.

3. In this analysis and others based on longitudinal data, Time 1 scores on the target variable (here, self-reliance) were controlled statistically. Thus, the effects reported are independent of any initial differences on the target variable that might antecede employment and lead to selective work experiences.

4. They recommended more extensive employment in the naturally occurring workplace and in work programs deliberately designed to foster young people's development.

5. Generally, job stressors affect boys and girls in similar ways, but a few sex differences did emerge. For example, boys' alcohol and marijuana use were more strongly predicted by amount of exposure to restrictive (autocratic) supervision than was girls' substance use (Greenberger, Steinberg, and Vaux 1981). The greater vulnerability of boys to a job characteristic that poses threats to autonomy is consistent with developmental theory and research on sex differences in adolescent development (e.g., Douvan and Adelson 1966). Along related lines, Mortimer et al. (1986) found that work autonomy plays a larger role in men's job satisfaction than that of women.

6. For an account of how these job characteristics are related to adolescents' physical and mental health, see Greenberger and Steinberg (1986).

7. Alcohol and drug use on the job are not, of course, a uniquely adolescent phenomenon. More than a decade ago, a special task force studying the quality of work in America commented that alcohol and drug use at work may constitute a "special means of coping" with job related pressure and boredom (Special Task Force 1973). It is of considerable interest that this means of coping appears among school-going adolescents in the part-time labor force, while employed in their first job.

8. Analyses of the effects of employment on standardized achievement scores would be preferable.

9. Studies reviewed in this chapter do not furnish any clues concerning the assets that youth who work intensively may bring to the marketplace.

46

REFERENCES

Bachman, Jerald G., Lloyd D. Johnston, and Patrick
    O'Malley. In press. "Recent Findings from Monitoring
    the Future: A Continuing Study of the Lifestyles and
    Values of Youth." In Frank Andrews (ed.), Research on
    the Quality of Life. Ann Arbor, Mich.: Institute for
    Social Research.
Bronfenbrenner, Urie. 1961. "Some Familial Antecedents of
    Responsibility and Leadership in Adolescents." Pp. 239-
    271 in Luigi Petrullo and Bernard M. Bass (eds.),
    Leadership and Interpersonal Behavior. New York: Holt,
    Rinehart & Winston.
Cloward, Richard A., and Lloyd E. Ohlin. 1960. Delinquency
    and Opportunity: A Theory of Delinquent Gangs. Glencoe,
    Ill.: Free Press.
Cobb, Stanley, and Stanislav V. Kasl. 1977. Termination:
    The Consequences of Job Loss. Cincinnati: Ohio National
    Institute for Occupational Safety and Health, Behavioral
    and Motivational Factors Research.
Coleman, James S. 1972. "The Children Have Outgrown the
    Schools." Psychology Today 5 (February):72 ff.
D'Amico, Ronald. 1984. "Does Working in High School Impair
    Academic Progress?" Sociology of Education 57:157-164.
Dooley, David, and Ralph R. Catalano. 1980. "Economic
    Change as a Cause of Behavioral Disorder." Psychological
    Bulletin 87:450-468.
Douvan, Elizabeth, and Joseph Adelson. 1966. The
    Adolescent Experience. New York: Wiley.
Durkheim, Emile. 1951. Suicide: A Study in Sociology.
    Glencoe, Ill.: Free Press.
Elder, Glen H., Jr. 1974. Children of the Great
    Depression. Chicago: University of Chicago Press.
Finch, Michael D., and Jeylan T. Mortimer. 1985.
    "Adolescent Work Hours and the Process of Achievement."
    Pp. 171-196 in Alan C. Kerchoff (ed.), Research in
    Sociology of Education, Vol. 5. Greenwich, Conn.: JAI
    Press.
Freeman, Richard B., and David A. Wise. 1979. Youth
    Unemployment. Washington, D.C.: National Bureau of
    Economic Research Summary Report.
_____. 1982. The Youth
    Labor Market Problem: Its Nature, Causes, and
    Consequences. Chicago: University of Chicago Press.

Ginzberg, Eli. 1977. "The job problem." Scientific
American 237:43-51.
Goldstein, Bernard, and Jack Oldham. 1979. Children and
Work. New Brunswick, N.J.: Transaction Books.
Gottfredson, Denise C. 1985. "Youth Employment, Crime, and
Schooling: A Longitudinal Study of a National Sample."
Developmental Psychology 21:419-432.
Greenberger, Ellen. 1984. "Defining Psychosocial
Maturity." Pp. 3-39 in Paul Karoly and John J. Steffen
(eds.), Adolescent Behavior Disorders: Foundations and
Contemporary Concerns. Lexington, Mass.: Lexington
Books. (Revised copy of chapter available from author.)
Greenberger, Ellen, and Lloyd Bond. 1976. User's Manual
for the Psychosocial Maturity Inventory. Irvine,
Calif. University of California (mimeo).
Greenberger, Ellen, Ruthellen Josselson, Claramae Knerr, and
Bruce Knerr. 1975. "The Measurement and Structure of
Psychosocial Maturity." Journal of Youth and Adolescence
4:127-143.
Greenberger, Ellen, and Aage B. Sorensen. 1974. "Toward a
Concept of Psychosocial Maturity." Journal of Youth and
Adolescence 3:329-358.
Greenberger, Ellen, and Laurence Steinberg. 1983. "Sex
Differences in Early Labor Force Participation:
Harbinger of Things to Come." Social Forces 62:467-486.
_____. 1981. "The
Workplace as a Context for the Socialization of Youth."
Journal of Youth and Adolescence 10:185-210.
_____. 1986. When
Teenagers Work: The Psychological and Social Costs of
Adolescent Employment. New York: Basic Books.
Greenberger, Ellen, Laurence D. Steinberg, and Mary
Ruggiero. 1982. "A Job Is a Job Is a Job...or Is It?
Behavioral Observations in the Adolescent Workplace."
Work and Occupations 9:79-96.
Greenberger, Ellen, Laurence Steinberg, and Alan Vaux.
1981. "Adolescents in the Workplace: Health and
Behavioral Consequences of Job Stress." Developmental
Psychology 17:691-703.
Johnston, Lloyd, Jerald Bachman, and Patrick O'Malley.
1982. Monitoring the Future: Questionnaire Responses
from the Nation's High School Seniors, 1981. Ann Arbor,
Mich. Institute for Social Research.
Kasl, Stanislav. 1974. "Work and Mental Health." Pp. 171-
196 in James O'Toole (ed.), Work and the Quality of
Life. Cambridge, Mass.: MIT Press.

Kohn, Melvin L. 1969. Class and Conformity: A Study in Values. Homewood, Ill. Dorsey Press.

Kohn, Melvin L., and Carmi Schooler. 1973. "Occupational and Psychological Functioning: An Assessment of Reciprocal Effects." American Sociological Review 38:97-118.

_____. 1978. "The Reciprocal Effects of the Substantive Complexity of Work and Intellectual Flexibility." American Journal of Sociology 84: 24-52.

Kohn, Melvin L., Kazmierz M. Slomczynski, and Carrie Schoenbach. 1986. "Social Stratification and the Transmission of Values in the Family: A Cross-National Assessment." Sociological Forum, 1:73-102.

Lewin-Epstein, Noah. 1981. Youth Employment During High School. Washington, D.C.: National Center for Education Statistics.

Lumpkin, Katharine DuPre, and Dorothy Wolff Douglas. 1937. Child Workers in America. New York: International Publishers.

McNeil, Linda. 1984. "Lowering Expectations: The Impact of Student Employment on Classroom Knowledge." Madison, Wisc.: Wisconsin Center for Education Research.

Miller, Joanne, Kazimierz M. Solmczynski, and Melvin L. Kohn. 1986. "Continuity of Learning-Generalization: The Effect of Jobs on Men's Intellective Process in the United States and Poland." Pp. 79-107 in Jeylan T. Mortimer and Kathryn M. Borman (eds), Work Experience and Psychological Development Through the Life Span. Boulder, Colo.: Westview Press.

Mortimer, Jeylan T., and Michael D. Finch. 1986. "The Effects of Part-Time Work on Adolescent Self-Concept and Achievement." Pp. 66-89 in Kathryn M. Borman and Jane Reisman (eds.), Becoming a Worker. Norwood, N.J.: Ablex Publishing Corporation.

Mortimer, Jeylan, Michael D. Finch, and Geoffrey Maruyama. 1986. "Work Experience and Job Satisfaction: Variation by Age and Gender." Pp.   in Jeylan T. Mortimer and Kathryn M. Borman (eds.), Work Experience and Psychological Development Through the Life Span. Boulder, Colo.: Westview Press.

Mortimer, Jeylan T., and Jon Lorence. 1979. "Work Experience and Occupational Value Socialization: A Longitudinal Study." American Journal of Sociology 84:1361-1385.

National Center for Education Statistics. 1982
(November). Bulletin. Washington, D.C.: U.S.
Department of Education.

National Panel on High School and Adolescent Education.
1976. The Education of Adolescents. Washington, D.C.:
U.S. Government Printing Office.

President's Science Advisory Committee. 1973. Youth:
Transition to Adulthood. Chicago: University of Chicago
Press.

Ruggiero, Mary. 1984. "Work as an Impetus to
Delinquency: An Examination of Theoretical and Empirical
Connections." University of California, Irvine:
Unpublished doctoral dissertation.

Ruggiero, Mary, Ellen Greenberger, and Laurence Steinberg.
1982. "Occupational Deviance Among First-Time
Workers." Youth and Society 13:423-448.

Sewell, William, Robert A. Hauser, and David L.
Featherman. 1976. Schooling and Achievement in American
Society. New York: Academic Press.

Shannon, Lyle W. 1982. Assessing the Relationship of Adult
Criminal Careers to Juvenile Careers. Washington,
D.C.: U.S. Department of Justice. (Microfilm N. NCJ
77744 available from the National Juvenile Justice
Clearinghouse of the National Criminal Justice Reference
Service, Washington, D.C.)

Special Task Force to the Secretary of Health, Education,
and Welfare. 1973. Work in America. Cambridge,
Mass.: MIT Press.

Steinberg, Laurence, Ellen Greenberger, Laurie Garduque, and
Sharon McAuliffe. 1982. "High School Students in the
Labor Force: Some Costs and Benefits to Schooling and
Learning." Educational Evaluation and Policy Analysis
4: 363-372.

Steinberg, Laurence D., Ellen Greenberger, Laurie Garduque,
Mary Ruggiero, and Alan Vaux. 1982. "Effects of Working
on Adolescent Development". Developmental Psychology
18:385-395.

Steinberg, Laurence, Ellen Greenberger, Maryann Jacobi, and
Laurie Garduque. 1981. "Early Work Experience: A
Partial Antidote for Adolescent Egocentrism." Journal of
Youth and Adolescence 10:141-157.

Steinberg, Laurence, Ellen Greenberger, and Mary Ruggiero.
1981. "Early Work Experience: Effects on Adolescent
Occupational Socialization." Youth and Society 12:403-
422.

50

Vaux, Alan. 1981. "Adolescent Life Stress, Work Stress, and Social Support: Psychological, Somatic, and Behavioral Consequences." University of California, Irvine: Unpublished doctoral dissertation.

Yovovich, B. G. 1982. "A Game of Hide and Seek." Pp. 17 and ff in Advertising Age (2 August).

3. The Process of Becoming a Worker[1]

Entry into the labor market following high school constitutes a process of personal mobility through a series of transitional experiences. Finding and settling into a job or, more typically, a number of different jobs, mark the process of becoming a worker as an especially important period in the life cycle. It is a frustrating and difficult time for those who lack supports to ease the movement from a nonwork to a work status (Williams and Kornblum 1985). Without the benefit of experience, many youth fail to find meaningful work, and do not possess "personal resources and sponsorships, qualifications, aspirations, expectations, and knowledge" to enable them to slip easily into the role of a good, dedicated employee (Piker 1968:3). Further, there are few institutional arrangements and organizational policies and practices designed to assist their job-seeking efforts (Corwin 1986).

During this period in the life cycle, finding work is only one of the major tasks facing the young who are at the same time concerned with developing intimate relationships, achieving legal statuses, and moving away from home. With a formidable list of demanding developmental tasks confronting adolescents, the wonder is that some appear to make the transition with relative ease. In discussing adult socialization to work roles, Mortimer and Simmons (1978) posit a four-stage process by which the work role incumbent moves to an adjustment or fit with work responsibilities in an organization. The individual must first reconcile expectations with the realities of work, next survive a "hazing" period, third recover from the shock of disillusionment in being on one's own, and finally develop a sense of community or shared misery with others (generally co-workers) who are enduring similar adjustments. It is likely that adolescent workers make parallel transitions which may be all the more painful given their lack of experience and the existence of competing developmental tasks.

Although it is important to consider labor market entry from the perspective of personal mobility and development through the life cycle, the problem of matching workers and jobs is also a societal dilemma. Unemployment figures for the young tell the story in stark terms. According to data released by the Bureau of Labor Statistics in December 1985, more than 8 million Americans were unemployed. Almost 40% were under age 25. The unemployment rate for 16-19 year olds stood at 18.8%. Most dismal were the data for minority youth who suffered unemployment at the rate of 41.6% percent. In concluding his survey of young persons' job search activities, Charles Dayton notes:

> Persons between the ages of 16 and 19 years constitute only 10 percent of the work force but over 20 percent of the unemployed. Nonwhites have unemployment rates more than double those for whites. Thus, unemployment in the United States falls heavily on the shoulders of youth and particularly minority youth. (Dayton 1981:321)

In sum, unemployment among all youth constitutes a major social issue, with the problem of unemployed minority youth especially acute.

In seeking and locating work, the job-seeker typically utilizes a number of strategies. Among the job seeking activities ranked as most helpful by Dayton's respondents were "writing up and sending out a resume," "seeking help from friends," "searching the classified want ads," "registering with a private employment service," "knocking door to door at potential employers' work places," and "seeking help from family."

Dayton examined the extent to which background features such as race, sex, and ability influenced job finding success. The important predictors of employment were gender and socio-economic status. These findings strengthen Steinberg et al.'s (1981) claim that sex and social class are the major influences upon the occupational course taken by an individual. It is important to note that these characteristics are regarded as socially significant by parents, peers, teachers, and employers who continually shape young peoples' destinies throughout the adolescent and early adult years   (Steinberg, et al. 1981:418).

　　To understand how young people locate and settle into regular jobs after high school is a problem of great practical significance in counseling and vocational guidance, as well as a critical area of theoretical concern. Becker argues that the "social processes" by which jobs are allocated to youth are pertinent to three major domains of social science research: "the status attainment research tradition within sociology, the vocational psychologists' study of personal-vocational goals, and work by economists relating economic conditions to youths' labor force behavior" (Becker 1977:1).

　　It should be noted that labor market conditions facing young workers are bleak in large part because employers often view them as deficient in their willingness to work and as lacking understanding of the demands of workplaces. Employers, therefore, engage in relatively uninspired hiring campaigns when seeking adolescent workers (Hollenbeck and Smith 1984; Murphy and Jenks 1982). For example, when an opening occurs, employers in small businesses, although they may rely on contacts such as teachers or trainers in specific vocational high school settings, rarely recruit graduating seniors needing jobs. Shapiro notes that employers frequently view young workers as labor market transients "who will stay on the job only long enough to attain short term goals" (1983:40). It has been estimated that less than one-third of all employers in the United States give serious consideration to hiring an individual under the age of 21 for a full-time job (Sorrentine 1981). Given this stance, young workers are likely to be provided less benefit of the doubt in hiring, promotion, and firing decisions than would be the case for workers in older age groups (Reisman 1985).

　　This chapter investigates the job search activities undertaken by adolescents who have left school. It also examines the nature of their subsequent relationships at work, particularly with supervisors, and their ongoing friendships and kinship ties.

　　The initial concern in this chapter is to describe adolescents' job search activities and their results. Special attention will be given to gender differences in job search and subsequent success in locating and settling into a job. Because most earlier work has focused on young male job seekers, we know relatively little about the parallel processes of job seeking pursued by young women. A second concern is the social context of the transition to

work, particularly as defined by family support and
mentoring on the job.

In addition, I will discuss the nature of adolescents'
work experience. Jahoda (1982) argues that engagement in
work performs a range of important functions for the
individual. Work structures time, provides opportunities
for social interaction and job satisfaction, and
contributes the basis for a work role identity.
Adolescence is a period in which formulating a rudimentary
sense of one's identity is the paramount developmental
task. Making a meaningful personal contribution through
work is an important component in the construction of a
positive occupational identity.

However, the workplaces in which adolescents are
employed are likely to inhibit the development of positive
work identities. Opportunities and incentives are highly
limited in the secondary labor market, the largest employer
of young workers. Not only are jobs within this labor
market sector highly unstable (Edwards 1979), but employers
and supervisors are likely to be rigid and autocratic,
perhaps as a result of their powerlessness to reward
subordinates with promotions or salary increases (Kanter
1977). In turn, attitudes held by young workers toward
their jobs are less positive than those expressed by older
workers. In a survey of a representative sample of the
civilian labor force employed in 1972-73, Kalleberg and
Loscocco (1983) compared job rewards and work values across
age groups. Their findings revealed that in comparison to
older workers, younger workers were more concerned with
both intrinsic rewards, such as the degree of challenge,
meaning and fulfillment obtained from work, and financial
rewards, such as pay, job security, and benefits.
Ironically, these rewards become increasingly available as
workers age and hence are less problematic generally for
older workers. The dissatisfaction expressed by younger
workers is partially a response to age differences in
occupational rewards. It is important to recognize,
however, that young workers also want more out of work --
especially in the areas of challenge, meaning, and
fulfillment -- than older workers. Unfortunately, perhaps
due to young workers' inexperience, powerlessness, and
reticence, these positive orientations are frequently
unexpressed. Youth may perceive leaving an awkward or
dissatisfying job situation as a better alternative than
hashing out their problems with a remote employer (Reisman
1985).

It is also clear that young workers desire to work.
In an analysis of data from the 1979 National Longitudinal

Survey of Youth Labor Market Experience (NLS), Borus (1982) considered the willingness of various groups of young workers to work for different rates of pay. Borus concluded that large proportions of youth representing various race and gender configurations were willing to accept work at less than the minimum wage.

Research Setting, Participants, and Data Sources

Data reported in the remainder of this chapter come from a larger project, "The Adolescent Worker Study" (Borman 1984), which focused on the linkages between youths' values and personality development and their labor market experiences. The research settings were Columbus and Cincinnati, two midwestern cities of similar size. Columbus, unlike its neighbor 100 miles to the south, is experiencing population growth and limited economic expansion. Both cities, however, have been faced with problems of restricted development in manufacturing, as have virtually all population centers in the North and Midwest.

During the course of the study, we recruited 25 participants who worked in a total of 46 different job settings during the period of the research. Young workers who were entering their first jobs following high school were targeted during initial interviews with employers in businesses representing the labor market sectors traditionally employing youth. It should be emphasized that while the research sample was small and thus precludes generalization to a larger population, participants were recruited in a manner that took current national youth labor market conditions into account. Thus, although workplace settings typical of jobs in manufacturing, retail sales, and entertainment were included, positions in the service sector are overrepresented in the study as they are in the working lives of youth.

The recruitment procedure generally followed in gaining access to the sample involved first obtaining permission from a potential employer and later securing the cooperation of an appropriate newly hired employee. Efforts were made to balance the sample by gender -- there were 11 males and 14 females. All participants were out of school and seeking full-time work. The process of securing a sample in this manner took approximately six months. Of the 25 participants selected for the study, only one withdrew after the study began and two moved out of town during the course of the research. There were no refusals to participate.

The first observations were made in May 1983, and observations continued through May of the following year. Subsequent checks were made to determine the full duration of employment up to two years from the initiation of the research. Some participants in the research were systematically observed for 12 months during full- and half-shifts at work, while others were involved in the study for shorter periods of time.

Most of the adolescent workers came from working-class or lower middle class family backgrounds, as indicated by their parents' occupations. Four had upper middle class family backgrounds. All but one of these were enrolled in college preparatory courses while in high school. However, the majority of the participants were enrolled in either general track or vocational courses during high school. Seven participants attended vocational schools, while two attended parochial (Catholic) schools.

A wide range of grade point averages was reported by the participants. A few received mostly A's during their school careers, while the majority reported their average grade as C. Our participants ranged in age from 18 to 22 at the start of the study. Most were 18 years of age and graduated from high school in June 1983.

Although most of these young workers eventually changed employers during the course of their participation, several were still employed by the same companies that had initially hired them, and were working at jobs similar to those in which they had been hired when we withdrew from the field. In all these cases, with one exception, the workers had received at least one salary increase during the period of their employment.

While 11 young workers were employed full-time, the majority were employed part-time. Not only was their work limited to partial employment, but their hours were frequently scheduled at variable times during the week. In many cases, workers' schedules were not posted by employers until the beginning of the week in question.

The jobs themselves can be characterized as entry-level, low-skill, or in many cases, dead-end positions. Some had possibilities for enlargement and advancement. For example, a shop hand in a sheet metal shop can eventually become a foreman. A mail clerk in a bank can advance to the position of department supervisor with minimal additional training. However, most jobs provided occupants with limited opportunities to take on

additional responsibilities and advance to another position
in the organization. Although the job of health spa
instructor held by three participants included collateral
responsibilities, these were considered demeaning and,
worst of all, boring by the young workers, and they did not
enable workers to become promotable.

While wages varied, most jobs paid the minimum wage
($3.35/hr.) to start. Raises of a few cents per hour were
contingent upon favorable evaluations after a 30-, 60-, or
90-day probation period.

The primary source of information used in this study
is field note data covering literally hundreds of worksite
observations. Each participant was observed for at least
one full shift at the time of hiring, and subsequently at
least twice a month in the workplace during the period of
study. If the individual quit a job or were fired and
later found other work, contact was made with the new
employer, and arrangements were made for observations to
begin in the new work setting.

In addition to workplace observations, a series of
systematic interviews were conducted with each participant.
These interviews included an initial life history
interview, covering prior work experience, education,
family background, use of leisure time, and other topics.
Monthly current events interviews were conducted with each
participant probing attitudes toward work, activities with
friends and family, current aspirations, and the like.
Finally, a work history was compiled for each participant
detailing features of earlier jobs such as rates of pay,
methods for obtaining jobs, and the like.

FINDINGS RELATED TO THE PROCESS OF BECOMING A WORKER

Locating a Job

Traditionally, job search strategies have been seen as
falling into one of two broad categories, formal and
informal. Formal methods include utilizing employment and
placement services, taking a civil service exam, or
applying through a union hall, while informal methods
include contacting friends or relatives about jobs,
applying directly to an employer, or asking teachers and
others for job related information. In virtually all
previous research, informal methods have been viewed as
most effective in obtaining jobs (Wielgosz and Carpenter
1984). Effective job search activities are those that
result in locating work. According to Wielgosz and

Carpenter (1984), effectiveness has been measured in one of
two ways: either a ratio is estimated between the number
of job seekers who obtain jobs by the method and the number
who mentioned using that method, or a ratio is estimated
between the number who obtain jobs by the method and the
number who used the method most.

Another indicator of the effectiveness of a job search
strategy is the length of time the successful young seeker
spends in the job he or she obtains. This measure has not
been used in prior research, although it seems likely that
the length of time invested in a particular job is likely
to be an indicator of the job holder's interest in the
position as a vehicle for mobility in his or her field of
interest. Because the average time on the job for workers
under 25 is 9.6 months (Borus 1982), a figure less than
one-third the amount of time on the job for the next
closest age group (26-34), a period of nine months or more
was considered to be indicative of the worker's minimal
commitment to a particular job.

As indicated in Table 3.1, adolescent males and
females in the study used a variety of job search methods.
Although there is some overlap, there are several points of
contrast for the two groups of job seekers. These young
male workers were more likely than their female
counterparts to obtain jobs through contact with friends or
relatives who possess job-related information. In fact,
all of the adolescent boys for whom data were complete used
this method at least once compared to only 20 percent of
the adolescent girls. Moreover, a relatively large
proportion, 38 percent of the male job seekers, remained on
jobs located by this method for nine months or more. Young
female workers, on the other hand, were more likely to
respond to help wanted ads in local newspapers, or to apply
directly to employers, strategies that were not
particularly effective in obtaining jobs or staying in
positions.

Furthermore, young women in the study used a greater
variety of job search strategies, and were therefore likely
to expend a greater effort in locating work than young men,
who relied on fewer strategies with generally more
favorable results.

The advantage in locating work through a friend or
relative, particularly if this contact is employed in the
work setting where the job is available, was apparent to
adolescent workers in the study. One young man with no
prior related vocational training got a job in an appliance
repair shop where his brother worked as the parts manager.
He was well aware of his good fortune, but rationalized it

Table 3.1

Job Search and Job Finding Methods Used by Adolescent Boys and Girls

	Adolescent Boys Base N = 8		
	Number using method (job search) at least once	Number finding job by this method	Number staying in job at least 9 mos.
Direct application to employer	4	2	1
Ask friends or relatives	8	8	3
Answer ads	1		
Inquire door-to-door in neighborhood households	2	1	
Check with employment service	1		
Use school placement service	2	2	2
Ask teachers			
Civil service exam			

Table 3.1 (Cont'd.)

Job Search and Job Finding Methods Used by Adolescent Boys and Girls

	Adolescent Girls Base N = 10		
	Number using method (job search) at least once	Number finding job by this method	Number staying in job at least 9 mos.
Direct application to employer	8	4	
Ask friends or relatives	2	2	1
Answer ads	2	1	
Inquire door-to-door in neighborhood households			
Check with employment service	2	1	
Use school placement service	3	3	3
Ask teachers	1		
Civil service exam	1		

as the company's advantage in being able to train him to
suit shop needs. It was Pat's[2] perception that the company
usually hired only those who had had some training in
appliance repair. However, Pat's brother, who was in
charge of placing orders for parts and keeping an
inventory, "talked them into hiring" Pat despite his lack
of previous training. Pat asserted that he "had learned a
lot in three months." He believed that one learns more on
the job because employers "teach you to do it their way."
Thus, good connections and trainability were perceived as
more crucial in the process of gaining and keeping a job
than prior related training and experience.

Another young male worker found a job as a materials
handler in an industrial fastener factory where his mother
had worked for 13 years. His employers readily
acknowledged that he was an attractive candidate for the
job because of his mother's employment, and also because
many other employees from his small rural town had
successful work records with the firm. For his part, Jerry
acknowledged his success in light of unfavorable economic
conditions and job shortages.

> Interviewer: When you were in high school, did
> you have a notion about what you wanted to do
> when you finished? Jerry: I didn't know what I
> was going to do when I got out. I had no idea.
> I kept hearing on the radio that there weren't no
> jobs. That puts you depressed. It surprised me
> that I got a job that quick. Really, I guess if
> it wasn't for mom and all those guys down at the
> Personnel Department, I wouldn't have got a job
> down here more than likely.
> Interviewer: You have a few friends there, I know.
> Jerry: All of those guys in that office--I know a
> lot of them, especially that one, Johnny
> Knight...He helped me out a lot. I think he
> pulled a lot of strings

Among the participants in this study, the young males who
had siblings or other relatives in the work force, or who,
like Jerry, had built reputations in the community through
their involvement in high school athletics, were more
likely than the young women to be successful in informal
job search strategies.

The females, on the other hand, often relied on more
formal, time-consuming, and generally less successful
routes to jobs. They were more likely than males in the
study to check with employment offices, to use school

placement services, or to take a civil service exam. Two
highly talented dancers were assisted by their schools in
locating auditions, which resulted in jobs at a large
entertainment complex similar to Disneyland. Two others
were assisted by participation in the Job Training
Partnership (JTP) program, a job assistance program
cooperatively administered by the federal government and
local businesses. They found clerical positions in a large
bank participating in the JTP effort. All four of them
remained in their positions for more than a year. However,
only the dancers saw their positions as representing
career-related opportunities.

Even though informal job search methods provide direct
access to employers and jobs, they were generally not
effective for the young women in the study. One of the
participants, Laurie, gave a painful account of an
ultimately unsuccessful job search that was not only costly
in her investment of time but that also caused her
considerable stress. The full text of her remarks is
included here because it reflects the anxiety and frequent
futility suffered by job seekers attempting to locate jobs
such as clerical positions for which employers appear to
demand evidence of commitment and past related experience.
Since young women were the frequent seekers of such
positions, they appeared to have experienced these kinds of
difficulties more frequently than boys.

> I have been at Skiff's warehouse so many times.
> Like I think I have been there so far like four
> times already. The first time I went it was just
> to fill out an application and to meet Bill
> Roberts, the guy in personnel, because they were
> interviewing Tom. . . [Laurie's boyfriend] and
> they wanted him to come back to the job, and at
> the time they also had a position open. So I
> went in and filled out an application and they
> said 'Well, you can go back in and fill out an
> application today.' So I said, 'Ok.' So I go
> back and he talks to me a little bit, and he
> doesn't have that much time to talk to me. So I
> go back and take a typing test, talk to him
> again. And then I go back and take another one
> and talk to another man. And so this is where I
> am today, waiting to see if I have a job. I am
> really scared because . . . it all depends on
> whether it is part-time or full-time. If it is
> part-time, it is just copying and making
> blueprints and all of this kind of stuff which

they know I can handle. But if it is a full-time
job, then it is a lot more typing. He told me
that I would have to take typing classes, and I
said, 'No problem.' So I have a feeling that
this girl ... [another applicant] is just a
little more qualified than I am. If they do pick
me it is just because they like me and they think
I will work for the company. They said 'We want
somebody who will grow in our company.' Now,
when he says that, that is really what gets me
scared. Because if you want someone to grow in a
company, you would think that they would want
somebody who is obviously better qualified and
they wouldn't have to go to school or anything
like that. But who knows, it is kind of an iffy
situation, but I have to prepare myself that I
might not get it.

Although Laurie's job-hunting activities included the
frequently effective job search method of direct
application on the basis of information obtained about the
job informally from her boyfriend, she was not hired by
this employer, and remained jobless for 9 months.

   With one exception, the young women whose informal job
search strategies resulted in obtaining work located
employment in fast food establishments, health spas, and
other industries characterized by rapid employee turnover,
little opportunity for advancement, and low level skill
demands. All but one of those locating these jobs remained
in their positions for six months or less.

   The exception to this general pattern was Betty, a
customer service representative at a large bank in Columbus
who found work through a friend employed at the same firm.
However, the conditions of her work led to considerable
dissatisfaction and a decision to leave the bank. During
the course of her work day, Betty handled between 20 and 26
calls per hour from bank customers requesting information
on their accounts which was available to Betty on
microfiche or through the bank's computerized system which
she operated.

   Although Betty's job demanded fairly extensive
clerical skills, her work was tightly regulated by
technology and by the bank's rigorous lateness and absence
rules. Betty perceived her employers to be strict and
lacking in trust. She observed: "Employees are assigned
to seats at work like in school. Employees are not
permitted to receive personal telephone calls, and
telephone lines are monitored."

Indeed, calls <u>were</u> unobtrusively monitored by
supervisors who explained, "In monitoring, we pick up
different things, such as the type of call, her answer to
the call, the timing, her voice, tone, the service she
gives. Then we have what we call a miscellaneous category
such as using correct procedures." This latter category
included gaining proper identification from the caller
before providing information on the account, maintaining an
"appropriate" number of pauses, and so forth.

Occupation and industry variables have an important
effect on job involvement and the likelihood of a young
person locating a position on a career ladder. In the
current study, jobs in the entertainment sector provided
workers with the clearest career trajectory. "Pounding the
boards" as a dancer at King's Island led to employment on
cruise ships, in night spots in Nevada, and for the
fortunate, in shows in New York City. At the other end of
the spectrum, least job involvement and career commitment
were fostered among workers in fast food restaurants or
large banking institutions who never saw themselves as
waitresses, busboys, or clerical workers, but rather saw
themselves in terms of other facets of their current lives.
For example, Betty, the bank worker, most closely
identified with her talents as a singer and light show
artist. Although she had received favorable performance
reviews, Betty quit her job after 8 months to pursue her
options in a rock band with which she had been performing
without much pay for more than two years.

Betty was well aware of both differential
opportunities for men and women to advance at the bank, and
differential enforcement of policies regulating employees'
hours and lateness. Fearing reprisals for requesting two
days off, Betty walked off the job one sunny spring
afternoon. In explaining her action, Betty characterized
management's interaction with the employees in the
following way:

> Betty: Before Bill quit a few weeks ago he had said,
> I'll work from 10:00 until 2:00 and that's it.' And he
> did it no problem. They scheduled him 10:00 until
> 2:00 every day. I imagine that if I were a guy they
> would do it for me.
> Interviewer: Why do you think your sex makes a
> difference?
> Betty: It does because at the bank, if you're a
> guy, you go places. You get out of the
> department. They pick you for management
> training. If you're a guy you don't need a

college education. If you are a girl, you need a
college education to go anywhere and even then
you don't go very far. The guys get treated well
in our department because they...[ie. management]
know they are going to go somewhere in the bank.
When you come into the department, they tell you
you'll get training to go far. What they don't
tell you is that...[those people] are all
guys...If you are a girl, they tend to give you a
bad review when you are trying to go to another
department in the bank.

Betty's perceptive account of the bank's sexist practices
were reflected in our observations of the uneven support
given to male and female employees in the large
institutional settings of our study. Few of our
participants, however, were as aware of differential
opportunities across an organization's departments as was
she.

Making the Transition to Work: The Importance of Family Support and Mentoring on the Job

The social context of young workers' job experiences
is largely defined by their relationships with family and
co-workers. Material and moral support from family members
and mentoring from co-workers or supervisors were crucial
in the successful transition to work experienced by
adolescents who stayed on the job for nine months or more.
Betty's shift from working in a bank as a customer service
representative to doing light shows for a band suggests the
importance of work relations and the strength of individual
values and personality in shaping the work experience of
young people. Personality and work-related behavior reflect
the social relationships formed and maintained during this
period.
In Betty's case, a change of jobs was associated with
a decision to set up housekeeping with her boyfriend, a
musician in the band for which she did light shows. This
decision was based on her increasing discomfort with living
conditions at home. Betty lived with her mother,
stepfather, younger sister and two older brothers. Since
all of them shared a single bathroom, Betty was forced to
get up at 5:00 AM to shower and prepare for work. However,
her biggest difficulty was her worsening relationship with
her stepfather.

Family difficulties impelled several participants in
the study to leave home to establish their own households
if financial circumstances allowed. However, not all
decisions to leave the family to set up independent living
arrangements were preceded by strained relations with
parents. Val and a close friend from high school, Mary,
got an apartment together immediately after Val found work
as a clerk in an insurance office. Her relationship with
her parents continued to be good. Not only did they supply
furnishings from their home to help the girls set up
housekeeping, but they maintained daily contact by
telephone to exchange news, provide guidance, and give
support. Although she was able to be self sufficient and
did not receive financial support from her parents, Val was
forced to modify her spending habits, as she indicates in
an interview:

> Interviewer: What do you need money for?
> Val: Clothes.
> Interviewer: Clothes. Okay. About how much money
> a month?
> Val: Uh, well lately it's about really cut in
> half... I'd probably say I spend between fifty
> and a hundred, depending on my financial status
> that month.

Val's household expenses included $75 for rent, about $40
for utilities, and about $75 for food each month. Her
roommate contributed the same amount in each category.
These expenses were considerably more than costs for room
and board paid to parents by the young workers who lived at
home. However, Val's earnings per month were considerably
higher than the average salary of $624. In fact her
monthly pay of $876 ranked second in the range of salaries
earned by young workers in the study, a range that extended
from a low of $141 to a high of $1296. Typically, those who
lived at home paid their parents about $100 per month for
room and board.

Though most of the young workers remained at home with
their families during this period, all of them talked about
moving out, and frequently complained about the burden of
remaining in the family. For example, John, who was often
unemployed and had no prospect of leaving home for some
time, expended time, money, and energy outfitting his room
with stereo equipment, carpeting, and other furnishings.
His parents assisted him by providing transportation to
pick up the carpeting, purchase the sound system, and so
forth. Yet, he believed his parents, and especially his

dad, "don't make no sense." His father had bought John a
22 rifle, but then had forbidden him to use it because, "It
would get scuffed up and look ugly in my dad's gun rack."
John felt he enjoyed no status in the household. He was
not allowed to use the kitchen after 6:00 in the evening
because his parents worked an early shift and were asleep
in a room adjoining the kitchen at that hour.

Moving away from home was a more important priority
than owning and driving a car or attending college or
vocational school for virtually all the young workers in
the study. Most remained financially or materially
dependent upon their families whether they lived at home or
not. Providing rides to and from work was one aspect of
this dependency. Clyde's father drove him around town to
apply for jobs, and Andy's financial contributions to the
household were made with the understanding that his mother
would give him a lift to work. None of the young women and
only three of the young men had cars. Two others had owned
cars previously, but had demolished them in accidents.
Some young workers rode the bus to work, a process that
took as long as an hour and a half one way. A few got
lifts from friends.

Relying on the family for material support was evident
in the "loans" parents and other family members provided.
They were always interest-free, and were most often paid
back, if at all, at the convenience of the debtor. Betty
borrowed money from a brother and from her mother. Her
brother was a source of support for large or "extravagant"
expenses. For example, he loaned Betty $1600 while she was
in high school to tour Europe with a singing group who
performed to raise money for the American Cancer Society.
The more typical loan was a much smaller amount for an
immediately needed item:

> Interviewer: What do you do with money you earn,
> and what do you do when you need money?
> Betty: Well, I borrow small loans from my
> mother. Like when I was sick, I needed $20 for
> bills. Sometimes my mom says to forget it.
> Other times she says she wants me to pay her
> back. If I need a lot of money, say to buy a
> guitar with, then I borrow that from my brother.
> He likes to get that money paid back as soon as
> possible. I pay for all my own makeup and
> clothes. Once in a while if my mom sees
> something I use on sale, she'll pick it up...like
> Noxema. She bought me this big jar.

Most loans and gifts came from family members and appeared to be extensions of provisions made to adolescent workers by adults still invested in their offspring or their kin's well being and upkeep. Borrowing money from adults who are "near-kin," such as the mothers of steady boyfriends or girlfriends, also occurred. For example, Andy owed his ex-girlfriend's mother money she had lent him to buy a car, a car he subsequently wrecked.

> Interviewer: Name the things and expenses that you spend money on.
> Andy: Cigarettes.
> Interviewer: Anything else?
> Andy: Bills.
> Interviewer: What kind of bills?
> Andy: I owe my ex-girlfriend's mother money, some money we borrowed to buy a car, and bills around the house.
> Interviewer: How much was the loan?
> Andy: Two hundred and fifty.
> Interviewer: How much do you pay her?
> Andy: I go weeks without paying. I give her $20 a week...when I do pay.

The financial support of family and individuals who were like family members was instrumental in allowing young people to begin to achieve some measure of autonomy, although paying back loans placed a lid upon personal mobility for those like Andy and Betty whose debts were large.

Inside the workplace, relationships with supervisors and co-workers were important to the young worker's job stability. Those young workers who consistently received high performance reviews and stayed on the job for longer periods than others usually developed close work relations with a mentor/supervisor. These relationships, however, were relatively rare, and seemed to evolve when supervisors possessed an unusually strong helping orientation to their young workers. Rod developed especially close emotional ties to the manager/owner of the coin and stamp store where he worked as salesperson and "management trainee" for more than a year. Rod was dismissed when his employer, Jim, discovered that he had stolen cash and articles from the shop over a period of two or three months. Jim maintained his friendship with Rod during the three-month period that Rod remained unemployed after being fired. Eventually, Jim hired Rod back, convinced that he understood the consequences of his actions and would not steal again.

Jim's support of Rod was undiminished despite his violation of his employer's trust.

Poor health, trouble with the law, or consumption of drugs and alcohol were the major individual factors associated with a poor transition to the workplace. Rod's pot smoking and drinking had escalated prior to his dismissal. Rod, however, was convinced that his habits had not been excessive:

> Interviewer: Do you think that you were doing more drugs or drinking than you ought to?
> Rod: Not really. Maybe, I was drinking one night and the next day I would be 15 minutes late for work and he would make a big deal out of it. But I tried to be on time after that. When I started making it on time, he started leaving that alone.

After getting fired, Rod couldn't afford to do much partying. However, he admitted to still drinking "pretty much," enabled by a fake ID to get into bars where he consumed as many as 16 drinks during the evening three or four times a week. He did begin to restrict his dope smoking: "It's just something like I don't wake up every morning and need to get high, you know. I used to. If somebody is smoking a joint, I can take it or leave it."

During the interval that Rod was unemployed, Jim acquired a second store, and was determined to give Rod another chance. Jim and Rod eventually reached an understanding, settling on a set of expectations for Rod. In turn, Rod was given the position of manager in one of the stores. Jim described the terms of their agreement in an interview during this period.

> Jim: I had to explain one thing to him. I said, 'Rod, you must not confuse me as your friend and as your boss. There are two different sets of circumstances.' I went into detail. I said that there are things that I will forgive you for doing as your friend, but the things that I cannot forgive as a permanent employee is drug- or alcohol- impaired performance...[and] drug- or alcohol-impaired learning ability...I cannot have you being late. Not only must you be here and learn, but you must also generate revenue...You are not peripheral any more. You are now in the core of decision making. You can do severe harm. There ain't no games any more. I am never going

> to allow you to endanger the corporation. This is
> where the limit is. You cannot be forgiven for
> that.
> Interviewer: You mean...[endanger] you, his boss?
> Jim: Well, it really rises above me, see,
> because I have a duty to perform. The duty is to
> go and to support my family, and if he endangers
> that base, I have no choice but to remove the
> danger, period.

In his conversations with Rod, as he described them in the
preceding passage, Jim defined his relationship with Rod as
complex but differentiated. Jim was his friend, but he was
also Rod's boss, and certain behaviors tolerated in the
context of his friendship were out of line in the work
setting. Moreover, Jim characterized the ethic governing
their relationship at work as grounded in his duty to his
family, above and beyond the responsibilities and
allegiances he might have in his role as Rod's boss.

In order to meet Jim's expectations before being
rehired, Rod was expected to give up dope. Jim issued a
firm set of guidelines, and a rationale to support his
expectations:

> I said, 'You have to choose by March 1, 1984--Do
> you want your marijuana, your booze, and your
> freedom? Then take it. But if you want to work
> here, then you must satisfy me that in the next
> three months, you are controlling your drugs.
> This is how I am going to judge--how you talk,
> how you behave, how you manage your personal and
> financial affairs, how you settle debts, and all
> that. I will watch how you are doing--how you
> solve your problems, how you make decisions, how
> you save money, how you think of the future...all
> this changes as you get off drugs.'

Rod cut back on his smoking by 75% according to his own
estimate, began to see new friends, particularly Sam, a
friend who had recently completed a rehabilitation program
for substance abuse and was now holding a job. Eventually,
Rod went back to work for Jim.

Although this case presented the most dramatic example
of a close mentoring relationship, like the others observed
in the study, the relationship was structured not simply to
foster and develop job skills in the novice, but also to
engender dependability and abiding loyalty and trust,
important job-related traits in the coin and stamp

business. All instances of mentoring were characterized by the same set of components. First, the mentor saw the success of the organization intimately tied to the success of the trainee. Second, the mentor took time "after hours" and usually outside the work setting to interact with the young worker socially. Third, the mentor encouraged the trainee to take on values similar to those of the mentor, as if the mentor saw the novice literally following along in his or her footsteps. Mentoring is a process only infrequently observed in the day-to-day operations of workplaces where youth are employed. It places extraordinary demands on the employer. When loyalty and dependability over a long period of time are not demanded by the nature of the work, however, they will not be nurtured in young workers. Most jobs held by adolescents demand a willingness to tolerate boredom, lengthy and tightly structured systems of rules, and little sustained personal contact with co-workers and supervisors.

CONCLUSION

Among the concerns surrounding the transition from school to work for youth seeking jobs after high school, the most immediate are finding a job, and then, once work is located, managing time and resources outside work and negotiating personal relationships, particularly with supervisors and co-workers inside the workplace. This and the following generalizations stem from the findings of the admittedly highly limited set of studies discussed in this chapter. Qualitative research, while restricted in its scope to a relatively small number of cases, does allow for close, extensive examination of critically important social processes.

In sum, results from the set of case studies reviewed here show that those who locate regular jobs to which they form commitments generally find work through close friends or relatives, while young workers who leave jobs after less than nine months find work through other means. Moreover, the young women in this study expended more energy in locating work, and more frequently had disappointing outcomes in their job search activities compared to the young male participants. Those adolescents who stayed on the job for more than 9 months had families to whom they could turn for advice and occasional monetary loans or gifts, while those who left jobs early tended to have antagonistic relations with their families. In addition, while those who stayed on the job for relatively longer periods of time usually had developed close work relations

with a mentor/supervisor, those who left jobs typically
failed to form such relationships.

While relationships with family members and co-
workers, especially supervisors, are crucial in easing the
school-to-work transition, the personality of the young
worker, and particularly the ascribed status accorded by
gender, also have a bearing on job finding and acclimation
to work. Poor health and drug and alcohol abuse were the
chief culprits in the failure of young men to make an easy
transition. However, at least in this sample, the young
men in each circumstance tended to be rescued by a caring
mentor or another job. The young women, none of whom had
problems of ill health or substance abuse, were simply less
likely to get good, career-related jobs in the first place.
Without rescuers, the only option was to quit and locate
other work. Thus, far from being a peripheral matter,
relationships with a supportive network of family and
supervisors appear to be critical for the labor market
success of young workers. Their lack of experience and the
distractions of life outside work make adolescents
especially vulnerable, particularly in work environments
which devalue their efforts.

NOTES

1. The work reported in this paper was sponsored by the
   National Institute of Education (Grant NIE-G-83-0005).
   Opinions expressed here do not necessarily reflect
   those of either NIE or the Department of Education.
   The author acknowledges the useful comments of Jeylan
   T. Mortimer on an earlier draft of this chapter.

2. The names of all participants (and persons referred to
   by the respondents) have been changed to protect their
   anonymity. All participants agreed to have their
   remarks quoted (anonymously) in publications from this
   study.

REFERENCES

Becker, H.J. 1977. How Young People Find Career-entry Jobs: A Review of the Literature. Baltimore, Md: Center for Social Organization of Schools, Johns Hopkins University.

Bishop, J., J. Brown, and K. Hollenbeck. 1983. "Recruiting Workers: How Recruitment Policies Affect the Flow of Applicants and Quality of Workers." Columbus, Ohio: The National Center for Research in Vocational Education, Ohio State University.

Borman, K.M. (ed.). 1984. The Adolescent Worker Study. Columbus, Ohio: The National Center for Research in Vocational Education, Ohio State University.

Borus, M.E. 1982. "Willingness to Work Among Youth." The Journal of Human Resources XVII:581-593.

Corwin, R. 1986. "Organizational Skills and the Deskilling Hypothesis." Pp. 221-243 in K. Borman & J. Reisman (eds.), Becoming a Worker. Norwood, N.J.: Ablex Publishing Corporation.

Dayton, C.W. 1981. "The Young Person's Job Search: Insights from a Study." Journal of Counseling Psychology 28:321-333.

Edwards, R. 1979. The Transformation of the Workplace in the Twentieth Century. New York: Basic Books.

Hollenbeck, K., and B. Smith. 1984. "Selecting Young Workers: The Influence of Applicants' Education and Skills on Employability Assessment by Employers." Columbus, Ohio: The National Center for Research in Vocational Education, Ohio State University.

Horvath, F.W. 1982. "Job Tenure of Workers in January 1981." Monthly Labor Review 105:34-36.

Jahoda, M. 1982. Employment and Unemployment: A Social-Psychological Analysis. Cambridge, England: Cambridge University Press.

Kalleberg, A., and K.A. Loscocco. 1983. "Age Differences in Job Satisfaction." American Sociological Review 48:78-90.

Kanter R.M. 1977. Men and Women of the Corporation. New York: Basic Books.

Miguel, R.J., and R.C. Foulk. 1984. "Youth's Perceptions of Employer Standards." Columbus, Ohio: The National Center for Research in Vocational Education, Ohio State University.

Mortimer, J.T., and R.G. Simmons. 1978. "Adult Socialization." Annual Review of Sociology 4:421-454.

Murphy, C., and L. Jenks. 1982. "Getting a Job: What Skills Are Needed?" In Research Brief. San Francisco: Far West Laboratory.

Piker, J. 1968. Entry into the Labor Force. Ann Arbor, Michigan: Institute of Labor and Industrial Relations, University of Michigan, and Detroit, Michigan: Wayne State University.

Reisman, J. 1985. "Quits and Firings Among Adolescent Workers." Paper presented at the American Sociological Association Annual Meeting, Washington, D.C.

Shapiro, D. 1983. "Working Youth." PP. 23-58 in M.E. Borus (ed.), Tomorrow's Workers. Lexington, Mass.: Lexington Books.

Sorrentine, C. 1981. "Youth Unemployment: An International Perspective." Monthly Labor Review 104:3-15.

Steinberg, L., E. Greenberger, M. Jacobi and L. Garduque. 1981. "Early Work Experience: A Partial Antidote for Adolescent Egocentrism." Journal of Youth and Adolescence 10:141-157.

Wielgosz, J., and S. Carpenter. 1984. "The Effectiveness of Job Search and Job Finding Methods of Young Americans." Chapter 3 of Pathways to the Future, Vol IV. Columbus, Ohio: Center for Human Resource Research, The Ohio State University.

Williams, T., and W. Kornblum. 1985. Growing up Poor. Lexington, Mass.: Lexington Books.

Part 2

The Influence of Work on the Psychological Development of Men and Women in Adulthood

Joanne Miller, Kazimierz M. Slomczynski,
Melvin L. Kohn

4. Continuity of Learning-Generalization: The Effect of Job on Men's Intellective Process in the United States and Poland

There is an accumulating body of evidence that job
conditions affect adult personality mainly through a
direct process of learning and generalization--
learning from the job and generalizing what has been
learned to other realms of life. People who do
intellectually demanding work come to exercise their
intellectual prowess not only on the job, but also in
their nonoccupational lives (Kohn and Schooler 1978,
1981; J. Miller, Schooler, Kohn, and K. Miller 1979);
they even seek out intellectually demanding activities
in their leisure-time pursuits (K. Miller and Kohn
1983). More generally, people who do self-directed work
come to value self-direction more highly, both for
themselves and for their children, and to have
self-conceptions and social orientations consonant with
such values (Kohn 1969; Kohn and Schooler 1969; Coburn
and Edwards 1976; Hoff and Gruneisen 1978; J. Miller et
al. 1979; Mortimer and Lorence 1979a,b; Slomczynski, J.
Miller, and Kohn 1981; Grabb 1981; Naoi and Schooler
1985; Kohn and Schooler 1983a). All these findings are
consistent with the theoretical expectation that
"transfer of learning" extends to a wide spectrum of
psychological functioning (Gagne 1968; see also Breer
and Locke 1965). The findings are also consistent with
the sociological premise that experience in so central a
domain of life as work must affect orientations to and

79

behavior in other domains as well (Marx 1964, 1971; Kohn
and Schooler 1973).

In this chapter, we ask whether learning-
generalization continues throughout men's working
lives. Recent work in developmental and social
psychology suggests that learning, particularly as
represented in "crystallized" (or synthesized)
intelligence, continues throughout the life-span (for
reviews and assessments of this literature, see Baltes
and Labouvie 1973; Horn and Donaldson 1980:
468-476; Baltes, Dittmann-Kohli, and Dixon 1984). In
principle, since "transfer of learning" is "an essential
characteristic of the learning process" (Gagne 1968:
68), not only initial learning but also the
generalization of what has been learned should continue
as workers grow older. It is nevertheless possible that
learning-generalization does not occur at the same rate
or to the same extent at all ages. The process may be
especially pronounced in younger workers, who are at
early stages of their occupational careers, before they
are preoccupied with family responsibilities, but may
diminish as workers grow older, advance in their
careers, and have changing family responsibilities. It
is also possible that either learning or generalization
diminishes as workers grow older, simply because of
biological decrements (Horn and Donaldson 1980:
476-481; Jarvik and Cohen 1973:227-234; but see
Labouvie-Vief and Chandler 1978; Riley and Bond 1983).
To see whether learning and the generalization of
learning continue unabated throughout adult life
requires an analysis of how job conditions affect the
psychological functioning of workers at different ages,
or stages of career, or stages of life-course.

In this chapter, we focus on what we regard as a
prototypic example of learning-generalization: the
relationship between occupational self-direction and
intellective process. By occupational self-direction we
mean the use of initiative, thought, and independent
judgment in work. We focus on occupational
self-direction--or, more precisely, the job conditions
that facilitate or inhibit the exercise of occupational
self-direction--because prior analyses have
demonstrated that the experience of occupational
self-direction is at the heart of what is learned from
the experience of work (Kohn and Schooler 1973, 1982).
We focus on intellective process because it offers a

clearcut instance of what we mean by learning-generalization: Thinking on the job is carried over to thinking off the job.

The analysis is cross-national: It examines the continuity of learning-generalization in two countries, Poland and the United States. For both Poland and the United States, we do separate analyses of job conditions and intellective process for younger, middle-aged, and older men. For each country, our analysis asks: Is the relationship of job to intellective process consistent for all three age-groups? Cross-national comparative analysis has the utility of ascertaining whether the findings in any one country are specific to the culture and to the economic and political system of that country. In an analysis of people of differing ages, there is the further advantage that even the "same" cohorts have had different experiences in different countries. When the two countries are Poland and the United States, we also have the opportunity of seeing whether the findings are consistent for a socialist and a capitalist society.

METHODS OF DATA COLLECTION AND CHARACTERISTICS OF AGE SUBSAMPLES

The original U.S. survey was based on interviews carried out in 1964 with 3101 men, representative of all men in the United States, 16 years of age or older, who were currently employed in civilian occupations. (For detailed information, see Kohn 1969, Appendix C.) These data provide the primary base for the U.S. analyses in this chapter. In addition, for analyses of the reciprocal effects of occupational self-direction and intellective process, we utilize a ten-year follow-up study of a representative subsample of 687 of those men originally interviewed (Kohn and Schooler 1983: Appendix A).

The Polish survey, conducted in 1978 with a sample of 1557 men, was an exact replication of the main parts of the original U.S. survey (Slomczynski et al. 1981). Questions pertaining to occupational self-direction were directly adopted from the U.S. study, while those pertaining to intellective process required some modification to provide cross-cultural equivalence. The Polish sample was a multistage probability sample, designed to represent men, aged 19 to 65, living in urban areas and employed in civilian occupations (Slomczynski et al. 1981).

In our analyses for both Poland and the United States, we distinguish three age groups: 30 years of age or younger, 31 through 45, and 46 or older. Given the age-distributions of our total samples, such a division is optimal for achieving subsamples of relatively equal size. If it were possible to do so, we would consider not only age, but also stage of career and stage of life course, both of which are defined by sequences of events rather than by chronology (Elder 1981).

From a historical perspective, the three Polish cohorts have had unique generational experiences. The majority of men in the oldest age-group completed their elementary educations before the Second World War, and entered the labor force before the rapid industrialization of the 1950s had begun. A critical experience for this generation was the Nazi occupation and, later, the Stalinist era, terminated by the national upheaval of the "Polish October" in 1956. Men in the intermediate age-group were just entering their adult lives in the mid-1950s; at the early stages of their occupational careers, they experienced the post-October economic and political stabilization, which ended with the students' protests in 1968 and the workers' revolt in 1970. The youngest group came of age under the relative prosperity of the Gierek regime, which started showing visible cracks in 1976 during the workers' riots.

Although both the middle and the youngest age-groups were educated in the common-school system introduced under the socialist regime, they differ with respect to their vocational preparation. The transition from more general to more specialized education experienced by these two age-groups paralleled the economic development of the country. Forced industrialization of the 1950s—when the majority of the middle age-group started to work—provided many new job opportunities for persons without specialized education. In contrast, the youngest group entered a more competitive labor market created by a declining rate of new industrial positions and a structural shift from the industrial to the service sector.

Since the U.S. men had been interviewed fourteen years before the Polish men, the experiences of all three U.S. age-groups are of a rather different historical era from those of their Polish counterparts. The oldest group (born in 1918 or before) had experienced the Great Depression and World War II as adults. The middle age-group (born between 1919 and 1933) includes both those for whom World War II was a childhood experience and those whose young adult lives were disrupted by wartime experience. The youngest men (born between 1934 and 1948) are essentially a post-World War II generation. As in Poland, educational requirements for many jobs increased greatly from cohort to cohort.

It is apparent that in distinguishing the same three age-groups for Poland and the U.S., we are in fact comparing age-cohorts from markedly dissimilar historical periods. This means that if we discover a different relationship between age and learning-generalization in the two countries, it will be difficult to assess precisely what explains the divergence. But if, in both countries, we find the effects of job conditions on intellective process to be similar for all three age-groups, this will provide powerful evidence for the continuity of learning-generalization.

MEASUREMENT OF INTELLECTIVE PROCESS

We examine two aspects of intellective process: ideational flexibility and authoritarian conservatism. These offer two distinct vantage points for looking at intellective process. Ideational flexibility is a measure of intellectual performance in the interview situation, reflecting the use of logical reasoning, ability to see both sides of an issue, and independent judgment. As such, it is a measure of how effectively a person uses his intellect in a relatively demanding situation; it is the thinking process, rather than the content of the task, that is at issue. Authoritarian conservatism, by contrast, is explicitly meant to measure the content of one's normative beliefs—namely, obeisance to authority and intolerance of nonconformity to the dictates of authority—rather than the process by which one came to hold those beliefs. Yet, authoritarian conservatism also reflects intellective process, for the opposite pole of

intolerance is openmindedness in one's orientation to
the social world (Kelman and Barclay 1963; Kohn 1969:
189, 201-203; Gabennesch 1972; Roof 1974; J.
Miller, Slomczynski, and Schoenberg 1981). By looking
at both ideational flexibility and authoritarian
conservatism, we assess the continuity of
learning-generalization with respect to conceptually
distinct, albeit closely related, aspects of
intellective process.

Ideational Flexibility

In analyzing both the U.S. and the Polish data, we
follow the strategy of measuring intellectual
flexibility that was developed in Kohn and Schooler's
(1978) longitudinal analysis of the U.S. data. We rely
on a variety of indicators--including men's answers to
seemingly simple but highly revealing cognitive
problems, their handling of perceptual and projective
tests, their propensity to "agree" when asked
agree-disagree questions, and the impression they made
on the interviewer during a long session that required a
great deal of thought and reflection. None of these
indicators is assumed to be completely valid, but we do
assume that all the indicators reflect, to some
substantial degree, men's flexibility in attempting to
cope with the intellectual demands of complex tasks. An
index based on such measures reflects men's actual
intellectual functioning in a nonwork situation that
seemed to elicit considerable intellectual effort from
nearly all respondents. Such an index also transcends
the criticism that "the perseverance of a youth-centric
...measurement of intellectual aging has demonstrated,
most conspicuously by its very existence, a serious gap
in age- and cohort-fair assessment" (Baltes et al. 1984:
36); our measures are decidedly not "youth-centric."
The original U.S. measurement model of
intellectual flexibility was based on seven indicators:

1. The Goodenough estimate of the respondent's
    intelligence (see Witkin et al. 1962), based
    on a detailed evaluation of the Draw-A-Person
    test;
2. The appraisal of Witkin et al. (1962) of the
    sophistication of body-concept in the Draw-A-
    Person test;

3. A summary score for his performance on a portion
   of the Embedded Figures Test (see Witkin et al.
   i1962);
4. The interviewer's appraisal of the respondent's
   intelligence;
5. The frequency with which he agreed when asked
   the many agree-disagree questions included in
   ithe interview;
6. A rating of the adequacy of his answer to the apparently simple cognitive problem: "What are
   all the arguments you can think of for and
   against allowing cigarette commercials on TV?"
7. A rating of the adequacy of his answer to
   another relatively simple cognitive problem,
   "Suppose you wanted to open a hamburger stand
   and there were two locations available.
   What questions would you consider in deciding
   which of the two locations offers
   a better business opportunity?"

In the Polish study, the last two questions have been
modified. Since there are no hamburger stands in
Poland, answering this question would require a
different level of knowledge by Poles than by Americans.
For this reason, "kiosk" (newsstand) was substituted for
"hamburger stand" in the Polish interviews, kiosks being
at least as familiar to Poles as are hamburger stands to
Americans. Similarly, "advertisement of goods" was
substituted for "cigarette commercials" as an equivalent
debatable issue. The pilot study, the field work, and
subsequent statistical tests indicate that Polish men
react to the modified questions much as do their
American counterparts to the original questions.
     The original U.S. model of intellectual
flexibility, a longitudinal model, contained two
underlying dimensions, one ideational, the other
perceptual. We cannot apply this instrument for
subgroup analyses of the Polish data, for in the Polish
study, both indicators of the perceptual dimension--the
Draw-A-Person Test and the Embedded Figures Test--were
administered to only a randomly chosen subsample of 400
men, too few to divide into three age-groups. We have
therefore developed measurement models for both Poland
and the United States using only those indicators that
are related to ideational flexibility (see Table 4.1).
Factor scores based on these one-dimensional models of

ideational flexibility correlate near unity with factor scores based on the ideational dimension of the two-dimensional models (for the United States, r=0.97; for Poland, r=0.96). This justifies using the simpler, one-dimensional model.

A rigorous test of between-group similarities should allow the possibility that men of differing age-groups vary in how their answers to the interview questions relate to the underlying concepts we wish to measure (Baltes and Labouvie 1973:174-176; Labouvie 1980). Thus, we construct separate measurement models of ideational flexibility for the three age-groups. The resulting models are very similar to each other, and to those for the total samples of both the United States and Poland (Table 4.1). All these models fit the data well, the chi-squares per degree of freedom ranging from 0.40 to 1.00. Such differences as do exist among age-groups in the relative strength of the paths from concepts to indicators are somewhat larger in Poland. To evaluate the extent to which these differences disturb the formal equivalence of measurement across age-groups, we developed three models for each age-group. The first is the best-fitting model for that age-group (as presented in Table 4.1); the others impose on a particular age-group the solutions for the other two age-groups. We then computed factor scores for each group from its best-fitting model and from the imposed models. The correlations between these factor scores range from 0.88 to 0.94, indicating that the idiosyncratic differences in measurement among age-groups are not of any great importance for causal analysis.

Authoritarian Conservatism

Authoritarian conservatism is measured by responses to questions assessing agreement or disagreement with statements advocating obeisance to authority or intolerance of nonconformity to authority. For both the United States and Poland, the indicators were selected from a set of 57 interview questions, including items taken from a short version (Srole 1956) of the California F-scale (Adorno et al. 1950) and from a scale of obeisance to authority (Pearlin 1962). Exploratory factor analyses of the U.S. and Polish data differentiated those items indicative of authoritarian

TABLE 4.1

MEASUREMENT MODEL OF IDEATIONAL FLEXIBILITY FOR THREE AGE-GROUPS: UNITED STATES AND POLAND
(Standardized Path: Concept to Indicator)

	U.S. Men (1964 Data)				Polish Men (1978 Data)			
	Age-Group				Age-Group			
	≤30	31–45	>46	All Men	≤30	31–45	>46	All Men
Reasons for location of a small business	.21	.29	.23	.30	.41	.49	.28	.32
Reasons for and against commercials on TV	.29	.36	.27	.32	.39	.29	.32	.31
Tendency to agree with agree-disagree questions	-.42	-.47	-.41	-.46	-.20	-.45	-.30	-.35
Interviewer's estimate of overall intelligence	.68	.66	.63	.64	.48	.43	.80	.61
Figures identified in Embedded Figures Test	.50	.56	.62	.60	.51	.62	.53	.58
N	711	1,209	1,171	3,101	452	575	530	1,557
χ^2/df	.83	.50	1.00	.42	.84	.40	.77	.57

conservatism from items indicative of other related
dimensions of orientation (Slomczynski et al. 1981). A
detailed, cross-national analysis comparing the
measurement instruments and their validity in each
country is presented in J. Miller et al. 1981 (see also
Schoenberg 1982). That analysis demonstrates that there
are both shared and nation-specific indicators of
authoritarian conservatism, but that the Polish and U.S.
indices of authoritarian conservatism are conceptually
equivalent, and thus can be used for comparative
analysis.

     We have constructed age-specific measurement models
for Poland and the United States, using the same sets of
indicators for all three age-groups as for the total
sample of that country. The patterns of responses for
the separate age-groups, presented in Table 4.2, show that
although there is some variation in the relative
importance of particular indicators in the several
age-groups, all indicators are statistically significant
for all groups. For each age-group, there is a good fit
of model to data, the chi-square per degree of freedom
ranging from 0.65 to 1.19. Correlations between factor
scores based on the best-fitting model for each
age-group and scores based on models imposed from other
age-groups are very high in both countries, ranging from
0.97 to 0.99. For both Poland and the United States, the
measurement of authoritarian conservatism is nearly
invariant across age groups.

MEASUREMENT OF OCCUPATIONAL SELF-DIRECTION

     Opportunities for occupational self-direction are
largely determined by the substantive complexity,
closeness of supervision, and routinization of the work
one does (Kohn 1969). For both the United States and
Poland, information about the substantive complexity of
work is based on detailed questioning of each respondent
about his work with things, with data or ideas, and with
people. These questions provide the basis for seven
ratings of each man's job: appraisals of the complexity
of his work with things, with data, and with people; an
evaluation of the overall complexity of his work,
regardless of whether he works primarily with data, with
people, or with things; and estimates of the amount of
time he spends working at each of the three types of

TABLE 4.2

MEASUREMENT MODEL OF AUTHORITARIAN CONSERVATISM FOR THREE AGE-GROUPS: UNITED STATES AND POLAND
(Standardized Path: Concept to Indicator)

	U.S. Men (1964 Data)				Polish Men (1978 Data)			
	Age-Group				Age-Group			
	≤30	31–45	≥46	All Men	≤30	31–45	≥46	All Men
The most important thing to teach children is absolute obedience to their parents*	.55	.73	.61	.65	.66	.66	.73	.73
In this complicated world, the only way to know what to do is to rely on leaders and experts†	.48	.48	.53	.52	.50	.46	.57	.53
It's wrong to do things differently from the way our forefathers did†	.50	.46	.43	.44	.48	.49	.35	.40
Any good leader should be strict with people under him in order to gain their respect	.41	.48	.50	.46	.48	.57	.60	.53
No decent man can respect a woman who has had sex relations before marriage	.28	.35	.38	.37	.39	.44	.40	.42
Prison is too good for sex criminals; they should be publicly whipped or worse†	.32	.44	.36	.39	…	…	…	…
Young people should not be allowed to read books that are likely to confuse them	.33	.44	.36	.44	…	…	…	…
There are two kinds of people in the world: the weak and the strong	.53	.54	.58	.62	…	…	…	…
People who question the old and accepted ways of doing things usually just end up causing trouble†	.55	.60	.48	.51	…	…	…	…
One should always show respect to those in authority	…	…	…	…	.50	.63	.65	.62
You should obey your superiors whether or not you think they're right	…	…	…	…	.50	.51	.55	.50
Do you believe that it's all right to do whatever the law allows, or are there some things that are wrong even if they are legal?†	…	…	…	…	.46	.44	.40	.42
N	711	1,209	1,171	3,101	452	575	530	1,557
χ^2/df	.89	1.19	.87	.68	.82	.92	.65	.72

* A high score on the indicator generally implies agreement or frequent occurrence; where alternatives are posed, the first alternative is scored high.
† Slight modification in wording of American question in the Polish interview.

activity. These seven ratings are treated as indicators
of the underlying construct, the substantive complexity
of that job.

In both studies, closeness of supervision is
measured by a worker's subjective appraisals of his
freedom to disagree with his supervisor, how closely he
is supervised, the extent to which his supervisor tells
him what to do rather than discussing it with him, and
the importance in his job of doing what one is told to
do.

We use slightly different measures of routinization
for the United States and Poland. For the United States,
respondents' work was coded from most variable (the work
involves doing different things in different ways and
one cannot predict what may come up) to least variable
(the work is unvaryingly repetitive). For Poland, we do
not include predictability in the index, since it adds
nothing to variability.

Age-specific measurement models of occupational
self-direction for each country are presented in Table
4.3. For each age-group, there is a good fit of model
to data, the chi-square per degree of freedom varying
between 0.72 and 2.78 for the United States and between
1.21 and 1.78 for Poland. The relative strengths of
indicators as measures of the underlying constructs are
similar for all age-groups, and all are statistically
significant. Correlations between factor scores based
on the best-fitting model for a particular age-group (as
presented in Table 4.3) and those based on measurement
models derived from the other age-groups are in all
cases near unity.

LEARNING-GENERALIZATION AMONG YOUNGER,
MIDDLE-AGED, AND OLDER MEN

The principal issue is whether the
learning-generalization process continues at more or
less the same rate throughout the lifespan. As
evidence of learning-generalization, we look to see
whether occupational self-direction affects intellective
process in the predicted direction. Doing substantively
complex work should result in greater ideational
flexibility and a more openminded orientation; close
supervision, by contrast, should diminish ideational
flexibility and be conducive to a rigid orientation;

TABLE 4.3

MEASUREMENT MODEL OF OCCUPATIONAL SELF-DIRECTION FOR THREE AGE-GROUPS: UNITED STATES AND POLAND
(Standardized Path: Concept to Indicator)

	U.S. Men (1964 Data)				Polish Men (1978 Data)			
	Age-Group			All Men	Age-Group			All Men
	≤30	31–45	≥46		≤30	31–45	≥46	
Substantive complexity:								
Complexity, work with data	.83	.85	.80	.82	.80	.89	.93	.87
Complexity, work with people	.76	.79	.75	.78	.86	.89	.87	.89
Complexity, work with things	.24	.21	.11	.25	.20	.27	.34	.25
Hours, data	.49	.47	.44	.44	.58	.62	.55	.59
Hours, people	.44	.44	.46	.43	.20	.27	.33	.29
Hours, things	-.63	-.59	-.56	-.58	-.59	-.66	-.63	-.64
Overall complexity	.85	.83	.84	.86	.79	.90	.88	.85
Closeness of supervision:								
Freedom to disagree with supervisor	.44	.46	.45	.46	.25	.32	.20	.26
Respondent's assessment of closeness of supervision	.73	.62	.64	.65	.53	.55	.54	.55
Supervisor tells respondent what to do	.64	.56	.58	.59	.57	.56	.45	.58
Importance of doing what one is told	.69	.60	.66	.65	.30	.47	.35	.40
Routinization:								
Variability/predictability of tasks	1.00	1.00	1.00	1.00	1.00	1.00	1.00	1.00
N	711	1,209	1,171	3,101	452	575	530	1,557
χ^2/df	.72	1.18	2.78	3.82	1.21	1.40	1.78	2.29

routinization might be expected to dull intellective
functioning.

Since the Polish data are cross-sectional, we
initially assume unidirectional effects of occupational
self-direction on intellective process. Under the
assumption of unidirectionality, we perform
multiple-regression analyses, treating ideational
flexibility and authoritarian conservatism as the
dependent variables in parallel analyses. The
conditions that facilitate or interfere with the
exercise of occupational self-direction (i.e., the
substantive complexity of work, routinization, and
closeness of supervision) are the principal independent
variables in both analyses. To statistically control
social characteristics that affect both job conditions
and intellective process--and thereby might result in
spurious effects of job on intellective process--we
include education and other pertinent social
characteristics as additional independent variables.

These analyses (see Table 4.4) clearly show that
occupational self-direction affects intellective process
in both countries. Overall, the multiple-partial
correlations of occupational self-direction and
ideational flexibility (education and other pertinent
social characteristics statistically controlled) are
0.39 for the United States and a strikingly similar 0.41
for Poland. The comparable multiple-partial
correlations of occupational self-direction and
authoritarian conservatism are 0.22 for the United
States and a somewhat higher 0.29 for Poland. Of
crucial importance for this analysis: the magnitudes of
the multiple-partial correlations are about as great for
the older as for younger and middle-aged men--in both
countries and with respect to both ideational
flexibility and authoritarian conservatism.

In both countries, the substantive complexity of
work has the greatest effect on ideational flexibility
of any of the three job conditions (see the standardized
regression coefficients), with closeness of supervision
adding appreciably to its impact in Poland and modestly
in the United States, and with routinization adding
modestly (but significantly) in the United States.
These findings are generally consistent for all
age-groups. For example, the standardized regression
coefficients for the substantive complexity of work are
consistently larger than are those for closeness of

TABLE 4.4

EFFECTS OF OCCUPATIONAL SELF-DIRECTION ON INTELLECTIVE PROCESS FOR THREE AGE-GROUPS: UNITED STATES AND POLAND (with Education and Other Pertinent Social Characteristics Controlled)[a]

| | U.S. Men (1964 Data) | | | | Polish Men (1978 Data) | | | |
| | Age-Groups | | | | Age-Groups | | | |
	≤30	31-45	≥46	All Men	≤30	31-45	≥46	All Men
	Unstandardized Regression Coefficients							
Ideational flexibility:								
Substantive complexity	.022*	.021*	.027*	.028*	.090*	.040*	.055*	.040*
Closeness of supervision	−.009	−.034*	−.006	−.017*	−.118*	−.146*	.016	−.102*
Routinization	.007	−.006*	−.004*	−.013*	−.005	−.018	.004	−.006
Authoritarian conservatism:								
Substantive complexity	−.134*	−.130*	−.099*	−.121*	−.053	−.023	−.052	−.082*
Closeness of supervision	.032	.048	−.041	−.009	.614*	.661*	.991*	.644*
Routinization	.021	−.005	.039*	.058*	.045	.030	.071	.046
	Standardized Regression Coefficients							
Ideational flexibility:								
Substantive complexity	.248*	.214*	.333*	.267*	.514*	.250*	.631*	.378*
Closeness of supervision	−.041	−.105*	−.025	−.053*	−.124*	−.159*	.021	−.142*
Routinization	.076	−.046*	−.044*	−.060*	−.016*	−.043*	.018	−.022
Multiple-partial correlation	.326*	.381*	.404*	.393*	.478*	.299*	.466*	.407*
Authoritarian conservatism:								
Substantive complexity	−.264*	−.216*	−.201*	−.225*	−.097	−.055	−.120	−.174*
Closeness of supervision	.025	.025	−.028	−.005	.209*	.273*	.257*	.203*
Routinization	.039	−.006	.066*	.051*	.045	.027	.067	.041
Multiple-partial correlation	.244*	.187*	.192*	.215*	.274*	.273*	.318*	.292*
N	711	1,209	1,171	3,101	452	575	530	1,557

[a] For Poland, the social characteristics are age, urbanness of place raised, and father's education and occupational status. For the United States, social characteristics are age, urbanness and region of place raised, religious background, race, national background, father's education and occupational status, maternal and paternal grandfathers' occupational statuses, and number of siblings.

* Statistically significant at $P \leq .05$.

supervision and routinization for all three age groups
in both countries. Moreover, the unstandardized
regression coefficients show that, in both countries,
the magnitude of the effect of substantive complexity on
ideational flexibility is about as large for the older
men as for younger and middle-aged men. The one respect
in which the overall findings for ideational flexibility
do not hold for all age-groups is that the effect of
closeness of supervision on Polish men's ideational
flexibility does not seem to hold for the oldest
age-group, men 46 years of age and older. (The findings
for authoritarian conservatism, though, belie any
thought that closeness of supervision ceases to be
important for intellective process in older Polish men.)
This one discrepancy notwithstanding, the results for
both the United States and Poland generally indicate
consistent effects of job conditions on ideational
flexibility for men of all ages.

As for authoritarian conservatism, in the United
States, substantive complexity again has the strongest
effect, with closeness of supervision of trivial
importance and routinization having a statistically
significant but only modest impact. In Poland, however,
closeness of supervision assumes greater importance, its
effect surpassing those of both substantive complexity
and routinization. In principle, close supervision
should increase authoritarian conservatism in both
countries. In the social and political circumstances of
Poland, closeness of supervision does result in
authoritarian conservative beliefs, but somehow, in the
social and political circumstances of the United States,
closeness of supervision is overshadowed in importance
by the substantive complexity of work and even by
routinization. We shall return, at least
speculatively, to this cross-national difference. It
must be emphasized, though, that both the U.S. and the
Polish findings are entirely consistent with the
learning-generalization hypothesis, the only issue being
the relative importance of the substantive complexity of
work and closeness of supervision for that process.

For this analysis, the focal question is whether,
within each country, the pattern of relationships
between job conditions and intellective process is
consistent for men of different ages. The findings for
both U.S. and Polish men vis-a-vis authoritarian
conservatism are generally consistent for younger,

middle-aged, and older men. Thus, the substantive complexity of work is of primary importance for authoritarian conservatism among U.S. men, albeit with somewhat diminished effect for the oldest men, for whom routinization has assumed increased importance. For Polish men, closeness of supervision has a statistically significant effect on authoritarian conservatism in all three age-groups, the magnitude of that effect being even greater among the oldest men than among younger and middle-aged men (see the unstandardized regression coefficients). Moreover, in all three age-groups, the effect of close supervision surpasses those of substantive complexity and routinization (see the standardized coefficients). Thus, the findings for authoritarian conservatism again show intra-nation, cross-age consistency.

The final finding of this analysis is decisive: The eighteen statistically significant regression coefficients are all consistent in sign with the learning-generalization hypothesis. We conclude that the effects of occupational self-direction on intellective process apply consistently to younger, middle-aged, and older men. This conclusion must be hedged, though, because our analyses have thus far been cross-sectional. The assumption of unidirectionality leaves open the possibility that our findings result not from job conditions affecting intellective process, but solely from intellective process affecting selection into and modification of job conditions. For example, if younger men have less choice of job and less control over their conditions of work, they may be especially reactive to job conditions; if older men have greater job security, they may have more opportunity to affect their conditions of work. To examine such possibilities, we turn to an analysis of reciprocal effects, which requires longitudinal data. These we have for the United States, but not for Poland.

LONGITUDINAL ANALYSES OF RECIPROCAL EFFECTS

The longitudinal analyses are based on a subsample of 687 men, representative of those men in the 1964 U.S. cross-sectional survey who were aged 26-65 at the time of the ten-year follow-up survey in 1974. For this analysis, we have divided the men into only two

age-groups, those 25 through 45 at the time of the
follow-up survey (N=282), and those 46 through 65 at
that time (N=405). We have deliberately used the same
cutting point, age 46, to define "older" men.

Measurement Models

The measurement models on which the longitudinal
analyses are based are similar to those previously
discussed for the cross-sectional analyses, the
principal differences being that the models are
longitudinal, using data from both 1964 and 1974, and
that we are able to use the original two-dimensional
measurement model of intellectual flexibility. We still
focus our attention on the ideational component. In
developing the longitudinal measurement models for older
and younger men, we followed as closely as possible the
models previously developed for all men in the follow-up
study (Kohn and Schooler 1982). We estimated the
models for younger and for older men independently,
retaining wherever possible the same parameters as in
the corresponding longitudinal model for all men, but
re-estimating the magnitudes of those parameters. In
general, the measurement parameters for all three models
--occupational self-direction, ideational flexibility,
and authoritarian conservatism--are very similar for
all men, younger men, and older men; moreover, the
parameters for the 1964 portions of the models are very
similar to those of the cross-sectional models presented
earlier in this chapter.

Causal Models

To identify the models, we treat all effects of
job conditions on intellective process and of
intellective process on job conditions as if
contemporaneous, using the cross-lagged effects as
instruments. This does not mean that we believe that
the effects of job conditions on intellective process
and of intellective process on job conditions are
necessarily contemporaneous. On the contrary, past
research (Kohn and Schooler 1978, 1982) suggests that,
although the effect of the substantive complexity of
work on intellective process is indeed contemporaneous,

the effect of intellective process on substantive
complexity is actually lagged. It is nevertheless
legitimate to use the cross-lagged paths as instruments
to assess the total effects of job
conditions on intellective process and the reverse.
(For a discussion of the rationale and also the dangers
of this procedure, see Heise 1975:184-185.)
Further identification is provided by allowing all of
the social characteristics that were included in the
cross-sectional analyses of the U.S. data (footnote 2)
to affect intellective process; only those social
characteristics (namely age, race, national and
religious background) that might be seen as credentials
for a mid-career job are allowed to affect current
occupational self-direction. To keep the analysis from
being needlessly complex, we deliberately do not model
the effects of job conditions on one another; instead, we
simply allow their residuals to be correlated. The
models thus enable us to assess the direct reciprocal
effects of job conditions and intellective process,
while statistically controlling the prior states of both,
as well as other pertinent variables.

A prototypic model of the reciprocal effects of
occupational self-direction and ideational flexibility
for the older men in the follow-up sample is presented
in Figure 4.1. In this and subsequent models, the
residual of each job condition is allowed to correlate
with that for intellective process if that correlation
proves to be statistically significant; otherwise, it is
fixed at zero. In this instance, the residuals of both
the substantive complexity of work and of routinization
prove to be significantly correlated with that for
ideational flexibility.

The most important findings of this analysis are
the substantial reciprocal effects of the substantive
complexity of work and ideational flexibility: The
substantive complexity of work decidedly affects
ideational flexibility, and ideational flexibility has
an even more decided impact on the substantive
complexity of work. The longitudinal analysis thus
strikingly confirms the main finding of the
cross-sectional analysis, that the substantive
complexity of work continues to affect the ideational
flexibility of older men, adding that older men's
ideational flexibility, in turn, affects both the
substantive complexity of their work and how closely
they are supervised.

98

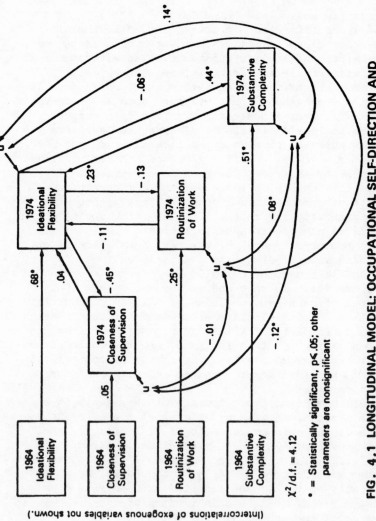

(Intercorrelations of exogenous variables not shown.)

$\chi^2/d.f. = 4.12$

• = Statistically significant, p ≤ .05; other parameters are nonsignificant

FIG. 4.1 LONGITUDINAL MODEL: OCCUPATIONAL SELF-DIRECTION AND IDEATIONAL FLEXIBILITY, OLDER U.S. MEN (Paths from social characteristics and "early" substantive complexity not shown)

Comparing this model to an exactly parallel model
for younger men (Table 4.5) shows that the reciprocal
effects of the substantive complexity of work and
ideational flexibility are not only as strong for older
as for younger men, but may even be stronger for older
men. (The unstandardized coefficients bear out what is
apparent in the standardized coefficients shown in Table
4.5: The unstandardized effect of the substantive
complexity of work on ideational flexibility, for
example, is 0.40 for older men and 0.06 for younger
men.) Since these models are based on relatively small
numbers of cases, and are not entirely robust under
alternative specifications, we are loathe to claim an
increased effect for older men, but certainly there is
nothing here to suggest a diminished effect.

Similar models for authoritarian conservatism
(again, see Table 4.5), estimated independently for older
men and younger men, are entirely consistent in showing
the undiminished, perhaps even stronger, effect of the
substantive complexity of work for older as compared to
younger men. As with ideational flexibility, the
relationship between the substantive complexity of work
and authoritarian conservatism, for both older and
younger men, is reciprocal. In the case of
authoritarian conservatism, though, the effect is
predominantly from substantive complexity to
authoritarian conservatism.

Thus, the models for both ideational flexibility
and authoritarian conservatism confirm the central
finding of the cross-sectional analyses--that the
impact of the substantive complexity of work on
intellective process continues unabated in older men.
As anticipated, the longitudinal analyses do show that
the effects of "earlier" intellective process are very
strong; these are highly stable aspects of personality,
ideational flexibility especially so. Nevertheless, the
longitudinal analyses strikingly affirm the causal
effects of occupational self-direction, most notably
that of the substantive complexity of work, on both
ideational flexibility and authoritarian conservatism in
older men. Job conditions contribute not only to change,
but also to stability (or maintenance) of personality.
The longitudinal models for older men demonstrate that
these processes continue to have their effects, with
undiminished--perhaps even greater--magnitude, well
into men's occupational careers.

TABLE 4.5

LONGITUDINAL ANALYSES: RECIPROCAL EFFECTS OF OCCUPATIONAL SELF-DIRECTION AND INTELLECTIVE PROCESS

	SUBSTANTIVE COMPLEXITY OF WORK		CLOSENESS OF SUPERVISION		ROUTINIZATION OF WORK	
	Path to Intellective Process	Path from Intellective Process	Path to Intellective Process	Path from Intellective Process	Path to Intellective Process	Path from Intellective Process
Ideational flexibility:						
Older men (46–65)	.23*	.44*	.04	−.45*	−.11	−.13
Younger men (26–45)	.19*	.34*	−.04	−.11	−.01*	.12[a]
All men	.23*	.48*	.03	−.32*	−.14*	−.09
Authoritarian conservatism:						
Older men (46–65)	−.33*	−.09*	...[b]	...[b]	−.02	.05
Younger men (26–45)	−.22*	−.15*	−0.04	.22*	−.02	−.02
All men	−.28*	−.09*	...[b]	...[b]	−.03	.01

NOTE.—For older men, $N = 405$; for younger men, $N = 282$.

[a] Estimate of this parameter uncertain. (The correlation of residuals is fixed at zero; allowing a correlation of residuals—as in the models for all men and older men—creates statistical anomalies.)

[b] Not possible to disaggregate correlation between closeness of supervision and authoritarian conservatism; modeled instead as a correlation of their residuals.

* Statistically significant at $P \leq .05$.

SUMMARY AND DISCUSSION

The main conclusion of this research is that job
conditions affect intellective process in older men just
as much as in younger men. In particular, job
conditions facilitative of the exercise of
self-direction in work continue to enhance ideational
flexibility and an open-minded, non-authoritarian
orientation, even in the oldest segment of the
workforce, that is, among men aged 46 to age 65. These
findings are shown both in cross-sectional and in
longitudinal analyses for the United States. For
Poland, cross-sectional analyses indicate that the
findings apply as well to that country. What makes us
confident, albeit not certain, that our conclusion
applies as well to Poland is the consistency of the U.S.
longitudinal and cross-sectional findings.

There is thus a notable continuity not only of
the effects of job conditions on intellective process,
but also of the effects of intellective process on job
conditions. Men continue to learn from their jobs and
to generalize those lessons to outside-of-job reality,
and men continue well into their careers to select and
to mold their jobs to fit their intellective
proclivities.

The one non-negligible, cross-national difference
applies to all age-groups. In the United States,
uniformly for younger, middle, and older men,
authoritarian conservatism is most strongly affected by
the substantive complexity of work. In Poland, however,
uniformly for younger, middle, and older men,
authoritarian conservatism is more strongly affected by
closeness of supervision. Any explanation of this
cross-national difference must refer not simply to the
characteristics of individuals, but to characteristics
of the countries in which these individuals live. Thus,
we ask which characteristics of the political and
economic systems and of the national cultures facilitate
the impact of closeness of supervision on authoritarian
conservatism in Poland, and deter its impact in the
United States? It seems to us likely that the societal
authority structures and culturally grounded reactions
to those structures may be crucially at issue. In
Poland, because of the predominant state bureaucracy and
the powerful Catholic church, the authority structure is
more salient than in the United States. It is in the

self-interest of both the state bureaucracy and the
church to support all those elements of traditional
Polish culture that encourage people at the bottom of
the social hierarchy to obey all forms of authority; the
work setting is no exception. In the United States, by
contrast, it is in the self-interest of those who have
institutionalized economic and political power to
de-emphasize even to deny, the existence of authority
structures. The impact of closeness of supervision on
authoritarian conservatism may be greater in Poland than
in the United States because Poles have a keener
awareness of and are more receptive to hierarchical
structure.

Finally, we can consider the findings of this
chapter from the perspective of what they tell us about
the generality of the effects of occupational
self-direction on psychological functioning. These
findings add to the body of evidence in support of the
generality of those effects (for a review of that
evidence, see Kohn and Schooler 1983b; Kohn 1983). We
have learned that occupational self-direction,
particularly the substantive complexity of work, has a
decided effect on ideational flexibility in Poland--a
new and important piece of evidence. More generally,
the findings tell us that the relationship between
occupational self-direction and intellective process
holds for six groups of men who have had decidedly
different generational and historical experiences. The
generality of the relationship is thus extended not only
with respect to age, but also with respect to diversity
of experience.

NOTES

1. Earlier versions of this chapter were presented
to the World Congress of the International Sociological
Association (Mexico City, August 1982) and the Annual
Convention of the American Sociological Association (San
Francisco, September 1983). The Polish survey was
carried out under the auspices and with the financial
support of the Polish Academy of Sciences. We are
indebted to Wlodzimierz Wesolowski, who initiated the
Polish study and encouraged the investigators throughout
the inquiry; to Krystyna Janicka and Jadwiga
Koralewicz-Zebik for collaboration in the design and

administration of the Polish survey; to Bruce Roberts, Margaret Renfors, and Diane Mueller for conscientious and thoughtful research assistance; to Virginia Marbley for effectively and uncomplainingly transcribing many revisions of this paper; and to Carrie Schoenbach, Karen A. Miller, Carmi Schooler, Ronald Schoenberg, Matilda Riley, Paul Baltes, Jeylan T. Mortimer, and John A. Clausen for critical readings of earlier versions of this paper. The models in this paper were estimated by MILS, an advanced version of LISREL (Joreskog and van Thillo 1972) developed by Ronald Schoenberg. Requests for reprints should be sent to Miller/Slomczynski/Kohn, Building 31, Room 4C-11, National Institutes of Health, Bethesda, MD 20205.

2. For the United States, the pertinent social characteristics are age, urbanness and region of place raised, race, religious and national backgrounds, mother's and father's educational levels, father's occupational status, maternal and paternal grandfathers' occupational statuses, and number of siblings. Some of the social characteristics in the U.S. analysis are omitted from the Polish analysis because they are nearly invariant in the culturally more homogeneous Polish society (namely, race, religious background, and national background), and others are omitted because the pertinent information was not collected. The social characteristics included in the Polish analysis are age, urbanness of place raised, father's educational level, and father's occupational status.

3. One might think that closeness of supervision is more pertinent to authoritarian conservatism in Poland than in the United States, because the indicators of authoritarian conservatism specific to Poland emphasize the centrality of authority relations (see Table 4.2). But if we repeat the multiple-regression analyses, using indices of authoritarian conservatism based on the same questions in both countries, the cross-national difference persists.

4. Both occupational self-direction and cognitive functioning are generated by dynamic processes. It has been shown (Schoenberg 1977) that a static model of what, in reality, is an underlying dynamic process will underestimate the parameters, but will not otherwise be misleading.

104

REFERENCES

Adorno, T. W., Else Frenkel-Brunswik, Daniel J. Levinson, and R. Nevitt Stanford. 950. The Authoritarian Personality. New York: Harper.

Baltes, Paul B., Freya Dittmann-Kohli, and Roger A. Dixon. 1984. "New Perspectives on the Development of Intelligence in Adulthood: Toward a Dual-Process Conception and a Model of Selective Optimization with Compensation." Pp. 33-76 in Paul B. Baltes and Orville G. Brim (eds.), Life-Span Development and Behavior. New York: Academic Press.

Baltes, Paul B., and Gisela V. Labouvie. 1973. "Adult Development of Intellectual Performance; Description, Explanation, and Modification." Pp. 157-219 in Carl Eisdorfer and M. Powell Lawton (eds.), The Psychology of Adult Developmemt and Aging. Washington, D.C: American Psychological Association.

Breer, Paul E., and Edwin A. Lock. 1965. Task Experience as a Source of Attitudes. Homewood, Ill.: The Dorsey Press.

Coburn, David, and Virginia L. Edwards. 1976. "Job Control and Child-Rearing Values." Canadian Review of Sociology and Anthropology 13(3):337-344.

Elder, Glen H., Jr. 1981. "Social History and Life Experience." Pp. 3-31 in Dorothy H. Eichorn, John A. Clausen, Norma Haan, and Marjorie P. Honzik (eds.), Present and Past in Middle Life. New York: Academic Press.

Gabennesch, Howard. 1972. "Authoritarianism as World View." American Journal of Sociology 77(March):857-875.

Gagne, Robert M. 1968. "Learning: Transfer." Pp. 168-173 in David I. Sills (ed.), International Encyclopedia of the Social Sciences, Vol. 9. New York: Macmillan and Free Press.

Grabb, Edward G. 1981. "The Ranking of Self-Actualization Values: The Effects of Class, Stratification, and Occupational Experiences." The Sociological Quarterly 22(Summer):373-383.

Heise, David R. 1975. Causal Analysis. New York: John Wiley & Sons.

Hoff, Ernst-Hartmut, and Veronika Gruneisen. 1978. "Arbeitserfahrungen, Erziehungseinstellungen, und Erziehungsverhalten von Eltern." Pp. 65-89 in H. Lukesch and K. Schneewind (eds.), Familiare Sozialisation: Probleme, Ergebnisse, Perspektiven. Stuttgart: Klett-Cotta.

Horn, John L., and Gary Donaldson. 1980. "Cognitive Development in Adulthood." Pp. 445-529 in Orville G. Brim and Jerome Kagan (eds.), Constancy and Change in Human Development. Cambridge, Mass.: Harvard University Press.

Jarvik, Lissy F., and Donna Cohen. 1973. "A Behavioral Approach to Intellectual Changes with Aging." Pp. 220-280 in Carl Eisdorfer and M. Powell Lawton (eds.), The Psychology of Adult Development and Aging. Washington, D.C: American Psychological Association.

Joreskog, Karl G., and Marielle van Thillo. 1972. "LISREL: A General Computer Program for Estimating a Linear Structural Equation System Involving Multiple Indicators of Unmeasured Variables." Research Bulletin 72-56. Princeton, N.J.: Educational Testing Service.

Kelman, Herbert C., and Janet Barclay. 1963. "The F Scale as a Measure of Breadth of Perspective." Journal of Abnormal and Social Psychology 67 (December):608-615.

Kohn, Melvin L. 1969. Class and Conformity: A Study in Values. Homewood, Ill.: The Dorsey Press. (Second edition, 1977, published by the University of Chicago Press.)

-----. 1983. "Unresolved Interpretive Issues." Pp. 296-312 in Melvin L. Kohn and Carmi Schooler, Work and and Personality: An Inquiry into the Impact of Social Stratification. Norwood, N.J.: Ablex Publishing Corporation.

Kohn, Melvin L., and Carmi Schooler. 1969. "Class, Occupation, and Orientation." American Sociological Review 34(October):659-678.

-----. 1973. "Occupational Experience and Psychological Functioning: An Assessment of Reciprocal Effects." American Sociological Review 38 (February):97-118.

-----. 1978. "The Reciprocal Effects of the Substantive Complexity of Work and Intellectual Flexibility: A Longitudinal Assessment." American Journal of

Sociology 84(July):24-52.
-----. 1981. "Job Conditions and Intellectual
Flexibility: A Longitudinal Assessment of their
Reciprocal Effects." Pp. 281-313 in David J.
Jackson and Edgar F. Borgatta (eds.), Factor
Analysis and Measurement in Sociological Re-
search: A Multi-Dimensional Perspective.
London: Sage.
-----. 1982. "Job Conditions and Personality: A
Longitudinal Assessment of their Reciprocal Effects."
American Journal of Sociology 87(May):1257-1286.
-----. 1983a. Work and Personality: An Inquiry into
the Impact of Social Stratification. Norwood, N.J.:
Ablex Publishing Corporation.
-----. 1983b. "The Cross-National Universality of the
Interpretive Model." Pp. 281-295 in Melvin L. Kohn and
Carmi Schooler, Work and Personality: An Inquiry
into the Impact of Social Stratification. Norwood,
N.J.: Ablex Publishing Corporation.
Labouvie, Erich W. 1980. "Identity Versus Equivalence
of Psychological Measures and Constructs." Pp. 493-502
in Leonard W. Poon (ed.), Aging in the 1980s:
Psychological Issues. Washington, D.C.: American
Psychological Association.
Labouvie-Vief, Gisela, and Michael J. Chandler. 1978.
"Cognitive Development and Life-Span Developmental
Theory: Idealistic Versus Contextual Perspectives."
Pp. 181-210 in Paul B. Baltes (ed.), Life-Span
Development and Behavior, Volume 1, New York: Academic
Press.
Marx, Karl. 1964. Early Writings. Edited and trans-
lated by T. B. Bottomore. New York: McGraw-Hill.
-----. 1971. The Grundrisse. Edited and translated by
David McLennan. New York: McGraw-Hill.
Miller, Joanne, Carmi Schooler, Melvin L. Kohn and
Karen A. Miller. 1979. "Women and Work: The Psycho-
logical Effects of Occupational Conditions." American
Journal of Sociology 85(July):66-94.
Miller, Joanne, Kazimierz M. Slomczynski, and Ronald J.
Schoenberg. 1981. "Assessing Comparability of
Measurement in Cross-National Research: Authoritar-
ian-Conservatism in Different Sociocultural Settings."
Social Psychological Quarterly 44(September):178-191.
Miller, Karen A., and Melvin L. Kohn. 1983. "The
Reciprocal Effects of Job Conditions and the Intel-

lectuality of Leisure-Time Activities." Pp. 217-241
in Melvin L. Kohn and Carmi Schooler, Work and
Personality: An Inquiry into the Impact of Social
Stratification. Norwood, N.J.: Ablex Publishing
Corporation.

Mortimer, Jeylan T., and Jon Lorence. 1979a. "Work
Experience and Occupational Value Socialization: A
Longitudinal Study." American Journal of Sociology
84(May):1361-1385.

------. 1979b. "Occupational Experience and the Self-
Concept: A Longitudinal Study." Social Psychology
Quarterly 42 (December):307-323.

Naoi, Atsushi, and Carmi Schooler. 1985. "Occupational
Conditions and Psychological Functioning in Japan."
American Journal of Sociology 90(January):729-752.

Pearlin, Leonard I. 1962. "Alienation from Work: A
Study of Nursing Personnel." American Sociological
Review 27(June):314-326.

Riley, Matilda White, and Kathleen Bond. 1983. "Beyond
Ageism: Postponing the Onset of Disability." Pp. 243-
252 in Matilda White Riley, Beth B. Hess and Kathleen
Bond (eds.), Aging in Society: Selected Reviews of
Recent Research. Hillsdale, N.J.: Lawrence Erlbaum
Associates.

Roof, Wade Clark. 1974. "Religious Orthodoxy and
Minority Prejudice: Causal Relationship or
Reflection of Localistic World View?" American
Journal of Sociology 80(November):643-664.

Schoenberg, Ronald. 1977. "Dynamic Models and Cross-
Sectional Data: The Consequences of Dynamic Misspec-
ification." Social Science Research 6(June):133-144.

------. 1982. "Multiple Indicator Models: Estimation
of Unconstrained Construct Means and their Standard
Errors." Sociological Methods & Research 10(May):
421-433.

Slomczynski, Kazimierz M., Joanne Miller, and Melvin L.
Kohn. 1981. "Stratification, Work, and Values: A
Polish-United States Comparison." American Socio-
logical Review 46(December):720-744.

Srole, Leo. 1956. "Social Integration and Certain
Corollaries: An Exploratory Study." American
Sociological Review 21(December):709-716.

Witkin, H. A., R. B. Dyk, H. F. Faterson,
D. R. Goodenough, and S. A. Karp. 1962. Psycho-
logical Differentiation: Studies of Development.
New York: Wiley.

Jeylan T. Mortimer, Michael D. Finch,
Geoffrey Maruyama

5. Work Experience and Job Satisfaction: Variation by Age and Gender[1]

What has come to be called the "fit hypothesis" is a central organizing principle in much of the vast literature on job satisfaction (Locke 1976). According to this hypothesis, the essential meaning of job satisfaction lies in the "fit" or congruence of the worker and the job. Workers are expected to respond differently to their job experiences depending on their particular needs, prior experiences, and orientations to work, and these will be determined largely by their structural locations in society. This perspective stresses the differences in how workers react to their jobs, and the preponderant importance of these variations in influencing their satisfaction and dissatisfaction with work. The compatibility of external work features and individual characteristics is thus considered to be the central determinant of job satisfaction.

While the fit hypothesis is quite plausible, there is another reasonable point of view. According to the major alternative perspective in the job satisfaction literature, the features of work itself are of preeminent importance as causes of job satisfaction; the attributes of the individual are said to make little difference. That is, certain attributes of work are universally satisfying or dissatisfying irrespective of the particular incumbents of the job. For example, Herzberg et al. (1959) have argued that only "motivators," or features of work that are intrinsically gratifying, generate job satisfaction, without adding any qualifications with regard to the characteristics of workers. Consistent with this position, Kohn and Schooler's (1973) research has shown that the components of what they call "occupational self-direction" had the

strongest effects on job satisfaction when several other
important features of jobs were controlled (see also
Gurin et al. 1960), and these effects were not contingent
on worker values. Considerable evidence documents the
importance of autonomy and "job scope" for satisfaction
(Shepard 1973; Stone 1976; Tannenbaum et al. 1974;
Seashore and Taber 1975; Locke 1976). Still, Herzberg's
thesis cannot be said to be fully confirmed. There is
impressive evidence that pay and other extrinsic concerns
are also of importance in fostering job satisfaction and
dissatisfaction (Locke, 1976:1323; Fein 1976; Strauss
1974a and b; Tannenbaum et al. 1974; Voydanoff 1978).

This chapter investigates whether there are
differences in the determinants of job satisfaction
depending on the age and sex of the worker. Age and
gender are two of the most central bases of social
structural differentiation (Linton 1936). The prior
experiences of men and women and persons of different
age, as well as their current situations, could foster
distinctive outlooks, values, and needs, which could
generate variant reactions to the very same work
experiences. We will consider whether age and gender
interact with work experiences in influencing job
satisfaction.

The relationship between job satisfaction and age
has become an increasingly popular focus of attention
(Wright and Hamilton 1978; Janson and Martin 1982;
Kalleberg and Loscocco 1983; Glenn and Weaver 1985),
partly because of its pertinence to major theoretical
issues in social psychology. The extent to which
individual psychological attributes remain the same or
change through the course of life is of central
importance in the study of life span development (Brim
and Kagan 1980). Are people equally responsive in
different phases of their lives to the impacts of
environmental conditions, such as those encountered at
work? There is evidence that external forces have the
strongest implications for personal change immediately
after the acquisition of new social roles (Van Maanen and
Schein 1979; Hall 1971; Nicholson 1984). According to the
"aging stability hypothesis" (Glenn 1980), individual
attitudes become more stable with age. This increasing
attitudinal constancy may be partially attributable to
the fact that the social environment also is typically
less likely to change as people grow older (at least
until the transitions of later life, such as retirement
and the death of a spouse). As people move through the

periods of youth and middle age, they become less likely
to have to adapt to roles and social conditions that are
new and unfamiliar to them. Their attitudes therefore
become more stable. If this is the case, differences in
job conditions at any given time might be expected to
have stronger impacts on psychological change for younger
workers--those who are relatively new to the occupational
role--than for older workers who have occupied it for a
longer period of time. Therefore, we might find
increasing stability in job satisfaction with age, with
occupational conditions having diminishing effects on
such satisfaction with longer experience on the job or
with longer tenure in the workforce.

Increasingly, however, development is seen "as a
life-long process" (Baltes et al. 1980:70), with great
potential for change and redirection even in the later
years of life (Brim and Ryff 1980). If people remain
equally responsive to occupational conditions throughout
their lives, no matter how long these conditions have
been experienced, one might expect to find that work
experiences will have the same effects on job
satisfaction irrespective of length of time in the work
force.[2] If such experiences are stable over time, and
continue to have constant effects on attitudes through
the work life, the degree of stability of job
satisfaction would likely be constant across age groups.

Alternatively, the associations between occupational
conditions and psychological variables might even become
stronger as people grow older. Encountering a persistent
work environment over a long period of time could
engender an increasing, cumulative psychological effect.
Frese (1984) refers to this possibility as the "exposure
time position." If work experiences were to have a
stronger influence on the satisfaction of older than
younger workers, the stability of this psychological
dimension might even decline as workers age.

But despite the enormous literature on job
satisfaction (see Locke 1976; and Mortimer 1979 for
reviews), empirical data that could be used to examine
these possibilities are lacking. Very little attention
has been given to the stability of job satisfaction over
time among persons of different age, or to the differing
levels of psychological responsiveness of age groups to
the varying conditions and rewards of their work (for an
exception, see Lorence and Mortimer 1985).

There is another reason to expect that younger and
older workers would react differently to their jobs. Age

could affect the ways people respond to their jobs,
because it is such a central marker of life circumstances
and needs. In fact, age has been found to be associated
with different patterns of occupational reward values,
with younger workers, faced with the prospect of
increasing financial need as their families grow,
stressing promotional opportunities. Older workers place
greater emphasis on retirement benefits and interpersonal
relationships in the workplace (Wright and Hamilton
1978). Kalleberg and Loscocco (1983) report that both
financial and intrinsic values are stronger in younger
age groups, perhaps resulting from the disinctive life
experiences of the "baby boom" cohort. Given these value
differences, one might expect to find that the job
satisfaction of older workers is less responsive than
that of younger workers to both income and the intrinsic
rewards of jobs. Janson and Martin (1982) report that
while the effects of intrinsic rewards on job
satisfaction decline with age, extrinsic rewards have the
same effects across age groups. Cohn (1979), however,
using a different data set, finds that age neither
interacts with the intrinsic nor the extrinsic qualities
of jobs in predicting satisfaction.

There is also reason to believe that there will be
gender differences in the determinants of job
satisfaction. Of foremost importance, men and women have
been exposed to distinctive socialization experiences
which could foster different reactions to experiences in
the work setting. Whereas young women are increasingly
expecting to combine family and work roles (Regan and
Roland 1982), in the past, they have been led to
deemphasize and underestimate their future participation
in the labor force (Sexton 1977). Adolescent girls'
gender role socialization, oriented to their future
family roles as wives and mothers, greatly influences
their occupational decision making (Aneshensel and Rosen
1980). Women's commitment to these family roles
generates role conflicts and difficulties in accomodating
to the requirements of the work role (Laws 1976; Osipow
1975; Card et al. 1980; Falk and Cosby 1978). Women's
family situations are still of predominant importance in
determining their work behavior, as marriage and
especially children disrupt the continuity of their labor
force participation and encourage part-time work (Card et
al. 1980; Sewell et al. 1980; Falk and Cosby 1978;
Felmlee 1984; Moen 1985).
Recent time-use studies show that employed women

still hold major responsibility for housework and childcare (see, for example, Pleck and Rustad 1980). Part time and intermittent work experience are commonly used by employed women to accommodate to their families' demands (Felmlee 1984; Moen 1985). These considerations point to the hypothesis that women's work orientations, including their job satisfaction, may be substantially determined by the compatibility of their work with family needs. Andrisani (1978) has reported that a negative husband's attitude has a significant depressant effect on the wife's job satisfaction. Quinn et al. (1974) find that the presence of a preschool-age child similarly dampens women's job satisfaction. If women's work orientations are substantially affected by family variables such as these, it might be the case that women's job satisfaction is less responsive than that of men to important features of work like autonomy and extrinsic rewards.

Consistent with this hypothesis, significant gender differences in work values have been reported. Women have been found to place greater importance than men on hours of work and travel time from home, which can make work more compatible with family responsibilities (Quinn et al. 1974). Miller (1980) reports that job pressures, how tiring the work is, and hours are more salient occupational concerns for women, whereas men stress factors relating to positional authority (leadership, opportunities for advancement, and decision-making ability).

However, such value differences do not necessitate that men and women will have distinctive responses to their experiences in the work setting. Miller (1980) reports that the work values of men and women are generally very much alike. That is, in her study, there were no significant gender differences in the importance of pay, fringe benefits, opportunities for interesting and exciting work, and several other value dimensions. Kanter (1976, 1977) expects similarities, not differences between women and men, in the causal processes by which work influences psychological functioning. She and others (see, for example, Weaver 1978) have argued that differences in work experiences, not unique socialization experiences or special nonwork situations, account for gender differences in work attitudes. According to Kanter, the most important determinants of attitudes in the work setting are opportunity, power, and the proportional representation of women. Though women's

disadvantages with respect to opportunity and power--and
their minority status in male-dominated occupational
positions--often foster distinctive orientations to work,
Kanter's research in a large firm indicates that employed
men and women respond quite similarly when they encounter
the same job conditions. Weaver (1978), using data from
three National Opinion Research Center surveys
(1972-1974), finds that occupational prestige and work
autonomy have about the same predictive power with
respect to the job satisfaction of men and women.

Similarly, Miller (1980) found no evidence that
women's job satisfaction is less responsive to work
experiences than that of men, though some particular
features of work differed, by sex, in the extent to which
they fostered job satisfaction. In her study of a
nationwide panel of male workers and their wives, the
substantive complexity of work and job pressures were
more potent determinants of women's satisfaction.
Consistent with their higher evaluation of factors
related to positional authority, closeness of supervision
was of greater significance for men's satisfaction.
(Glenn and Weaver 1982 also report that job authority,
defined by the supervision of others, and job autonomy,
defined by the lack of a supervisor for oneself,
significantly predicted men's, but not women's, job
satisfaction when they pooled data from four NORC surveys
from 1974 to 1980.) But Miller concluded, in view of the
many features of work that were considered in her study,
that the reactions of men and women to their jobs are
very much the same.

Martin and Hanson (1985), using cross-sectional data
from the 1972-3 Quality of Employment Survey, also
examined gender differences in the determinants of job
satisfaction. They compared men with women separated
into two groups, depending on the importance of their
work for their families' economic sustenance: women whose
income is the primary means of support for the family
(who they call "breadwinning women"), and women whose
income only supplements that of the primary breadwinner
("nonbreadwinning women"). In addition to constructs
representing extrinsic and intrinsic rewards, they
studied a third factor, related to the "comfort" and
"convenience" features of work. This factor encompassed
a range of issues: ease of travel, good hours, pleasant
physical surroundings, absence of excessive work and
conflicting demands, having enough time to complete
tasks, and being able to forget personal problems while

at work. It had a significant effect on job satisfaction
only among the nonbreadwinning women. For those women,
the compatibility of their work with the needs of their
husbands and children is apparently a highly salient
concern. Because their employment may be considered the
most discretionary, they may be freer than other employed
wives and mothers to be actively concerned with this set
of issues, and to act on these concerns.

We have thus far examined some of the evidence related
to gender and age differences in the effects of work
experiences on job satisfaction, considering each
variable separately, as they have been treated in prior
studies. But given the cross-cutting nature of age and
sex, the situation is undoubtedly more complex. We must
consider the possibility that there are differences in
the determination of job satisfaction among men, as well
as women, of different ages. That is, age and sex might
reasonably be expected to interact with job conditions in
producing satisfaction. For example, young women, given
the fact that peak domestic responsibilities occur in the
early, child-bearing phase of the family life cycle, may
have quite different orientations to work, and responses
to the job, than young men. As family and work roles
become less conflictive for women as their children grow
older, the reactions of older men and women to their jobs
might perhaps become more similar.

While our research is mainly concerned with the
determinants of job satisfaction, most prior
investigations have been preoccupied with level
differences. That is, does job satisfaction increase or
decline with age? How do men and women compare in their
levels of job satisfaction? Groups defined by age and
gender may be considered "strata," with unequal access to
occupational rewards of both an intrinsic and extrinsic
character (see Riley 1985; Mortimer and Sorensen 1984).
In view of these differences, it becomes important to
ascertain whether the subjective gratification of work is
likewise unequally distributed.

Studies of the mean trend generally show that job
satisfaction is greater among older workers (Quinn et al.
1974; Campbell et al. 1976; Kalleberg 1977; Schwab and
Heneman 1977; Janson and Martin 1982; Rhodes 1983).
Kalleberg and Loscocco (1983) identify a curvilinear
trend within a general upward pattern--job satisfaction
increasing to age 40, leveling off and fluctuating until
the mid-fifties, and then rising in the older age groups.
They interpret this pattern in terms of both life cycle

and cohort effects.

As workers age, they generally come to have better, more rewarding jobs, as they accrue seniority and advance through the ranks of organizational hierarchies. (However, as retirement age approaches, declining physical capacities, outmoded skills, and age discrimination may decrease the rewards and opportunities available to the oldest workers.) Age stratification (Riley 1985) is thus expressed and actualized through the dynamics of careers. Young and middle-aged workers are also subject to economic pressures specific to their stages in the family life cycle. A pattern of increasing satisfaction with age could be the result of a closer "fit" between workers and jobs, in terms of economic need as well as in other ways. Older workers have had more time to change jobs, and to mold their work in ways that are compatible with their particular values and needs. Values may also change over time in response to work conditions (Mortimer and Lorence 1979a). However, age differences in job satisfaction may be substantially attributable to cohort effects (Glenn and Weaver 1985). The present cohort of younger workers may have unrealistic job expectations, stimulated by their high educational attainment relative to preceding cohorts. This cohort faces persistent disadvantages in the job market due to its large size, which would foster job dissatisfaction.

The central paradox in studies of gender and job satisfaction is that men and women tend to have quite similar levels of satisfaction, despite gross differences in their occupational rewards. Weaver (1978) reports that since 1962, at least 10 surveys of representative samples of the U.S. labor force failed to show a significant difference in job satisfaction between the sexes (see also Quinn et al. 1974; Mannheim 1983). The absence of consistent gender differences in satisfaction may result from women's lack of awareness of the deficiencies of their positions or their use of lower standards of comparison (Weaver 1978; Campbell et al. 1976). Andrisani (1978) speculates that the decline in women's job satisfaction between 1967 and 1972, observed in the NLS Surveys, may be linked to the women's movement, which has raised occupational goals and expectations.

Whereas a large number of studies have examined mean differences in job satisfaction, either by age or by sex, few have considered gender and age simultaneously. (In a

notable exception, Weaver [1978] reports that age has
relatively equal, positive effects on satisfaction among
both men and women.) Furthermore, most previous studies
are based on cross-sectional data (Kalleberg and Loscocco
1983; Janson and Martin 1982; Cohn 1979; Martin and
Hanson 1985) or repeated national surveys (Weaver 1978;
Glenn and Weaver 1982). Longitudinal data have marked
advantages for examining the questions at issue. With
data collected at only one point, it is impossible to
examine trends over time in the same people; the degree
to which a psychological phenomenon, such as job
satisfaction, is stable or changing.

Longitudinal data also permit more precise estimates
of the effects of work conditions on job satisfaction,
since the impact of prior satisfaction can be controlled.
Thus, processes of "selection" to work, on the basis of
prior attributes, can be separated from the influences of
work experiences on the individual (Mortimer and Lorence
1979a; 1979b). When workers are dissatisfied with their
jobs, they may attempt to change their positions or
employers. Alternatively, they may try to "mold" or
improve their jobs to make them more compatible with
personal needs. When workers are satisfied, they may
exert more effort, make a better impression on their
supervisors, and thereby be granted increasingly
rewarding positions over time. Thus, workers do not just
passively react to occupational conditions; they actively
choose, shape, and, perhaps, selectively perceive them.
Any of these possibilities, coupled with stability in
satisfaction, could render significant cross-sectional
associations between work conditions and job satisfaction
spurious. It is therefore necessary to control prior
levels of job satisfaction when estimating the effects of
job conditions.

The present study examines the interrelations of
work conditions and job satisfaction among persons of
different age and sex using longitudinal data from the
1973-1977 Quality of Employment Survey, a national panel
of men and women workers. We estimate a causal model of
the development of job satisfaction in six subgroups of
the panel--young, middle-aged, and older workers of each
sex. Whereas a large number of job conditions could have
been chosen for investigation, to simplify the models, we
confine our attention to three work conditions--work
autonomy, income, and work overload--because of the
demonstrated power of these variables in predicting job
satisfaction (Mortimer 1979; Locke 1976).

There is considerable evidence that work autonomy
has widespread implications for psychological change
(Mortimer, Finch, and Kumka 1982; Mortimer, Lorence, and
Kumka 1986; Mortimer and Finch 1986; Kohn and Schooler
1982, 1983). The related dimensions of work autonomy,
occupational self-direction, and job scope have been
found to have clear positive effects on job satisfaction.
However, there are reasons to expect gender and age
differences in the effects of autonomy on satisfaction.
For example, in accord with the "fit hypothesis," if
intrinsic values have greater salience for young workers,
one might expect that the effects of autonomy on job
satisfaction would decline with age. However, both
gender and age may have to be considered in interaction
with one another. For example, if young working women
are highly preoccupied with family responsibilities, the
degree of autonomy which they experience at work may have
less bearing on their job satisfaction.

Income and other extrinsic rewards have also been
found to be significant predictors of job satisfaction
(Kalleberg 1977; Locke 1976; Fein 1976; Strauss 1974a and
b; Tannenbaum et al. 1974), but the importance of income
may be greater at times of "life cycle squeeze," such as
when workers are supporting adolescent and college-age
children (Moen and Moorehouse 1983; Oppenheimer 1974).
Moreover, to the extent that traditional conceptions of
gender roles are accepted, income would be of greater
importance for men's job satisfaction, given their
central responsibility as family breadwinners. As we
have seen, Martin and Hanson's recent analysis (1985) of
the 1972-73 Quality of Employment cross-section showed
that extrinsic rewards were significant determinants of
job satisfaction for men and "breadwinning women."

In comparison to these two work dimensions, work
overload has been given less attention in the job
satisfaction literature, but deserves inclusion because
of our particular focus on age and gender differences.
Again, while conditions of overload on the job may be
expected to detract from job satisfaction in all groups
(Locke 1976), they may have special implications
contingent on age and sex. Women workers, who typically
shoulder major responsibility for family work even when
they are employed, may feel more burdened than men by
overload on the job. It is unclear which age group would
be the most strongly affected by this job condition, but
all have reason to be bothered by work overload. Younger
workers of either sex may not have yet acquired the

knowledge and coping mechanisms to adapt successfully to excessive amounts of work, and older workers are faced with declining stamina and increasingly outmoded knowledge and skills. Workers in their middle years are in the process of building their careers, and may likewise feel highly strained by time pressure and overload.

DATA SOURCE

The data were obtained from the 1972-73 and 1977 Quality of Employment Surveys (QES), through the Inter-University Consortium for Political and Social Research. The 1972-73 survey included a national sample of 1455 persons, chosen according to a multistage area probability design so as to be representative of the U.S. working population. To be eligible for inclusion, respondents had to be at least 16 years of age and employed 20 hours or more a week during the interview period. These 1455 persons constituted 75.5 percent of those originally chosen for participation (for further information concerning the sampling procedures, see Quinn and Staines 1979:Ch. 2). In 1977, 74.6 percent (N=1086) of persons from the 1972-73 sample were reinterviewed. Our analyses are based on the 884 workers (81 percent of the reinterviewed group) who were employed 20 or more hours per week in 1977. They received a "long form" questionnaire inquiring about their 1977 work experiences and job satisfaction. (It should be noted that among the workers included in our analyses, employment was generally considerably more than 20 hours. The men worked an average of 46.5 hours per week, the women, 39.3 hours.)

Kalleberg and Loscocco (1983) point out, quite correctly, that panel attrition may be dependent on prior level of job satisfaction if dissatisfied workers leave the labor force or reduce their level of participation below the requisite 20 hours per week. This attrition would be especially problematic if the intent were to register the absolute magnitude of, and changes in, job satisfaction in the work force over a given period of time. Such compositional changes would seem to be less consequential given our present focus, which is to investigate whether work experiences have distinct effects on job satisfaction among persons of different ages who maintain a substantial level of labor force participation over a period of time. (Lorence and Mortimer 1985:623 describe some differences between the 1973 cross-section and the 1973-1977 panel.)

The 1972-73 sample was weighted to correct for the number of eligible workers in each selected household. We use the weighted N of 1292 employed panel members. Furthermore, in the analyses to be reported, only respondents with complete data for each variable in the causal model are included (unweighted N=772; weighted N=1133). As a result, we lose 159 cases, or approximately 12 percent of the weighted panel available in 1977. To examine the implications of this procedure, we assessed the differences between those included in and those excluded from our analysis (on the basis of missing data). There were no differences between the two groups in gender composition, educational attainment, job satisfaction in 1973, or in work overload, work autonomy, and income in 1973 and 1977. However, those without missing data were significantly younger and lower in job satisfaction in 1977. While these differences are cause for concern, bias is also introduced when the matrix of associations between variables, to be used in multivariate analysis, is drawn from different cases (Finkbeiner 1979).

MEASUREMENT OF THE CONSTRUCTS

The 1973 measure of educational attainment follows: What was the highest grade of school or level of education you completed?
1. Grades 1-7 (some grade school),
2. Grade 8 (completed grade school),
3. Grades 9-11 (some high school),
4. Grade 12 (high school diploma, GED, or any high school equivalent),
5. Grades 13-15 (some college),
6. Grade 16 (college degree),
7. Graduate or professional education in excess of college degree.

In prior studies, work experiences indicative of autonomy have been measured in various ways. Kohn and Schooler's (1982:1259) approach emphasizes the job's objective structure as providing opportunities for "the use of initiative, thought, and independent judgment".

Their measures of "occupational self-direction" include
substantive complexity, routinization, and freedom from
close supervision. In our prior work (Mortimer and
Lorence 1979a,b; Mortimer et al. 1982), we have used the
term "work autonomy" to refer to reports of work
experiences that would likely accompany "occupational
self-direction"-- freedom to make decisions, innovative
thinking required by the job, and the level of challenge.
We chose three questions from a large number of available
items that appeared to represent this experience in work,
emphasizing decision-making latitude. (There are minor
variations in question wording in 1973 and 1977.)

1973: How much freedom does it [your job] allow you as to
how you do your work?
    1. Not at all,
    2. A Little,
    3. Somewhat,
    4. A lot.
1977: I am given a lot of freedom to decide how I do my
own work.
    1. Not at all true,
    2. A little true,
    3. Somewhat true,
    4. Very true.

1973: Here are some more things that might describe a
person's job. How much are these like your job?...[A
job] where you have a lot of say over what happens on
your job? [How much is your job like this?]
    1. Not at all,
    2. A Little,
    3. Somewhat,
    4. A Lot.
1977: I have a lot of say about what happens on my job.
    1. Strongly disagree,
    2. Disagree,
    3. Agree,
    4. Strongly Agree.

1973: [How much does your job] allow you to take part in
making decisions that affect you?
    1. Not at all,
    2. A little,
    3. Somewhat,
    4. A lot.
1977: It is basically my own responsibility to decide how

my job gets done.
1. Strongly disagree,
2. Disagree,
3. Agree,
4. Strongly agree.

The measure of extrinsic reward is total job income before taxes and other deductions. A probe added in 1977 may make the 1977 measure more accurate.

Three items were selected to represent work overload, the perception that the job is demanding and that one has excessive amounts of work to do. (Again, there are changes in question wording. Within each time period, response categories for the three questions are the same, and are therefore not repeated.)

1973: And finally, a job where there is not enough time to get things done? [How much is your job like this?]
1. Not at all,
2. A little,
3. Somewhat,
4. A lot.
1977: I never seem to have enough time to get everything done on my job.
1. Strongly disagree,
2. Disagree,
3. Agree,
4. Strongly agree.

1973: A job where there is always a great deal of work to be done? [How much is your job like this?]
1977: I have too much work to do everything well.

1973: [How much does your job] require you to work very hard?
1977: My job requires that I work very hard.

Following Locke (1976), we consider job satisfaction to be a "positive emotional state resulting from the appraisal of one's job or job experiences." In this study, we investigate the determinants of overall job satisfaction, rather than its facet-specific components (i.e., satisfaction with particular aspects of the job). Three questions, with identical wordings in 1973 and 1977, represent this dimension:

All in all, how satisfied would you say you are with your

job?
1. Not at all satisfied,
2. Not too satisfied,
3. Somewhat satisfied,
4. Very satisfied.

Knowing what you know now, if you had to decide all over again whether to take the job you now have, what would you decide?
1. Decide definitely not to take the job,
2.5. Have some second thoughts,
4. Decide without hesitation to take the same job.

In general, how well would you say that your job measures up to the sort of job you wanted when you took it?
1. Not very much like,
2.5. Somewhat like,
4. Very much like,

   Our age categories (16-29, 30-44, 45 and over) correspond roughly to those used in prior research (see, for example, Miller et al., Chapter 4 this volume; Gould 1979) and to Super et al.'s early (1957) classification of vocational life stages. During their "trial stage" (22-30), workers are trying out alternative positions and/or occupations; in the "stabilization stage" (31-44), the career is built; in the "maintenance stage" (45-65), the work continues without major change in direction.[3]

MEAN DIFFERENCES IN WORK AND JOB SATISFACTION BY AGE AND GENDER

   Gender and age inequalities in the labor force were initially investigated by assessment of mean differences in the work variables and job satisfaction. We use the F test to assess differences in unit weighted indices, and the Duncan multiple comparisons test to locate significant ($p < .05$) differences between categories (see Table 5.1; with the one exception designated, the lines below the means indicate those groups that were not significantly different from one another.)[4]
   Job satisfaction generally increases from the youngest to the oldest groups, with no clear trend manifested by gender. However, gender inequality is clear with respect to income and work autonomy. It is especially noteworthy that there are no significant

Table 5.1 Mean Differences in Education, Work, and Job Satisfaction by Age and Gender.

Education[1]
(F=5.67, df=5,1127)***

OF	OM	MF	YF	MM	YM
3.93	4.13	4.38	4.50	4.52	4.54

Work Autonomy 1972-3
(F=19.94, df=5,1127)***

YF	OF	MF	YM	OM	MM
7.85	8.51	8.83	8.85	9.56	9.85

Work Autonomy 1977
(F=12.11, df=5,1127)***

YF*	MF	OF	YM*	OM	MM
8.43	8.50	8.78	9.28	9.46	9.65

Income 1972-3
(F=60.68, df=5,1127)***

YF	OF	MF	YM	MM	OM*
$5,900	$6,200	$6,700	$8,400	$12,600	$14,100

Income 1977
(F=38.57, df=5,1127)***

MF*	OF*	YF*	YM*	MM*	OM*
$9,700	$10,100	$10,400	$15,000	$19,000	$19,900

Overload 1972-3
(F=1.97, df=5,1127)

YF	YM	OF	MF	OM	MM
9.28	9.41	9.57	9.70	9.73	9.74

Overload 1977
(F=3.21, df=1127)**

OF*	YF*	YM*	OM*	MF*	MM*
7.36	7.51	7.57	7.77	7.84	7.97

Job Satisfaction 1972-3
(F=5.93, df=5,1127)***

YF	YM	MF	MM	OM	OF
9.77	9.84	10.23	10.38	10.38	10.79

Job Satisfaction 1977
(F=3.62, df=5,1127)**

MF*	YM	YF	MM[2]	OF*	OM
9.52	9.78	9.80	10.21	10.22	10.24

[1]Education was coded on a scale from 1 to 7 with 1 being some grade school, 4, grade 12, and 7, graduate or professional education in excess of college degree.

[2]Middle age males are significantly different from middle aged females and young males and females.

*Denotes a significant change between 1973 and 1977.
**p < .01   ***p < .001

increments with age in women's income in 1973 or 1977,
while men's incomes show a consistent pattern of increase
from the youngest to the oldest age groups.

Among both men and women, the youngest workers
possess the least autonomy. Young females report the
least autonomy in their work in 1973, while middle-aged
and older men report the highest levels of autonomy. By
the second wave of the study, four years later, the three
groups of men clearly have more autonomy in their work.
With respect to work overload, there is no significant
difference among the age and gender subgroups, overall,
in 1973 (p > .05), and the pattern is rather mixed in
1977. Middle-aged workers, however, tend to have higher
overload. Following well-documented cohort trends
(Featherman 1980), educational attainment is lowest among
the oldest women and men (though women in the middle age
group do not differ significantly from the oldest men).

Over the period of observation (1973 to 1977), the
youngest male and female workers experienced greater work
autonomy. All groups increased in income and decreased
in overload. However, because of the differences in the
wordings of the questions in 1973 and 1977, these changes
should be viewed with caution. Job satisfaction, measured
identically in the two waves, appears to decline over the
four-year period among the middle-aged and older women,
perhaps continuing the pattern of decline in job
satisfaction between 1967 and 1972 noted by Andrisani in
the NLS cohort of women aged 30-44 (1978).

CAUSAL MODEL

The causal model is shown in Figures 5.1-5.4.
(Figures 5.1 and 5.3 present the unstandardized and
standardized solutions for males; Figures 5.2 and 5.4
present the same information for females.) Given the
importance of education as a determinant of occupational
achievement and income (Sewell and Hauser 1976; Spaeth
1976), there are paths from education to each of the
three work experiences in 1973 and 1977. One might
expect to find positive effects of education on job
satisfaction, because the more highly educated workers
tend to have the more rewarding jobs.[5] Direct paths from
education to 1973 and 1977 job satisfaction are also
estimated.

To the extent that the work variables influence job
satisfaction, we would expect to find significant

relationships among these constructs in both 1973 and 1977. However, because there is no measure of job satisfaction prior to 1973, we cannot estimate the effects of work experiences on satisfaction at that time, net of its stability. As discussed earlier, a large portion of the relationship between work and psychological variables may be attributable to the selection of work on the basis of the same stable characteristics. We therefore express the interrelations of the work and psychological constructs in 1973 as residual covariances, not as causal paths. (See Appendix A.)

There are stability paths connecting the same work experiences in 1973 and 1977. If workers tend to "settle down," making fewer job changes in the middle and later phases of their careers, these paths would likely become stronger in the older age groups. They may, however, be weaker among women if women's intermittent labor force participation leads to frequent job shifts and concomitant changes in work experiences. We also estimate the stability of job satisfaction over the four year period. According to the "aging stability hypothesis" (Glenn 1980), stability in this psychological dimension would increase as workers age. This could result from the decreasing probability of environmental change, and/or workers' diminishing reponsiveness as they age to differences and changes in their work environments.

Paths from 1973 job satisfaction to the 1977 work experiences signify the likelihood that workers actively choose and mold their jobs depending on their prior levels of job satisfaction. However, it is difficult to predict the direction of these effects. The more satisfied workers may have greater investment in the work sphere, and may strive to continuously improve the quality of their working lives. But alternatively, job dissatisfaction could motivate workers to change or alter their jobs in a manner that enhances job conditions. Differences in the magnitudes of these paths, across gender and age groups, may reflect inequalities in workers' power to select or to alter their jobs in accord with their prior dispositions.

Finally, and of greatest interest, we estimate the effects of the three work experiences on 1977 job satisfaction, net of 1973 satisfaction and education. Given the findings of prior research, we expected that autonomy and income would increase job satisfaction, and

that work overload would diminish it. However, these
effects could differ depending on age and gender. If
persons are more responsive to job conditions in the
early phases of their work careers, we would expect these
paths to be strongest in the youngest age group.
Moreover, if women's job satisfaction is largely
determined by family-related variables, one might expect
the intrinsic and extrinsic dimensions of work to have
weaker effects. The relations among the work
experiences, at each time, are specified in the model by
residual covariances (see Appendix A).

MODEL ESTIMATION

     To estimate the model, we used maximum likelihood
analysis of structural equations (Joreskog and Sorbom
1979; Long 1976). The analyses were performed by the
LISREL IV (International Educational Services 1972)
computer program, with variance-covariance matrices[6]
constituting the program input. We estimate the model in
six subgroups (men and women 16-29, 30-44, and 45 and
older).
     Initially, confirmatory factor analyses were
undertaken to develop measurement models for all
multiple-indicator constructs, representing each
construct with indicators found to have substantial
factor loadings in preliminary exploratory factor
analyses. (The measurement parameters are the lambda
coefficients or loadings from the constructs to the
indicators, the residuals of the indicators, and the
covariances among the residuals.) When the same measures
are repeated in multiple waves, residuals of the
identical indicators may covary as a result of their
unique variances (shared variance that is unrelated to
the construct) or measurement effects. Therefore, an
important feature of the measurement models for work
autonomy, work overload, and job satisfaction is the
inclusion of residual covariations for the same items
over time. (All of these measurement parameters were
simultaneously reestimated in the causal models.)   With
the exception of work overload in 1977,[7] there was little
difference in the lambda coefficients for the constructs
in the six subgroups. This pattern assured us that they
had the same general meaning irrespective of age and sex
(Mortimer et al. 1982).

FINDINGS

In Figures 5.1 and 5.2, the unstandardized solutions
are given. For comparisons across age and sex groups,
given possible differences in construct variances, the
unstandardized parameters are more appropriate. The
standardized parameters, which allow one to compare the
relative effects of variables within each group, are
given in Figures 5.3 and 5.4. For each model, all
designated parameters, as well as the measurement
parameters and the covariations of construct residuals,
were estimated. Retention of the same causal paths in
each model, irrespective of their statistical
significance, heightens their comparability.

Let us first examine the unstandardized parameter
estimates for men and women in each age group (Figures
5.1 and 5.2). Consistent with the findings of attainment
research, education has a positive effect on income for
men in all age groups in 1973, which tends to increase in
magnitude with age. Manifesting a similar pattern,
education significantly predicts the incomes of
middle-aged and older women workers, but its effect is
insignificant among the youngest women. The weaker
effects of education on 1973 income in the youngest
cohorts of men and women may be due to the fact that they
have not yet had enough time to reap the full economic
benefits of their education.[8] However, age differences
in the effects of education on income are also amenable
to a cohort interpretation. The high educational
attainment of young workers and the large size of the
"baby boom" cohort have led to a devaluation of higher
degrees in the job market (Freeman 1976; Featherman
1980).

Education significantly predicts 1973 work autonomy
in all age and gender groups, while the magnitudes of its
effects on autonomy are larger for women. Higher
education also fosters work overload, a concomitant of
many of the most highly autonomous and remunerative jobs,
among the youngest workers and oldest women (the
coefficient for the oldest men just fails to reach
statistical significance, t=1.94). Prior studies have
found rather inconsistent effects of education on job
satisfaction (cf. footnote 5). In this panel, education
has a significant positive effect on 1973 job
satisfaction only among the middle-aged men and women. In
general, with the exception of income, the effects of
education on the 1973 variables are somewhat stronger for

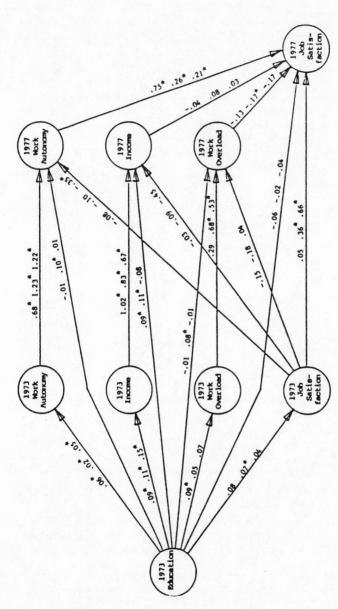

Figure 5.1 Causal Model of Job Satisfaction, Males
(unstandardized coefficients presented for young, middle-aged and older workers in that order).

young X^2= 327.35, df= 156, N= 254   Residual covariations of the constructs are
middle-aged X^2= 352.38, df= 156, N= 273   shown in Appendix A; construct residuals in
older X^2= 339.54, df= 156, N= 208   Appendix B.

*coefficient significant at a<.05

130

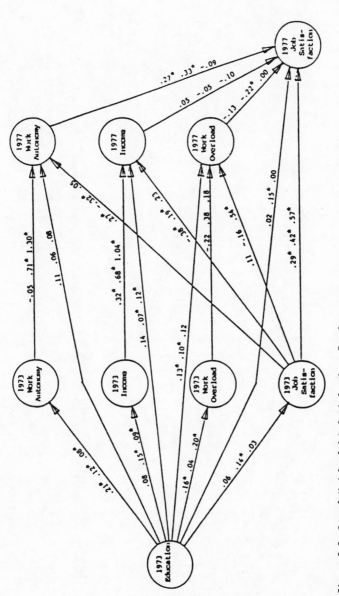

Figure 5.2 Causal Model of Job Satisfaction, Females
(unstandardized coefficients presented for young, middle-aged and older workers in that order).

young x^2= 390.02, df= 156, N= 162
middle-aged x^2= 412.07, df= 136, N= 124
older x^2= 331.05, df= 156, N= 112

*coefficient significant at a <.05

Residual covariations of the constructs are
shown in Appendix A; construct residuals in
Appendix B.

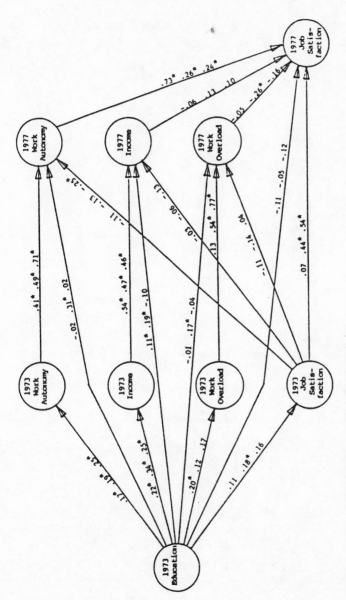

Figure 5.3 Causal Model of Job Satisfaction, Males
(standardized coefficients presented for young, middle-aged and older workers in that order).

*coefficient significant at α <.05

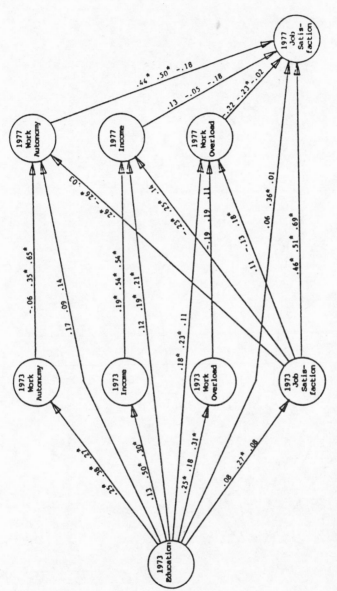

Figure 5.4 Causal Model of Job Satisfaction, Females
(standardized coefficients presented for young, middle-aged and older workers in that order).

* coefficient significant at α <.05

women than for men.

Because the estimates of the effects of education on the 1973 variables are not subject to controls, and the impacts of education on the 1977 constructs are estimated net of the variable stabilities, we would expect these coefficients to diminish in magnitude across time. This pattern was found in a several instances. But in some cases, education had equal or greater effects on the 1977 work constructs than on those measured in 1973. For example, the effect of education on overload was greater in 1977 than in 1973 for middle-aged men. Such patterns indicate the continuing importance of education for work experiences and attainments, net of job stability. It may take some time before educational credentials fully yield the more autonomous, remunerative, onerous, and satisfying jobs.

In comparing the youngest to the middle-aged group of men, we observe pronounced increases in the stability of work autonomy and overload. It is thus apparent that male workers in their early careers encounter greater change in these work experiences. In fact, the work overload construct is not even significantly stable among the youngest men. In comparison, there is rather little difference in the stability of these work experiences between the middle-aged and oldest men. These findings are consistent with the age-related pattern of job changes over the four-year period among the men (see Table 5.2). While only 46 percent of the young males are working for the same employer in 1973 and 1977, 81 and 85 percent, respectively, of the middle-aged and older male workers are. Similarly, among those working for the same employer, 52 percent of the youngest male workers held "roughly" the same job in both years. Seventy-three and 87 percent of the middle-aged and older workers did. (These age differences for men are statistically significant, $p < .0001$ for both variables, as indicated by chi square.)

Among women, work autonomy also increases in stability with age over the period of observation. Women's tendency to work for the same employer (see Table 5.2) likewise increases with age ($p < .0001$). But there is no significant age difference in women's reports that their jobs are "roughly the same" as the 1972-73 job. Moreover, the magnitude of the stability of work autonomy over the four-year period is considerably lower for young and middle-aged women than for their male counterparts. These patterns would suggest that in the youngest and

Table 5.2 Differences in Indicators of Job Stability by Age and Gender.

Percent working for the same employer in 1972-3 and 1977.

	Young			Middle Aged			Older		
	Men	Women	p	Men	Women	p	Men	Women	p
	46	42	ns	81	70	<.05	85	77	ns
N	204	147		226	107		152	99	

The present job is "roughly the same" as the 1972-3 job (% answering yes.)*

	Young			Middle Aged			Older		
	Men	Women	p	Men	Women	p	Men	Women	p
	52	69	<.05	73	79	ns	87	68	<.01
N	93	62		184	75		129	76	

*This question was only asked of self-employed persons and persons working for the same employer in 1972-73 and 1977.

middle age groups, women's work experiences are less
stable than those of men. Furthermore, the stability
coefficient for work overload among women fails to attain
statistical significance in any age group.

Table 5.2 shows that in each age group, women are
less likely than men to be working for the same employer
in both 1973 and 1977 (this difference reaches
statistical significance in the middle-aged cohort). For
those who remained with the same employer, among the
youngest and oldest men and women, there are significant
differences in the extent to which the present job is
"roughly the same" as the 1972-73 job, but men only show
greater stability in the oldest cohort. It may be that
men in their early careers move upward in rank even when
staying with the same firm, while women of the same age
are more likely to remain in place. By the age of 45,
men have stabilized their positions, but the tendency of
older women to change jobs in the same firm is roughly
the same as that of women of much younger age. The trend
shown in Table 5.2 is consistent with the fact that men
rise in occupational status as they go through their work
lives, while women tend to remain at approximately the
same level throughout their careers (Rosenfeld 1979; Wolf
and Rosenfeld 1978).

Income manifests a different pattern of stability
over time for men and women. For men, the greatest
stability is shown in the youngest group, and income
shows a continuing decline in stability among the
middle-aged and older workers. Among women, however, the
stability of income increases from the youngest to the
oldest group. Whereas most attainment research has
focused on the large gender gap in income, which we also
have observed (see Table 5.1), these differences in the
stability of income through the work life likewise
reflect inequality in the dynamics of careers, and
deserve further attention.

For both men and women, changes in the stability of
job satisfaction across age groups is highly consistent
with the "aging stability" hypothesis. That is, job
satisfaction stability is not statistically significant
among the youngest males over the four-year period, it
becomes quite stable in the middle-aged cohort, and
attains even further stability in the oldest segment of
the male panel. Among women, the stability of job
satisfaction is substantially higher than that of men in
the youngest age group, and shows the same pattern of
increase with age. It thus appears that the

psychological response to work becomes more constant over time as young workers, both male and female, move into their middle and later years.

Contrary to our expectations, job satisfaction has relatively little effect on subsequent work experiences for men, with only one of the nine relevant paths in the male models reaching statistical significance.[9] Five of the corresponding paths are significant among women. However, the different patterns of effects by age and gender manifest no clear and readily interpretable pattern. Though Miller (1980) reports no significant effects of earlier job satisfaction on income or occupational self-direction, she finds that the more satisfied male workers experienced less time pressure in the second wave of her study. (In the youngest QES male group, a negative effect of job satisfaction on work overload just fails to reach statistical significance, t=1.91.)

Turning to the effects of the work experiences on job satisfaction--the paths of greatest interest to us here--we find that work autonomy has a substantial effect on job satisfaction among the youngest male workers, while its effect diminishes considerably in the middle-aged and older cohorts of men. In fact, the unstandardized coefficient representing the effect of autonomy on job satisfaction is approximately three times greater in the youngest male cohort than in the middle and older cohorts. This pattern suggests that job satisfaction is most responsive to differences in autonomous work in the early phase of the career, the time of more frequent job changes and a period in which work autonomy itself is less stable. Thus, in this initial phase of the work career, men's job satisfaction is particularly reactive to the autonomy of their work. It should be noted that of the three work experience constructs, autonomy is the only one that significantly influences job satisfaction in all three male age groups. The significant influence of autonomy even in the oldest group of men--those whose employers and jobs manifest the least change over time--testifies to the continuing salience of this work experience for men's psychological well-being.

The findings for women indicate a quite different pattern. Most importantly, in comparison to men, young women's job satisfaction is much less responsive to the effects of work autonomy. In fact, the coefficient representing the effect of work autonomy on job satisfaction among women workers is only about one-third that of men. In the middle-aged group, the effect of autonomy on satisfaction is quite similar among women and men. However, in the oldest cohort, the causal pattern for men and women again diverges. Work autonomy significantly influences the job satisfaction of men, but not women. Thus, it is apparent that unlike men, the job satisfaction of women is not so strongly determined by their level of work autonomy in their early work lives, nor does the effect of autonomy plummet among women, moving from the youngest to the middle-aged group, as we observed for men (in fact, the effect of autonomy on satisfaction is slightly greater for middle-aged than for younger women). The effect of the level of autonomy at work on satisfaction does, however, fall in the oldest female cohort.

Income does not significantly predict satisfaction in any age group of men (though a positive effect among middle-aged men has a t value of 1.91) or women when the other work variables and prior satisfaction are controlled. It may seem contradictory that both Kalleberg (1977) and Janson and Martin (1982) report positive effects of extrinsic reward on job satisfaction, using the 1973 Quality of Employment cross-section. It should be noted, however, that in their studies, the measure of extrinsic reward is quite subjective. Their scale includes the respondent's level of agreement with the statement, "the pay is good," whereas our measure is actual pay. (Their extrinsic reward index also includes evaluations of fringe benefits and job security.) It is clear that both the objective and subjective features of jobs are of theoretical interest, and deserving of empirical investigation (Kohn and Schooler 1983; Mortimer and Finch 1983). Moreover, earlier studies have not controlled satisfaction at prior points in time. (It is interesting in this regard that net of the effects of education, there is a positive residual covariance in 1973 between income and job satisfaction among middle-aged men. See Appendix A.)

Work overload depresses job satisfaction only in the middle-aged cohorts of men and women. It may be that work overload is particularly distressing during this time of career building, when job responsibilities are likely to peak, especially for men.

In summary, for men, we find substantial support for the "aging stability" hypothesis. The increasing stability of job satisfaction across age groups corresponds to the greater stability of work autonomy and overload, and the decreasing frequency of job change, among the middle-aged and older workers. But what is of greatest significance for the aging stability model was the clear change in the effect of work autonomy on men's job satisfaction in different phases of the work career. Their responsiveness to work autonomy diminished drastically from the younger to the middle-aged group. Among women, we also find increasing stability of job satisfaction, work autonomy, and income (but not overload) with age.

Among women, the coefficient representing the effect of autonomy on job satisfaction also diminishes with age, but the timing of this change is different from that of men. For men, the coefficient falls drastically from the youngest to the middle-aged group. Among women, it decreases from the middle-aged to the oldest cohort of workers. It thus seems that although women's job satisfaction also becomes less responsive to the effects of work autonomy as they age, this decline in reactivity occurs for them at a later age than occurs among men.

Despite the apparent differences in the models for men and women, it may be that similar dynamics underlie the pattern of increasing stability of job satisfaction with age. That is, for both men and women there is evidence that reactivity to external conditions (such as autonomy) diminishes with longer incumbency of a role, after initial adjustments to it are made. Because of the intermittent patterning of women's labor force participation and frequent job shifts (see Moen 1985; Rosenfeld 1979; Andrisani 1978), there is a difference in tenure in the labor force between men and women workers of the same age. And this gender difference appears to increase with age. In 1977, the young men in this panel reported that they worked 11.6 years, on the average, since the age of 16; the young women worked 9.6 years. Thus, among the youngest workers in the panel, the men have been employed for 2 years longer than the women. In the middle-aged group, the difference increases to 6.3 years (23.9 vs. 17.6), and in the oldest group, it is 11.5 years (38.5 vs. 27.0). It is noteworthy that the older women in our panel are more similar, in terms of time in the labor force, to the middle-aged men than to the older men. In view of this fact, parallel declines in the impacts of external work conditions on job satisfaction between young and middle-aged men, and middle-aged and older women, are not surprising.

We have still not fully addressed the differences in the causal models for the younger men and women. Why would work autonomy be so much more important for young men's job satisfaction? The pattern we have observed (in both the youngest and the oldest cohorts) is consistent with Miller's (1980) observation that men value the dimensions of work associated with positional authority (such as decision-making latitude, tapped by our measure of autonomy) more than do women. Furthermore, it may be relevant that the phase of life from age 20-33, that of our youngest cohort in 1977, encompasses the period in which women are likely to have infants and preschool children in the home, which compete with the work role for their energy and time. It might be thought that in this youngest age group of women, work's compatibility with family roles may have the greatest relevance for job satisfaction. However, some further analyses did not support this interpretation.[10]

Considering all six models in tandem suggests a final observation. We find the smallest gender differences in the causal process by which job satisfaction is determined among workers of middle-age. In the 30-44 age group, the effects of autonomy and overload on men's and women's job satisfaction are approximately equal (income had no significant influence in either group), and the stabilities of this psychological dimension are also commensurate. The fact that the coefficients representing these effects are so similar would lead one to expect important equivalences in middle-aged men's and women's job situations, or perhaps in their nonwork lives. However, we found (Table 5.2) that middle-aged women have had more changes in employers over the four-year period. Middle-aged women have also worked, on the average, 6.3 years less than men of the same age. Further, middle-aged men manifest much greater stability in work autonomy, income, and work overload over the four-year period. It is likewise evident, from our inspection of mean differences in the work constructs (Table 5.1), that middle-aged men, in comparison to their female counterparts, are significantly advantaged with respect to work autonomy and income. The fact that the causal dynamics of job satisfaction are so much the same for middle-aged men and women, despite these important differences, is an intriguing problem.

DISCUSSION

Before proceeding further, an important, but unavoidable, limitation of the analysis should be made explicit. Our separation of the panel into three age groups, while indicative of career stages, is rather arbitrary. As we have seen, the differences in tenure in the labor force among our three groups of working women are smaller than those for men, since women tend to have less continuous work histories. Moreover, there is evidence that women and men of the same age do not have the same stability of work experiences.

Moreover, while there are socially-recognized age strata, they are defined differently in the various institutional and organizational complexes of the society (Riley 1985). The designation of age categories are likely geared to important turning points in the worklife, and these would differ in various occupational groups and work organizations. For example, in an academic career, the implications of work experiences for job satisfaction--rewards, as well as setbacks--might be expected to be quite different in the probationary and tenured periods. In a corporation, some persons may be recognized as "up and coming," others as having reached a "plateau," and still others as "kicked upstairs" or "awaiting retirement" (Kanter 1977:Chapter 6). To the extent that these designations are age-related, a meaningful age categorization of workers, corresponding to their work contexts, could be devised.[11]

In the absence of such a categorization, the differences in causal patterns by age that we have found have a number of reasonable interpretations. We anchored much of the discussion in the "aging stability hypothesis," that the stability of attitudes increases with age (Glenn 1980). While quite plausible, relatively little empirical research has been directed toward examining such an "aging stability" trend (Glenn 1980; Sears 1981; Costa et al. 1983).[12] If, in fact, attitudes do exhibit more constancy with age, this pattern may have two reasonable (and not mutually exclusive) interpretations. First, "aging stability" could occur because social roles also tend to be increasingly stable as one grows older, thus providing little impetus to personal change. Second, individuals may be more responsive to the effects of external forces, such as experiences encountered in the workplace, early in their lives.

Our findings provide evidence for both of these underlying dynamics of "aging stability." Both men and women manifested increases in the stabilities of both work autonomy and job satisfaction with age. (Work overload increased in stability with age only among men; income did so only among women.) Thus, the heightened stability of job satisfaction in the middle-aged and older groups occurs in a context of increasing stability in the work environment. The declines in the effects of work autonomy on job satisfaction across age groups indicate diminishing psychological responsiveness to job experiences as workers grow older, or as they spend longer amounts of time in their jobs, though the declines are patterned somewhat differently for men and women. To further understand gender differences in the dynamics of the "aging stability" pattern, it would be useful to compare the effects of work autonomy on job satisfaction in groups of men and women who have spent comparable amounts of time in particular types of jobs, with age controlled.

Before drawing any general conclusions about younger and older workers' psychological receptivity to job conditions, we should examine whether the pattern observed here can be replicated with other data sets and with different psychological variables. Kohn (personal communication, September 20, 1984) also finds evidence that substantive complexity is a more powerful correlate of younger workers' job satisfaction in his ten-year (1964-74) longitudinal study of a national sample of male workers. (However, Kalleberg and Loscocco [1983:82] report no significant interaction between age and occupational variables in the determination of job satisfaction.) Using the same Quality of Employment Survey data, a very similar "aging stability" pattern is manifest with respect to the effects of autonomy on job involvement (Lorence and Mortimer 1985). As in the present analysis, for both men and women, the stability of the work dimensions and job involvement increased after age 29, and the influence of autonomy on job involvement diminished with age.

However, a different pattern seems to emerge with respect to psychological variables that are more reflective of off-the-job intellectual functioning. In the panel studied by Kohn and his colleagues, the effects of substantive compexity on intellectual flexiblity were found to be approximately the same in three male age groups (Miller et al. Chapter 4 this volume). Moreover,

Miller et al. (1979), in examining a range of
psychological dimensions (e.g., intellectual flexibility,
social orientations, and self-conceptions) find that men
and women respond very similarly to the structural
imperatives of their work. It may be that psychological
orientations whose content directly pertains to work,
such as job satisfaction and involvement, are
crystallized during the early phase of the career in
response to salient job conditions. As they stabilize
thereafter, they may become increasingly impervious to
changes in work experiences. However, those
psychological characteristics that are more reflective of
psychological functioning off the job may be more
continuously influenced by work, through a more gradual
accretive process. Additional research is certainly
necessary to determine the generalizability of the
pattern we have observed, with respect to both
work-related orientations and to other psychological
variables.[13]

Furthermore, it is possible that cohort factors, not
age-related experiences, account for the patterns we have
described. Autonomy could be a more important
determinant of job satisfaction among the younger male
workers in our panel because of their distinctive
socialization experiences. These men, aged 20-33 in 1977
(16-29 in 1973), were born between 1944 and 1957, and
grew up in an expanding economic period. This economic
expansion during their formative years likely fostered
high intrinsic work expectations. For these individuals,
work autonomy may have particularly high salience.

The most important historical trends from the
standpoint of women who came to maturity during the same
period were the growing labor force participation of
women and the women's liberation movement, which
encouraged high aspirations and continuous employment.
But though these trends might lead one to expect greater
convergence on the part of young men and women in the
causal processes related to the development of job
satisfaction, we find the greatest gender similarity in
our causal models in the middle-aged cohort. Future
investigations should attend to both age and
cohort-related determinants of the processes by which
work affects job satisfaction. It is certainly premature
to decide between these differing, but surely not
mutually exclusive, kinds of explanations of the patterns
we have observed. We view this study as an exploratory
first step in the investigation of age, gender, work, and

job satisfaction.

Though we cannot fully explain the patterns of effects of work experiences on job satisfaction by gender and age, the differences found in this study support the "fit hypothesis" that workers' responses to their jobs are importantly affected by their personal characteristics. The effects of work autonomy on job satisfaction manifested interesting variations by gender and age. From this study, it would also appear that work overload is a significant determinant of job satisfaction only for middle-aged workers.

In conclusion, the findings suggest that both gender and age deserve consideration in future studies of workers' subjective responses to their jobs. Differences by gender and age are manifest not only in work conditions and rewards, but also in the causal processes through which job satisfaction is determined. There appear to be major variations in both the stability and the causal dynamics of job satisfaction across age and gender groups which merit further scrutiny. As long as investigators confine their attention to cross-sectional data, encompassing workers of all ages, or limit their research to studies of men, as has often been the case, important differences in causal influence will be obscured.

NOTES

1. Earlier versions of this chapter were presented at the 1985 Annual Meeting of the American Association for the Advancement of Science, the 1986 Meeting of the Midwest Sociological Society, and the 1986 World Congress of Sociology. The research was supported by a grant from the National Institute on Aging (AGO-03325) and by the University of Minnesota Computer Center. The data were made available by the Inter-University Consortium for Political and Social Research. The data for the Quality of Employment Surveys were collected by Robert P. Quinn and Graham L. Staines. Neither the original collectors of the data nor the Consortium bear any responsibility for the analyses or interpretation presented here. The authors would like to thank Ronald Abeles, Terry Baker, Melvin Kohn, Jon Lorence, Joanne Miller, Matilda W. Riley, and Ronald Schoenberg for their valuable comments

on earlier drafts of the manuscript.

2. In another psychological domain, Miller and her associates (Chapter 4, this volume) have reported that occupational self-direction influences intellectual flexibility in young, middle-aged, and older U.S. working men over a ten-year period. This occurred despite the exceedingly high stability of intellectual flexibility. Occupational self-direction also had a significant influence on intellectual flexibility in the same three age groups in a cross-sectional sample of Polish workers.

3. Workers were categorized on the basis of their ages in 1973. These categories are somewhat arbitrary, spanning about 14 (16-29), 15 (30-44), and 20 years each (45 to the time of retirement). The use of the terms young, middle-aged, and old only refer to these categories, and are not meant to imply any absolute characterizations. Workers of 45 are not "old" in any absolute sense.

4. We also analyzed the data by performing two-way analyses of variance, including tests for the direct effects of age and sex and the interaction of age and gender. These tests, and the assessment of mean differences described in the text, address the same problem in different ways. Since the mean differences among the six age by gender groups more clearly illustrate the inequalities of education, work, and satisfaction, they are presented in the text. The factors found to have significant effects in the ANOVAS are as follows: for education, age; for 1973 and 1977 autonomy, age (the middle-aged had highest autonomy) and sex; for 1973 and 1977 income, age, sex, and the age by sex interaction; for 1973 and 1977 overload, age (the middle-aged groups had highest overload); for 1973 satisfaction, age; for 1977 satisfaction, age and the interaction of age and sex.

5. However, when important job features are controlled, sometimes education has been found to have a positive effect (Miller 1980), sometimes a negative effect (Tannenbaum et al. 1974; Glenn and Weaver 1982), and sometimes no significant effect (Weaver 1978) on job satisfaction. In addition to providing the credentials for more satisfying jobs, education may sometimes raise workers' expectations. Seybolt (1976) reports that rewards of greater magnitude are required to satisfy the more highly educated employee.

6. Income was divided by 10,000 prior to constructing the variance-covariance matrix to make its

variance more comparable to that of the other variables.

7. The lambda coefficients for two 1977 overload indicators were not statistically significant among young males and middle-aged females. For them, the reference indicator, "I never seem to have enough time to get everything done on my job," in effect, defines the construct.

8. Among even younger workers, education has been found to have a negative effect on income. This pattern was present among men in the nationally representative Youth in Transition Study five years beyond high school (Maruyama et al. 1985; Mortimer and Finch 1986). At this age, persons with less education have accumulated more work experience and seniority, and therefore have the more remunerative jobs. Findings from the two panels, taken together, suggest a changing pattern of relationship between education and income through the worklife.

9. It could be argued that the four-year lag time is either too long or too short. That is, job satisfaction affects work experiences only over shorter or longer periods of time. While the length of the true causal lag is of crucial importance in interpreting a model of this kind, the present state of knowledge does not allow us to determine what this might be. Both Kohn and Schooler and their colleagues (1983) and our own prior studies (Mortimer and Lorence 1979a, 1979b; Mortimer et al. 1986) have demonstrated significant effects of psychological variables on work experiences over a period of ten years.

10. To investigate this possibility, we examined the same causal model, adding age as a predictor of 1977 job satisfaction, for men and women in different family situations, using OLS regression and unit weighted indices. There was no evidence that the pattern of causation of job satisfaction among women with more family responsibilities (e.g., married women with children under 6) diverged most strongly from that of men. Nor were the causal models for women without such responsibilities (e.g., single women without children) more similar to those of men.

11. Van Maanen and Katz (1976), in a cross-sectional study of the public sector, reported different patterns of relationship between job satisfaction and organizational tenure across major occupational categories (administrative, professional, clerical, and maintenance).

12.   Costa et al. (1983:246-249) examined
correlations of ten scale scores derived from the
Guilford-Zimmerman Temperament Survey over approximately
6 and 12 year intervals in three age groups, and found no
evidence for increasing personality stability with age.
It should be noted, however, that their youngest group is
20-44 years old.   This category encompasses both our
young and middle-aged workers.   If the major
developmental changes in psychological features in
response to work occur in the earlier phases of the
career, prior to age 30, their age categorization would
obscure the trends we have observed.

13.   It should also be noted that the differences in
the findings reported in Chapters 4 and 5 could be
attributable to variation in the measurement of work
experiences.   The indicators of work autonomy, used here,
are more subjective than the indicators of substantive
complexity.   It might be argued that job satisfaction
influences the subjective perception of work autonomy.
Prior job satisfaction, measured in 1973, had
significant, though inconsistent, effects on 1977 work
autonomy in some subgroups.   Similarly, 1977 job
satisfaction could influence the contemporaneous
perception of the 1977 job as autonomous.   However, given
the absence of appropriate instrumental variables, we did
not attempt to estimate reciprocal effects.

Appendix 5.A   Unstandardized Error Covariances for the Six Models
(standardized estimates in parentheses).

	Young		Middle-aged		Older	
	men	women	men	women	men	women
1973 Autonomy & 1973 Income	.01	.08	.01	.02	.11*	.02
	(.09)	(.15)	(.07)	(.08)	(.31)	(.15)
1973 Autonomy & 1973 Work Overload	.06*	-.18*	.05*	.02	.12*	-.01
	(.40)	(-.36)	(.54)	(.11)	(.46)	(-.03)
1973 Autonomy & 1973 Job Satisfaction	.17*	.25*	.05*	.07)	.06*	.03
	(.68)	(.47)	(.48)	(.19)	(.40)	(.21)
1973 Income & 1973 Work Overload	.03	.08*	.00	.03	.13*	.09*
	(.15)	(.20)	(.00)	(.24)	(.18)	(.40)
1973 Income & 1973 Job Satisfaction	.01	.06	.04*	.00	.04	.00
	(.04)	(.14)	(.16)	(-.01)	(.10)	(-.01)
1973 Work Overload & 1973 Job Satisfaction	.08*	-.01	.05	-.04	-.01	-.06
	(.23)	(-.02)	(.16)	(-.15)	(-.03)	(-.22)
1977 Autonomy & 1977 Income	-.01	.06	.05*	-.03	.04	-.06*
	(-.03)	(.09)	(.12)	(-.05)	(.04)	(-.16)
1977 Autonomy & 1977 Work Overload	.12*	.15*	.07	.07*	.05*	.12*
	(.22)	(.30)	(.23)	(.12)	(.16)	(.15)
1977 Income & 1977 Work Overload	.00	-.03	-.02	-.01	.10	.03
	(.00)	(-.03)	(-.03)	(-.04)	(.13)	(.03)

*   coefficient significant at α<.05

Appendix 5.B   Unstandardized Residual Variances for the Six Models
(standardized estimates in parentheses).

	Young		Middle-aged		Older	
	men	women	men	women	men	women
1973 Education	1.03*	.96*	2.09*	2.17*	2.93*	1.20*
	(1.00)	(1.00)	(1.00)	(1.00)	(1.00)	(1.00)
1973 Autonomy	.10*	.60*	.03	.18*	.12*	.10
	(.97)	(.94)	(.96)	(.85)	(.94)	(.93)
1973 Income	.17*	.42*	.21*	.15*	.99*	.10*
	(.95)	(.98)	(.89)	(.75)	(.94)	(.91)
1973 Work Overload	.20*	.36*	.30*	.10	.50*	.45*
	(.96)	(.94)	(.99)	(.97)	(.97)	(.91)
1973 Job Satisfaction	.55*	.44*	.30*	.51*	.18*	.16*
	(.99)	(.99)	(.97)	(.93)	(.97)	(.99)
1977 Autonomy	.27*	.42*	.13*	.74*	.21*	.20*
	(.89)	(.91)	(.67)	(.84)	(.58)	(.49)
1977 Income	.45*	1.06*	.52*	.14*	1.79*	.23*
	(.68)	(.91)	(.70)	(.44)	(.80)	(.57)
1977 Work Overload	1.03*	.48*	.31*	.36*	.10*	1.35
	(.98)	(.93)	(.67)	(.89)	(.42)	(.94)
1977 Job Satisfaction	.14*	.09*	.14*	.11*	.18*	.06*
	(.45)	(.52)	(.66)	(.31)	(.65)	(.56)

*   coefficient significant at α <.05

REFERENCES

Andrisani, Paul J. 1978. "Job Satisfaction Among Working Women." Signs 3:558-607.

Aneshensel, Carol S., and Bernard C. Rosen. 1980 "Domestic Roles and Sex Differences in Occupational Expectations." Journal of Marriage and the Family 42 (February):121-131.

Baltes, Paul B., Hayne W. Reese, and Lewis P. Lipsitt. 1980. "Life-span Developmental Psychology." Annual Review of Psychology 31:65-110.

Brim, Orville G., Jr., and Jerome Kagan (eds.). 1980. Constancy and Change in Human Development. Cambridge, Mass.: Harvard University Press.

Brim, Orville G., Jr., and Carol Ryff. 1980. "On the Properties of Life Events." In Paul B. Baltes and Orville G. Brim (eds.), Life-Span Development and Behavior Vol. 3. New York: Academic Press.

Campbell, Angus, Philip Converse, and Willard Rodgers. 1976. The Quality of American Life. New York: Sage.

Card, Josephina J., Lauri Steel, and Ronald P. Abeles. 1980. "Sex Differences in Realization of Individual Potential for Achievement." Journal of Vocational Behavior 17 (August):1-21.

Cohn, Richard M. 1979. "Age and the Satisfactions from Work." Journal of Gerontology 34 (No. 2):264-272.

Costa, Paul T., Jr., Robert R. McCrae, and David Arenberg. 1983. "Recent Longitudinal Research on Personality and Aging." Pp. 222-265 in K. Warner Schaie (ed.), Longitudinal Studies of Adult Psychological Development. New York: Guilford Press.

Falk, William W., and Arthur G. Cosby. 1978. "Women's Marital-Familial Statuses and Work Histories: Some Conceptual Considerations." Journal of Vocational Behavior 13 (August):126-140.

Fein, Mitchell. 1976. "Motivation for Work." Pp. 465-530 in Robert Dubin (ed.), Handbook of Work, Organization, and Society. Chicago: Rand McNally.

Featherman, David L. 1980. "Schooling and Occupational Careers: Constancy and Change in Worldly Success." Pp. 675-738 in Orville G. Brim, Jr., and Jerome Kagan (eds.), Constancy and Change in Human Development. Cambridge, Mass.: Harvard University Press.

Felmlee, Diane H. 1984. "The Dynamics of Women's Job Mobility." Work and Occupations 11 (August):259-281.

Finkbeiner, Carl. 1979. "Estimation for the Multiple Factor Model When Data Are Missing." Psychometrika 44 (December):409-420.

Freeman, Richard B. 1976. The Overeducated American. New York: Academic Press.

Frese, Michael. 1984. "Transitions in Jobs, Occupational Socialization, and Strain." Pp. 239-252 in Vernon L. Allen and Evert van de Vliert (eds.), Role Transitions. Explorations and Explanations. New York: Plenum.

Glenn, Norval D. 1980. "Values, Attitudes, and Beliefs." Pp. 596-640 in Brim, Orville G., Jr., and Jerome Kagan (eds.), Constancy and Change in Human Development. Cambridge, Mass.: Harvard University Press.

Glenn, Norval D., and Charles N. Weaver. 1982. "Further Evidence on Education and Job Satisfaction." Social Forces 61 (September):46-55.

--------. 1985. "Age, Cohort, and Reported Job Satisfaction in the United States." Pp. 89-109 in Zena Smith Blau (ed.), Current Perspectives on Aging and the Life Cycle, Vol. I. Greenwich, Conn.: JAI Press.

Gould, Sam. 1979. "Age, Job Complexity, Satisfaction, and Performance." Journal of Vocational Behavior 14:209-223.

Gurin, Gerald, Joseph Veroff, and Sheila Feld. 1960. Americans View Their Mental Health. New York: Basic Books.

Hall, Douglas T. 1971. "A Theoretical Model of Career Subidentity Development in Organizational Settings." Organizational Behavior and Human Performance 6:50-76.

Herzberg, Frederick, Bernard Mausner, and Barbara B. Snyderman. 1959. The Motivation to Work (Second edition). New York: Wiley. International Educational Services. 1972. Analysis of Linear Structural Relationships by the Method of Maximum Likelihood. Chicago: National Educational Resources.

Janson, Philip, and Jack Martin. 1982. "Job Satisfaction and Age: A Test of Two Views." Social Forces 60 (June):1089-1102.

Joreskog, Karl G., and Dag Sorbom. 1979. Advances in Factor Analysis and Structural Equation Models. Cambridge, Mass.: Abt Books.

Kalleberg, Arne L. 1977. "Work Values and Job Rewards: A Theory of Job Satisfaction." American Sociological Review 42 (February):124-143.

Kalleberg, Arne L., and Karyn A. Loscocco. 1983. "Aging, Values, and Rewards: Explaining Age Differences in Job Satisfaction." American Sociological Review 48 (February):78-90.

Kanter, Rosabeth Moss. 1976. "The Impact of Hierarchical Structures on the Work Behavior of Women and Men." Social Problems 23 (April):415-430.

-------. 1977. Men and Women of the Corporation. New York: Basic.

Kohn, Melvin L., and Carmi Schooler. 1973. "Occupational Experience and Psychological Functioning: An Assessment of Reciprocal Effects." American Sociological Review 38 (February):97-118.

-------. 1982. "Job Conditions and Personality: A Longitudinal Assessment of their Reciprocal Effects." American Journal of Sociology 87:1257-1286.

Kohn, Melvin L., and Carmi Schooler, with the collaboration of Joanne Miller, Karen A. Miller, Carrie Schoenbach, and Ronald Schoenberg. 1983. Work and Personality: An Inquiry into the Impact of Social Stratification. Norwood, N.J.: Ablex Publishing Corporation.

Laws, Judith Long. 1976. "Work Aspiration of Women: False Leads and New Starts." Signs 1 (Spring):33-49.

Linton, Ralph. 1936. The Study of Man. New York: Appleton.

Locke, Edwin A. 1976. "The Nature and Causes of Job Satisfaction." Pp. 1297-1349 in Marvin D. Dunnette (ed.), Handbook of Industrial and Organizational Psychology. Chicago: Rand McNally.

Long, J. S. 1976. "Estimation and Hypothesis Testing in Linear Models Containing Measurement Error." Sociological Methods and Research 2:157-206.

Lorence, Jon, and Jeylan T. Mortimer. 1985. "Job Involvement Through the Life Course: A Panel Study of Three Age Groups." American Sociological Review 50 (October):618-638.

Mannheim, Bilha. 1983. "Male and Female Industrial Workers: Job Satisfaction, Work Role Centrality, and Work Place Preference." Work and Occupations 10 (November):413-435.

Martin, Jack K., and Sandra L. Hanson. 1985. "Sex, Family Wage Earning Status, and Satisfaction with Work." Work and Occupations 12 (February):91-109.

Maruyama, Geoffrey, Michael D. Finch, and Jeylan T. Mortimer. 1985. "Processes of Achievement in the Transition to Adulthood." Pp. 61-87 in Zena Smith Blau (ed.), Current Perspectives on Aging and the Life Cycle. Greenwich, Conn.: JAI Press.

Miller, Joanne. 1980. "Individual and Occupational Determinants of Job Satisfaction: A Focus on Gender Differences." Sociology of Work and Occupations 7 (August):337-366.

Miller, Joanne, Carmi Schooler, Melvin L. Kohn, and Karen A. Miller. 1979. "Women and Work: The Psychological Effects of Occupational Conditions." American Journal of

Sociology 85 (July):66-94.

Miller, Joanne, Kazimierz M. Slomczynski, and Melvin L. Kohn. 1987. "Continuity of Learning-Generalization: The Effect of Job on Men's Intellective Process in the United States and Poland." This volume, Chapter 4.

Moen, Phyllis. 1985. "Continuities and Discontinuities in Women's Labor Force Participation." In Glen H. Elder, Jr. (ed.), Life Course Dynamics: 1960s to 1980s. Ithaca, N.Y.: Cornell University Press.

Moen, Phyllis, and Martha Moorehouse. 1983. "Overtime over the Life Cycle: A Test of the Life Cycle Squeeze Hypothesis." Pp. 201-218 in Research in the Interweave of Social Roles, Vol. 3. Greenwich, Conn.: JAI Press.

Mortimer, Jeylan T. 1979. Changing Attitudes Toward Work, Vol. 11, Work in America Institute Studies in Productivity. Scarsdale, N.Y.: Work in America Institute.

Mortimer, Jeylan T., and Michael D. Finch. 1983. "Autonomy as a Source of Self-Esteem in Adolescence." Paper presented at the annual meeting of the American Sociological Association, Detroit.

Mortimer, Jeylan T., and Michael D. Finch. 1986. "The Development of Self-Esteem in the Early Work Career." Work and Occupations 13 (May):217-239.

Mortimer, Jeylan T., Michael D. Finch, and Donald Kumka. 1982. "Persistence and Change in Development: The Multidimensional Self-Concept." Pp. 263-313 in Paul B. Baltes and Orville G. Brim, Jr. (eds.), Life-Span Development and Behavior, Vol. 4. New York: Academic Press.

Mortimer, Jeylan T., and Jon Lorence. 1979a. "Work Experience and Occupational Value Socialization: A Longitudinal Study." American Journal of Sociology 84 (March):1361-1385.

Mortimer, Jeylan T., and Jon Lorence. 1979b. "Occupational Experience and the Self-Concept: A Longitudinal Study." Social Psychology Quarterly 42:307-323.

Mortimer, Jeylan T., Jon Lorence, and Donald Kumka. 1986. Work, Family, and Personality: Transition to Adulthood. Norwood, N.J.: Ablex Publishing Corporation.

Mortimer, Jeylan T,. and Glorian Sorensen. 1984. "Men, Women, Work, and Family." Pp. 139-167 in Kathryn M. Borman, Daisy Quarm, and Sarah Gideonse (eds.), Women in the Workplace: Effects on Families. Norwood, N.J.: Ablex Publishing Corporation.

Nicholson, Nigel. 1984. "A Theory of Work Role Transitions." Administrative Science Quarterly

29:172-191.

Oppenheimer, Valerie. 1974. "The Life-Cycle Squeeze: The Interaction of Men's Occupational and Family Life Cycles." Demography 11 (May):227-246.

Osipow, Samuel H. 1975. "The Relevance of Theories of Career Development to Special Groups: Problems, Needed Data, and Implications." Pp. 9-22 in J. Steven Picou and Robert E. Campbell (eds.), Career Behavior of Special Groups. Columbus, Ohio: Charles E. Merrill Publishing Company.

Pleck, Joseph H., and Michael Rustad. 1980. "Husbands' and Wives' Time in Family Work and Paid Work in 1975-76 Study of Time Use." Unpublished paper. Wellesley College for Research on Women.

Quinn, Robert P., and Graham L. Staines. 1979. The 1977 Quality of Employment Survey. Ann Arbor, Mich.:Survey Research Center, University of Michigan.

Quinn, Robert P., Graham L. Staines, and Margaret R. McCullough. 1974. "Job Satisfaction: Is There a Trend?" Manpower Research Monograph No. 30. U. S. Department of Labor. Washington, D. C.: Manpower Administration.

Regan, Mary C., and Helen E. Roland. 1982. "University Students: A Change in Expectations and Aspirations over the Decade." Sociology of Education 55 (October):223-228.

Rhodes, Susan R. 1983. "Age-Related Differences in Work Attitudes and Behavior: A Review and Conceptual Synthesis." Psychological Bulletin 93(2):328-367.

Riley, Matilda White. 1985. "Age Strata in Social Systems." Pp. 369-411 in Robert H. Binstock and Ethel Shanas (eds.), Handbook of Aging and the Social Sciences (Second edition). New York: Van Nostrand Reinhold.

Rosenfeld, Rachel A. 1979. "Women's Occupational Careers: Individual and Structural Explanations." Sociology of Work and Occupations 6 (August):283-311.

Schwab, Donald P., and Herbert G. Heneman III. 1977. "Age and Satisfaction with Dimensions of Work." Journal of Vocational Behavior 10:212-220.

Sears, David O. 1981. "Life-Stage Effects on Attitude Change, Especially Among the Elderly." Pp. 183-204 in Sara B. Kiesler, James N. Morgan, and Valerie Kincade Oppenheimer (eds.), Aging: Social Change. New York: Academic Press.

Seashore, Stanley E., and Thomas D. Taber. 1975. "Job Satisfaction Indicators and Their Correlates." American Behavioral Scientist 18 (January-February):333-368.

Sewell, William H., and Robert M. Hauser. 1976. "Causes and Consequences of Higher Education: Models of the Status

Attainment Process." Pp. 9-27 in William H. Sewell, Robert M. Hauser, and David L. Featherman (eds.), Schooling and Achievement in American Society. New York: Academic Press.

Sewell, William H., Robert M. Hauser, and Wendy Wolf. 1980. "Sex, Schooling and Occupational Status." American Journal of Sociology 86 (November):551-583.

Sexton, Patricia C. 1977. Women and Work. Washington, D.C.: U.S. Department of Labor, Employment and Training Administration.

Seybolt, John W. 1976. "Work Satisfaction as a Function of the Person- Environment Interaction." Organizational Behavior and Human Performance 17 (October):66-75.

Shepard, Jon M. 1973. "Specialization, Autonomy, and Job Satisfaction." Industrial Relations 12 (October):274-281.

Spaeth, Joe L. 1976. "Characteristics of the Work Setting and the Job as Determinants of Income." Pp. 161-176 in William H. Sewell, Robert M. Hauser, and David L. Featherman (eds.), Schooling and Achievement in American Society. New York: Academic Press.

Stone, Eugene F. 1976. "The Moderating Effect of Work-related Values on the Job Scope-Job Satisfaction Relationship." Organizational Behavior and Human Performance 15 (April):147-167.

Strauss, George. 1974a. "Is There a Blue-Collar Revolt Against Work?" Pp. 40-69 in James O'Toole (ed.), Work and the Quality of Life: Resource Papers for Work in America. Cambridge, Mass.: MIT Press.

Strauss, George. 1974b. "Workers: Attitudes and Adjustments." Pp. 73-98 in Jerome M. Rosow (ed.), The Worker and the Job: Coping with Change. Englewood Cliffs, N.J.: Prentice-Hall.

Super, D. E., J. Crites, R. Hummel, H. Moser, P. Overstreet, and C. Warnath. 1957. Vocational Development: A Framework for Research. New York: Teachers College Press.

Tannenbaum, Arnold S., Bogdan Kavcic, Menachem Rosner, Mino Vianello, and Georg Wieser. 1974. Hierarchy in Organizations. San Francisco, Calif.: Jossey-Bass.

Van Maanen, John, and Ralph Katz. 1976. "Individuals and their Careers: Some Temporal Considerations for Work Satisfaction." Personnel Psychology 29:601-616.

Van Maanen, John, and Edgar H. Schein. 1979. "Toward a Theory of Organizational Socialization." Pp. 209-264 in Barry M. Staw (ed.), Research in Organizational Behavior. Greenwich, Conn.: JAI Press.

Voydanoff, Patricia. 1978. "The Relationship Between
    Perceived Job Characteristics and Job Satisfaction Among
    Occupational Status Groups." Sociology of Work and
    Occupations 5 (May):179-192.
Weaver, Charles N. 1978. "Sex Differences in the
    Determinants of Job Satisfaction." Academy of Management
    Journal 21 (June):265-274.
Wolf, Wendy C., and Rachel Rosenfeld. 1978. "Sex Structure
    of Occupations and Job Mobility." Social Forces 56
    (March):823-844.
Wright, James D., and Richard F. Hamilton. 1978. "Work
    Satisfaction and Age: Some Evidence for the 'Job Change'
    Hypothesis." Social Forces 56 (June):1140-1158.

Glorian Sorensen, Jeylan T. Mortimer

6. Implications of the Dual Roles of Adult Women for Their Health[1]

Since the turn of the century, there have been vast
changes in the work experiences of women, including recent
rapid increases in their labor force participation and
radical shifts in the distribution of their work through the
life span. The proportion of women in the U.S. labor force
has risen dramatically. In 1900, only 18 percent of females
over 14 years of age were employed (Smith 1979); they
comprised about one-fifth of the total work force (U.S.
Bureau of the Census 1975). By 1980, 60 percent of all
women between 16 and 64 were in the labor force, representing 43 percent of the total (National Commission on
Working Women 1982a).

The pre-World War II pattern of women's employment
through the life span meshed well with the traditional,
highly sex-typed division of family labor. Women worked
outside the home before marriage and childbearing, and then
dropped out of the labor force after having children. In
1900, in the 16 to 19 year age group, 27 percent of women
were employed; 32 percent of those 20-24 years old worked
outside the home. But in the 25-44 year age group, less
than 18 percent of women were employed; even fewer--14 per-
cent--of women aged 45-64 years were working[2].

In the post-war period, what has been called a "dual
peak" pattern of employment through the life cycle arose:
that is, women worked outside the home in the early years of
marriage, became full-time homemakers when their children
were born, and then returned to work sometime in middle age
when their children required less close supervision. This
"dual peak" pattern is also evident in the age-specific
labor force participation rates. For example, in 1955, 40

and 46 percent in the 16-19 and 20-24 year age groups were
employed, respectively; 35 percent of those in the 25-34
year age group, and 42 and 44 percent among those 35-44 and
45-54. Given the incompatibility of work and family obligations, this distribution of labor force participation
through the life course represented an accommodation to the
normative prescription that women should have primary
responsibility for the home and children.

More recently, women have pursued a more continuous
pattern of labor force participation throughout adulthood.
By 1977, the majority of women in all age categories between
16 and 54 were in the labor force. By 1983, in the 20-44
age group, more than two-thirds of women were employed; 62
percent were working in the 45-54 year old group. The most
rapid recent growth rates in employment have occurred among
women with very young children who have had relatively low
labor force participation rates in the past. At present,
half of mothers with children under four are in the labor
force. As a result, women are spending a longer period of
their lives in the workforce. It has been estimated that a
woman born in 1900 worked six years out of her 48-year life
expectancy. Women in 1980 will probably work 29 years of
their nearly 78-year life expectancy (McLaughlin et al.
1985; U.S. Department of Labor, Bureau of Labor Statistics
1982; see also Kreps and Clark 1975.)

Because of these changes, women today are more likely
to be simultaneously occupying demanding work and family
roles. For while they have entered the labor force in
increasing numbers, and the normative climate has become
increasingly favorable to their employment, women continue
to shoulder the major responsibility for household tasks and
children. It is often suggested that women's dual role
responsibilities and attendant role conflicts may have negative consequences for their health. But despite the rising
concern and the considerable speculation surrounding this
subject, relatively little is known about the implications
of the shifts in women's labor force participation and its
patterning through the life course for change in women's
physical and mental well-being. Systematic studies of the
impacts of women's job and family roles on their health have
yielded contradictory findings. In this chapter, we
describe four conceptual models that provide quite different
perspectives on the interrelationships of work and health
among women as they move through the life span.

THE FEATURES OF WOMEN'S WORK AND FAMILY ROLES

Despite the influx of women into the labor force in the twentieth century, and the increasingly continuous character of their labor force paticipation, the types of positions they hold and the relative salaries they earn have changed little. Women's jobs typically have less autonomy, authority, and advancement opportunity than the jobs occupied by men. In 1982, the median weekly earnings of women employed full-time was $241, compared to $371 for men; thus, women must work over seven and one-half days to gross what men gross in only five (U.S. Department of Commerce 1984). Over the course of their careers, men gain substantially more in terms of both income and prestige than do women, who tend to remain at the same occupational and earning levels as they grow older (Barrett 1979). Moreover, a man's income benefits far more from his education and work experience than does a woman's (Barrett 1979; Featherman and Hauser 1976). Several factors, related both to their traditional work and family roles, contribute to women's restricted mobility over the life span.

Sex role socialization certainly contributes to gender inequality. Young women have tended to underestimate their eventual labor force participation when compared with the actual labor force participation of adult women (Sexton 1977), and therefore have limited their investments in education, training, and work. However, recent evidence suggests that the aspirations and educational expectations of young women have been changing over the past decade. They are increasingly expecting to combine family and career. For example, in 1970 in one liberal arts college, only one-fourth as many women as men aspired to professional careers; in 1980, young women were almost as likely as young men to intend to pursue a profession (Regan and Roland 1982).

However, sex role socialization and differing human capital investments do not adequately account for the income gap between men and women (Kanter 1977a). Much of the income differential between men and women cannot be explained by differences in education, occupational prestige, and work experiences, and is probably due to discrimination (Featherman and Hauser 1976; Treiman and Terrell 1975; Corcoran et al. 1984). Women's occupational positions and economic rewards are determined not only by their socialization and educational investments, but by social expectations which restrict the opportunities available to them.

Much of the income differential is due to occupational segregation. Of the 441 occupations listed in the Census Occupational Classification System, the majority of employed women are found in only twenty. Eighty percent of women workers are concentrated in clerical, service, sales, factory, and plant jobs (National Commission on Working Women 1982b). In 1982, over one-third of all women workers were employed in clerical positions (U.S. Department of Commerce 1984). This sex typing of the labor force has been highly persistent, despite the increased numbers of women employed outside the home. According to Oppenheimer (1975), 14 out of 17 major jobs that were 70 percent or more female in 1900 continued to be occupied primarily by women in 1960. Because the number of jobs in this female sector has not kept pace with the number of women looking for employment, women's wages are further depressed and their unemployment increased (Barrett 1979). Since 1970, women have moved in significant numbers into some male-dominated areas, such as business management and law. Yet when women attempt to enter traditionally male positions, they frequently face sexual harrassment and a tightly-knit male buddy system (Barrett 1979). However, most women continue to work in female dominated fields (Beller 1985).

This segregated system is perpetuated by "statistical discrimination": employers assess individual job applicants on the basis of their categorical membership (Stevenson 1978), and assign women to positions which have little advancement opportunities and which do not require on-the-job training. Their assumption that women are unstable workers, likely to drop out of the labor force or to move depending on the requirements of their husbands' jobs, leads to a self-fulfilling prophecy, since persons working in simple, dead-end jobs are likely to have high absenteeism and turnover rates (Kanter 1977b). The concentration of women in such low-level jobs reinforces their image as unstable and uncommitted workers.

Women's advancement in the labor force is further restriced by traditional sex role assumptions, which shape the structure of work. Paid work is structured into discrete time blocks, allowing little flexibility for those women who must juggle work and family demands. The clockwork of the career system, which emphasizes the importance of achieving "on time," is designed for workers, usually male, who are free from family responsibilities to pursue this pressured course (Hochschild 1975; Fowlkes 1980). Unfortunately, this blueprint for the labor market is founded on the erroneous assumption that women are secondary earners receiving superfluous income. Such a perception overlooks the powerful economic incentive forcing many women to work. In fact, in 1978, 43 percent of working women were single, divorced, widowed, or separated; an additional 23 percent were married to men with earnings less than $15,000 per year (National Commission on Working Women 1982b).

This sex-typed division of labor, found in the occupational structure, also characterizes work in the home. The traditional family responsibilities of women persist despite women's expanding role in the labor force. Studies of time use indicate that while employed women spend about 28 hours on family work each week, their husbands contribute only about 13 hours (Pleck and Rustad 1980). When husbands do participate, they are more likely to care for children than to perform routine household tasks (Pleck 1977). Moreover, the amount of time husbands spend on family work does not vary significantly with the employment status of their wives (Pleck and Rustad 1980).

The nature of housework has changed dramatically in recent years, and the actual amount of time spent in household tasks has diminished (Pleck and Rustad 1980). Technology, urbanization, and demographic changes have done much to alter the character of housework. But today's housewife has less paid help than her 1900 counterpart. Her tasks have been complicated by higher standards and by the expectation that she also be household manager, planner, and record-keeper. And her role as consumer may be as time-consuming as her previous role as producer (Vanek 1978).

Traditionally, the wife also has had responsibilities related to her husband's career. Despite the cultural myth that individuals achieve on their own merits and efforts (Kanter 1977a), the role of wife frequently includes the expectation that she contribute to a "two-person career" headed by her husband (Papanek 1973). Her efforts, not only in maintaining the homefront, but also in direct and indirect support of her husband's work role, may contribute substantially to his career success (Mortimer 1980; Mortimer et al. 1978, 1982).

For women, family responsibilities may spill over into their own work lives. Because the boundaries between home and work are more permeable for women than men, the family role frequently is allowed to intrude on women's work role (Pleck 1977). As a consequence, many women choose to work part-time or intermittently. In 1978, only 44 percent of employed women worked full-time year round (U.S. Department of Labor 1980a, Table 19). Moen's (1985) analysis of data from the Panel Study of Income Dynamics showed that only 23 percent of women were continuously employed, full-time, over a five-year period (1972-76). Almost half of women under 62 changed their labor force status during this period. Children had a clear inhibiting effect on women's continuous full-time employment (see also Shaw 1985). Many women prefer to work close to home in jobs without overtime or travel commitments. Their need to locate employment that accommodates family demands is likely to constrict both their occupational opportunites and financial rewards.

MODELS OF WOMEN'S WORK AND HEALTH THROUGH THE LIFE SPAN

Given the potential for role overload and strain in the face of conflicting work and family demands, some have suggested that employed women's health is bound to suffer. However, since there are few available longitudinal studies on the relationship between health and employment, it is very difficult to determine whether their health is, in fact, threatened. Any differences in the health of employed and not employed persons may reflect the selection of healthy individuals into the labor force, those who can withstand the resultant strains (McMichael 1976). Moreover, although only six percent of women who are not in the labor force cite poor health as their main reason for not seeking employment (U.S. Department of Labor 1980b), as a group, employed women tend to be healthier than the non-employed. In a longitudinal study of married women, Waldron and her colleagues (1982) found support for the hypothesis that selection of healthy women into the labor force accounts for the fact that employed women are healthier than non-employed women. These researchers concluded that health has a strong impact on labor force participation, and that employment has few harmful or beneficial effects on women's health. Similarly, Jennings and her colleagues (1984) found that the "healthy worker effect" explained some of the association between employment status and several measures of health. However, these researchers have confined their attention to employment status; the characteristics of women's work experiences also must be considered. Although selection factors may influence entrance into the labor force as well as entry into specific jobs, it is likely that features of the work environment are powerful predictors of health. That is, selection and causal influence are not mutually exclusive processes; both may contribute to the relationships between women's work and health.

The great diversity of measures and definitions of health further complicates the relationship between work and health. Some investigators focus attention on mortality. Others have examined chronic disease incidence or precursors of chronic disease, such as blood pressure or smoking behavior. Morbidity rates may reflect true illness, as well as the perception of acute symptoms and the willingness to limit one's activities, seek help, and report symptoms. Finally, studies of mental health and well-being, as criterion variables, provide a different perspective from that of physical illness. Given these diverse measures, the findings of studies of the potential impact of job experiences on health have been far from consistent.

Investigators have made different assumptions about the relationship between women's work experience and their health status, and have developed varying explanatory frameworks. Interpretations of the varied--and often conflicting --empirical findings pertaining to this question may be subsumed under four general models. Thus, the reader may note that the results of studies presented under one model may contradict those included in another model.

First, according to the "stress model," work experiences threaten workers' health because of the demands and pressures work poses. A second "health benefits model" emphasizes the advantages of employment for health, reminding us that work experiences may provide opportunities for autonomy, social support, and satisfaction, all of which enhance health. Rather than examining job experiences, as the first two models do, a third "role expansion model" focuses on the number of roles a person occupies, such as worker, spouse, and parent. It suggests that multiple roles offer increased opportunities for building self-esteem and satisfactions from diverse sources, thus benefiting health. Finally, according to a fourth "person-environment fit model," health outcomes are predicted by the match or "fit" between worker characteristics and job demands rather than by job experiences alone.

None of the models were explicitly formulated to

address the relationship between work and health through the
life span. However, each directs our attention to particular questions and issues which have clear implications for
change over the life course. With respect to the "stress"
and the "health benefits" models, we might ask: How are the
stress-promoting and health-benefiting dimensions of work
and family roles distributed across age groups? The "role
expansion" model is highly applicable to a life course
perspective, for the number of role positions a woman
typically occupies expands and then contracts as she grows
older. Finally, indicators of position in the life course,
such as age, career phase, or stage in the family life
cycle, may be powerful determinants of the "fit" between
person and job.

The Stress Model

    Extensive empirical research has focused on the poten-
tially deleterious consequences of job stress.
Investigators have suggested that the stressful aspects of
the work environment may account for decrements in mental
well-being, increased physical morbidity, and heightened
rates of cardiovascular disease. Indeed, at any one time,
about five percent of the work force may be under work-
related strain severe enough to warrant help (Warr 1982).
The recent influx of women into the labor force has led some
investigators to suggest that women's exposure to the job
stressors previously confined to men is likely to increase
their risk of disease (Garbus and Garbus 1980; Lewis and
Lewis 1977; Nathanson 1980). The additional stress associated with dual responsibilities at home and on the job may
compound women's potential health risks.
    A common difficulty for research on job stress is the
failure to agree on the precise definition of "stress."
Some investigators have described job stress as occurring
when workers confront a situation for which the usual modes
of behavior are inadequate and for which the consequences of
not adapting are serious (House and Wells 1978). However,
the term "stress" is often used inconsistently to refer to
both environmental conditions and individual responses to
those conditions. In this review, the term "distress" is
used to refer to subjective responses to environmental conditions characterized by discomfort or negative affect.
Objective situations provoking distress are termed

"stressors."

Researchers have given considerable attention to the various objective conditions of the work environment that may cause distress; including work overload or underload (Frankenhauser 1977), role conflict or role ambiguity (Kahn et al. 1964), and role frustration (Hughes 1979). Time pressures related to both job and household tasks have been associated with mental strain, exhaustion, and depression (Karasek 1979; Schooler et al. 1983; Sorensen et al. 1985). In addition, cardiovascular symptoms and related premature death have been associated with fast-paced, demanding jobs, job deadlines, work overload, and a high level of job responsibility (House 1974; Karasek et al. 1981; Kasl 1978).

Interpersonal relationships on the job may provide social support or may produce distress, depending on their quality (House and Wells 1978). Close supervision has been found to be associated with distress, particularly among male workers (Kohn and Schooler 1982; Miller et al. 1979).

The experience of mobility may also constitute a stressor. It has been found, for example, that heart attack victims had more job changes prior to the coronary event than did matched controls (Syme et al. 1964; Jenkins et al. 1966). The "complexification" of the work environment, attendant on mobility, can tax the worker's coping abilities (House 1974). Furthermore, promotion beyond one's capabilities may diminish the perception of control over work, heightening distress (Matthews and Saal 1978).

In view of findings such as these, some investigators have raised concerns about the health consequences of some traditionally female occupations. For example, secretaries, 98 percent of whom are women, often are under considerable job pressure (Patterson and Engleberg 1978). Sixty percent of secretaries dislike their lack of advancement opportunities, and 55 percent are discontent with their salaries (National Commission on Working Women 1979). Haynes and Feinleib (1980) report that clerical workers are twice as likely as other employed women to develop coronary heart disease; they find that women clerical workers with nonsupportive bosses are at particularly high risk of heart disease.

From the perspective of the stress model, stressors on the job and in the home have a cumulative impact that may be particularly detrimental to women's health (Gore and Mangione 1983). The effect of job stressors on the health of both men and women is contingent upon the individual's

perceptual framework, personal resources, and the presence
of additional stressors outside the work setting. The
family may provide the social support needed to mitigate the
effects of distress or, when conflicts arise, may pose additional stressors with which the individual must cope. In
addition, family responsibilities may compound job-related
workloads. This perspective, derived from social role
theory, postulates that "having several roles with
conflicting obligations may cause distress" (Cleary and
Mechanic 1983). For women, marriage, motherhood, and
employment represent such potentially conflicting demands.

Certain stages of the life cycle and their accompanying
stressors may heighten the difficulties in juggling the dual
requirements of work and family roles. Although employment
often has positive consequences for married women, these
effects may be counteracted by the presence of children in
the home, which increases the woman's total work responsibility (Cleary and Mechanic 1983; Reskin and Coverman
1980; Johnson and Johnson 1977; Radloff 1975). The findings
of Baruch et al. (1983) suggest that motherhood, not
employment status, may be the most important correlate of
role strain. Gove and Geerken (1977) observed that women's
psychiatric symptoms were associated with the incessant
demands of young children, which prevented them from
spending time alone or with other adults. Ross et al.
(1983) reported that women who had full responsibility in
the home and whose husbands did not contribute to household
chores were more depressed than women whose husbands did
contribute, regardless of employment status. Other studies
suggest that psychological distress is high among women with
young children (Gove and Geerken 1977; Brown and Harris
1978), and that working women show more guilt and anxiety in
fulfilling their roles as wives and mothers (Burke and Weir
1976).

Similarly, childrearing has been correlated with risk
to physical well-being. Woods and Hulka (1979) report a
positive correlation between the number of reported symptoms
and the number of women's role responsibilities. (Family
pressures were more strongly associated with symptom
reporting than was the woman's employment status.) Thoits
(1984) reported that employment complicated the lives of
those occupying marital and parental roles. Age of the
children seems to be a primary factor. Women with preschool
children are more likely to adopt the sick role and to take
curative actions than are those with school-age children

(Verbrugge 1983; Geersten and Gray 1970; Thompson and Brown 1980; Woods and Hulka 1979; Brown and Harris 1978). Also, several studies have found that the more children a woman has, the greater her risk of coronary heart disease (Bengtsson et al. 1973; Haynes and Feinleib 1980). While family responsibilities represent role demands and socio-economic pressures that are likely to contribute to coronary heart disease risk, childbearing also may exert a strain on the circulatory system (Zalokar 1960).

Stress is also likely to be heightened during periods of major life transitions. For many women, midlife is asso-ciated with a return to the workforce, loss of a spouse, or children leaving home (Rubin 1979). Bart (1970) reports that compared to employed women, loss of the maternal role may be more acute for housewives, who may have been over-involved in their relationships with their children. And Welch and Booth (1977) found that wives in periods of tran-sition, such as beginning full-time work or leaving the work force, were under more stress than other married women, as reflected in alcohol and drug use, psychiatric symptoms, willingness to adopt the sick role, and the number of diseases uncovered in a physical examination.

The distress associated with women's multiple roles may spring from the particular character of their roles. Comparisons of mental and physical illness among men and women generally indicate that marriage is more protective of men's health than of women's (Berkman and Syme 1979; Nathanson and Lorenz 1982). The role of housewife is vague, unstructured, invisible, and of low prestige. Fulfilling nurturant roles also may interfere with women's self-care, contributing to fatigue and lowered bodily resistance to illness (Gove and Hughes 1979). Gove and Tudor (1973) suggest that housewives lack alternative sources of gratifi-cation available to men in their jobs. Yet even when women are employed, they often occupy less satisfactory jobs than do men, since society tends to define women's jobs as margi-nal and temporary. Thus, the frustrating and unsatisfactory character of housework in the absence of other, compensatory gratifications in the world of work, may contribute to women's distress (see also Bernard 1972; Bart 1970; Lopata 1971).

The quality of marriage may be an additional source of distress, adding to the stressors of work. Nonsupportive marital relationships result in higher rates of depression than do supportive marriages (Brown and Harris 1978;

Vanfossen 1981; Gove et al. 1983). In fact, Renne (1971) reported that individuals in unhappy marriages had even poorer mental health than those who were separated or divorced. Marital dissolution and the stressors associated with spouseless motherhood also have been related to increased physical morbidity (Berkman 1969).

In summary, particular work experiences may be especially powerful stressors, leading to distress and to decrements in health. Family demands and the workload in the home may also contribute to women's distress. At the same time, the perception of stressors, at home and on the job, and the resulting levels of distress, may be conditioned by events and circumstances in the other sphere. Since family demands tend to be greatest when young children are in the home, the "stress model" may be most applicable to the interrelations of work and health among women in early adulthood. Moreover, while women's career mobility is typically much more restricted than that of men, to the extent that women move to positions involving better working conditions or higher levels of job rewards over the course of their working lives, one might expect to find that job stressors and strains would be alleviated as they grow older. However, the findings supporting this stress model are contradicted by the results of other studies which confirm the "health benefits" and "role expansion" models.

Health Benefits Model

In contrast to the stressors it may pose, the job environment may offer the benefits of social support to otherwise isolated individuals, opportunities to build self-esteem and confidence in one's decision making, and experiences which enhance life satisfaction. Most investigations of these benefits, however, have focused on men. Indeed, separate research strategies for men and women have generally been applied to the study of the relationship between health and employment (Bronfenbrenner and Crouter 1981). Studies of men have followed a "work model," giving considerable attention to the variations in men's occupational experiences. However, a "gender model" has been applied to research on women, focusing on their employment status (i.e., employed vs. housewife), and giving little or no consideration to the amount of time they spend on the job, the nature of their work experiences, or even their occupational categories (Mortimer and Sorensen 1984; Nathanson and Lorenz 1982; Haw 1982). Thus, investigators have given more attention to the effects of women's employment status on their health, an issue of great relevance to the "role expansion" model, than to the impacts of the various dimensions of their work experiences. Nonetheless, there is evidence that comparable job conditions are likely to influence men's and women's psychological functioning in similar ways (Miller et al. 1979; Miller 1980; Sorensen et al. 1985). Comparability of the consequences of work for men's and women's physical well-being is less clear. Recent investigations of the health benefits of work have focused on three subjects: the extent to which work induces a sense of coherence, provides social support, and fosters job satisfaction.

Coherence is defined by Antonovsky as "a global orientation that expresses the extent to which one has a pervasive, enduring though dynamic, feeling of confidence that one's internal and external environments are predictable and that things will work out as well as can be reasonably expected" (Antonovsky 1979:123). The sense of coherence is associated with an internal locus of control, or the belief that success and failure are dependent on personal initiative and effort (Andrisani and Nestel 1976; Dubin et al. 1975). Antonovsky (1979) provides evidence that the sense of coherence fosters a wide range of mental and physical health outcomes.

In the workplace, it is plausible to suppose that occupational self-direction, the opportunity to exercise initiative and independent judgment (Kohn and Schooler 1982), would foster a sense of coherence, strengthening the worker's belief that the environment is controllable, predictable, and meaningful. For both men and women, self-direction in work has been found to influence numerous orientations to life:

> No matter what the sex of the worker, job conditions that directly or indirectly encourage occupational self-direction are conducive to effective intellectual functioning and to an open and flexible orientation to others. Job conditions that constrain the opportunity for self-direction or subject the worker to any of several types of pressures or uncertainties result in less effective intellectual functioning, unfavorable evaluations of self, and a rigid, intolerant social

orientation. (Miller et al. 1979:91).

Psychological distress is a likely outcome of jobs which lack opportunities for self-direction, as characterized, for example, by close supervision and highly routinized work (Kohn and Schooler 1982). Karesek (1979) found that decision making on the job presents the opportunity to exercise judgment and enhances feelings of efficacy. Rather than increasing distress, decision making promotes effectiveness in coping with the environment. Heightened risk of cardiovascular disease also has been related to low job decision latitude (Karasek et al. 1981).

The degree to which housework requires independent thought and judgment has similar psychological implications. Schooler et al. (1983) found that self-direction in housework is related to women's intellectual flexibility and a self-directed orientation. Similar relationships were not found among men, for whom housework generally is more discretionary.

A sense of coherence may promote effective coping with stress. Kobasa and her colleagues (1979) report that those who remain healthy under stress have a commitment to (rather than an alienation from) the various aspects of their lives, believe they have control over their lives, and seek novelty and challenge rather than familiarity and security. When exposed to stressors, such individuals tend to be exhilarated and energized rather than debilitated and worried.

Evidence that a sense of coherence fosters physical health is derived from studies of the "giving-up process," characterized by a loss of hope and a sense that the environment is meaningless and unpredictable. The "learned helplessness" model proposed by Seligman (1975) suggests that helplessness, a defining symptom of depression, is learned when one's actions are unrelated to rewards and punishments. The clinically depressed individual is convinced that any action would be ineffectual, and is thus unable to act. Giving up has been found to precede diseases of all kinds, ranging from degenerative to infectious (Engel and Schmale 1972; Antonovsky 1979). Furthermore, physical and mental health are affected by self-esteem (Coburn 1978), another by-product of self-directed jobs (Miller 1980; Miller et al. 1979; Mortimer and Finch 1986).

The sense of personal efficacy developed in jobs providing decision latitude and autonomy (Mortimer and Lorence 1979b) also may affect health knowledge and health-promoting behaviors. Seeman and Seeman (1983) found that those who thought health was not a matter of fate or luck were more likely to take preventive health action, including having a physical exam, changing the level of exercise or activity, diminishing or eliminating use of alcohol or tobacco, dieting for health reasons, and taking dietary supplements. Indeed, a high sense of personal control was related to higher self-reported health status and fewer reported episodes of chronic and acute illness. Seeman and Evans (1962) also found that powerlessness is inversely related to health knowledge among tuberculosis patients.

Social support arises from the interpersonal network of family, friends, co-workers, and acquaintances. The presence of social support is vital to the individual's ability to cope. Interaction with persons both on and off the job may change initial perceptions of potentially stressful objective stimuli. For example, the opportunity to discuss a stressful event with friends may diminish its importance in light of one's broader life context (House and Wells 1978; Cassel 1976). Furthermore, social support frequently alters the individual's response to the event even after it has been perceived as stressful.

Social supports are readily available within the work environment. Co-workers can fill the worker's needs for affiliation and stimulation, while also providing a frame of reference and a set of norms. Support from one's co-workers and supervisors thus may reduce role conflict and ambiguity and enhance self-esteem (House and Wells 1978). Indeed, some women workers report that a major benefit of employment is the establishment of close social ties with co-workers (Feree 1976; Jacobson 1974).

Research has linked social support to mental health. Roberts et al. (1982) found that both married and unmarried women who were employed had lower rates of psychiatric morbidity than those not employed. But when marital status, employment, and social contacts were considered together, only social contacts significantly predicted psychiatric morbidity. Pearlin and Johnson (1977) also reported that social isolation was an important predictor of depression. Sorensen et al. (1985) found that social support at work minimized distress symptoms among both men and women.

The protective impact of social support extends to self-reported physical well-being, coronary heart disease risk, and preventive health behaviors such as quitting smoking (Caplan et al. 1975; Cassel 1976). A classic longitudinal study followed men after the closing of two plants (Gore 1978). Men lacking social support evidenced significantly more illness symptoms and greater elevation of cholesterol levels than did those with social support. Similarly, Nathanson (1980) found that employment had the strongest health benefit for women having the fewest alternative sources of social support and self-esteem (i.e., divorced or separated women and women with less than a high school education), suggesting the importance of increased access to social ties and self-esteem through employment.

Job satisfaction may also influence health. Job satisfaction refers to a "positive emotional state resulting from appraisals of one's job or job experiences" (Locke 1976). In addition to satisfaction with one's job in general, specific facets of job satisfaction have been identified, including both intrinsic and extrinsic dimensions (Mortimer 1979). Extrinsic satisfactions refer to features of the job which are external to the work itself, including salary, benefits, and relations with one's supervisor. Intrinsic satisfactions include challenge, self-direction, creativity, and responsibility. A third dimension, which has received less attention in the literature, involves a people-oriented set of rewards: "the chance to work with people and to be useful to the society" (Mortimer and Lorence 1979a:1362).

The health benefits of job satisfaction are most notable in the deleterious effects of dissatisfaction with one's job. There is growing evidence that dissatisfaction, either with one's job in general or with specific facets of it, increases the risk of coronary heart disease as well as other symptoms of ill health (Kasl 1978; House 1974). For example, retrospective studies have suggested that, compared with persons without coronary heart disease, persons with heart disease were significantly more dissatisfied with their jobs or with certain aspects of them (e.g., lack of recognition, tedious work, or poor relationships with co-workers) (Jenkins 1971). Persons dissatisfied with their jobs report poorer health and take more curative actions, such as obtaining care from a physician, than do those who are satisfied with their work (Verbrugge 1982). And according to a study by Medalie et al. (1973), men who had problems with their supervisors were at higher risk for angina pectoris (chest pain). Bishop (1984) found that men and women military personnel reporting low job satisfaction also reported more symptoms of illness.

Kessler and McRae (1982) reported that women who were

very satisfied with their jobs derived significant health
benefits from employment, whereas among the dissatisfied,
employment increased distress. There is even evidence that
job satisfaction may contribute to longevity (Palmore 1969).
However, some studies have failed to show an association
between work satisfaction and physical well-being (Kasl
1978), and others have shown that the relationship may hold
only for specific groups (Sales and House 1971). For
example, the association between job dissatisfaction and
coronary heart disease has been found to be greater for
women than men (Verbrugge 1982).

In considering the implications of work for health
through the life span, it is important to take into account
the manner in which the health-promoting features of work
are distributed across age groups. Some relevant information is presented in Chapter 5 of this volume. Using data
from the 1973-1977 Quality of Employment Panel, Mortimer
et al. report that men generally have more work autonomy
than women. Middle-aged (30-44) and older men reported the
highest levels of autonomy. Within gender groups, the
youngest workers possessed the least autonomy. Job satisfaction tended to increase with age for both genders, consistent with the findings of a large number of prior studies
(Quinn et al. 1974; Rhodes 1983). From these findings, it
can be concluded that these health-promoting experiences of
work are more prevalent in middle-aged and older groups than
among the youngest workers. Thus, the "health benefits"
model may be more applicable to the experience of these
older workers as well.

As these studies indicate, more attention should be
paid to the objective and subjective features of women's
jobs, including the level of self-direction and autonomy,
and the sense of coherence thereby fostered; the opportunities they provide for social support; and the satisfactions they entail. These job experiences interact with
women's responsibilities in the home and the community. The
impacts of multiple roles on health are examined in the role
expansion model.

Role Expansion Model

In comparison to the health benefits model, the role
expansion model examines the number and types of roles a
person occupies. Rather than focusing on job character-

istics, employment status is a central concern. In direct
contradiction to the stress model, the role expansion model
posits that multiple roles and responsibilities, despite
their attendant conflicts and pressures, are health-
enhancing (or at least have no deleterious effects). As
women move through their lives, their role constellations
typically change. Even if they remain continuously employed
from young adulthood to the age of retirement (which is a
still unusual, but increasingly prevalent phenomenon, see
Moen 1985), they will experience a fluctuating sequence of
role responsibilities, rising in early adulthood, and then
contracting in middle age. At the onset of adulthood, the
woman is an unmarried student or worker (or sometimes,
student-worker). Upon marriage, she often takes on the role
combination of wife-worker. When children arrive, she
becomes a wife, parent, and worker. At mid-life, when
children leave home, her role obligations contract, and she
is again wife-worker. Finally, in the event of divorce or
widowhood, she reassumes the sole status of worker. Of
course, the sequence is usually much more complex, as additional roles are played (as volunteer worker, daughter of
aging parents and in-laws, friend, etc.), as women move in
and out of the labor force (and between part- and full-time
employment), and as they divorce, remarry, have children (or
obtain them through "reconstituted" marriages), and see
their children leave home. The role expansion model draws
our attention to the potential consequences of these fluctuating constellations of role statuses and obligations
through the life course for women's health.

From a symbolic interactionist perspective, the self is
defined by the multiple roles one holds. These role identities suggest norms for behavior, and give meaning, direction, and purpose to life (Thoits 1984). Group memberships
and their attendant role configurations help to maintain a
sense of personal identity and foster the reciprocal obligations between persons that contribute to social integration.
Thus, multiple role involvements may expand an individual's
resources and rewards, provide alternate sources of self-
esteem and satisfaction, and enhance physical and psychological well-being (Thoits 1984; Verbrugge 1985).

Turning first to employment, for those who occupy the
work role, time is structured, and income, activity, and
social contacts are provided. They also obtain a work
status and identity (Warr 1982). The unemployed lack these
rewards of work. Among men, unemployment has been asso-

ciated with increased risk of heart attack, ulcers, hyper-
tension, arthritis, diabetes, and elevations of serum
cholesterol, as well as feelings of self-blame, hopeless-
ness, depression, irritability, and malaise (Kahn 1981;
Warr 1982; Manuso 1977; Hepworth 1980; Stafford et al.
1980). It is evident, however, that these health and
psychological problems could also increase the likelihood of
unemployment.

Among women, the benefits of employment and the costs
of unemployment are less clear, and the difficulty of
establishing causal order is also present. Some studies
report that employment status makes no difference in women's
mental health (Newberry et al. 1979; Roberts and O'Keefe
1981). However, it is generally observed that compared with
housewives, employed married women report fewer psychiatric
symptoms, display better adjustment to their social roles,
and perform their roles more effectively (Gove and Geerken
1977; Gove and Tudor 1973; Newberry et al. 1979; Bart 1970;
Bernard 1972; Reskin and Coverman 1980; Kessler and McRae
1982; Burke and Weir 1976). Jennings et al. (1984) examined
numerous indicators of health, including self-reported
health status, health behaviors, and preventive health
actions, and found that employed women were most healthy,
unemployed women least healthy, and full-time homemakers of
intermediate health. In a similar comparison of part-time
and full-time workers, Herold and Waldron (1985) found the
relationship between employment and health varied by women's
marital status and race. For married black women and
unmarried women, part-time workers reported poorer health
than full-time workers, while the health differences between
part-time and full-time workers were generally nonsignificant for married white women.

Heavier role responsibilities may make women less
inclined to take action in response to symptoms. Thus,
employed women tend to report fewer chronic and acute symptoms, make fewer physician visits, and restrict their activities less often than housewives (Nathanson 1980; Welch and
Booth 1977; Finseth et al. 1975; Pope and McCabe 1975; Feld
1963; Verbrugge 1983, 1985, in press), although the evidence
here also is not entirely consistent (Radloff 1975; Wright
1978).

Findings on the risk of coronary heart disease are
likewise inconclusive. The prospective Framingham Heart
Study indicated no significant differences in the tendencies
of employed women and housewives to develop coronary heart

disease, although women with the longest job tenures--single women--had the lowest risk (Haynes and Feinleib 1980). Similarly, Hauenstein et al. (1977) found few differences in women's blood pressure levels according to employment status. In the San Antonio Heart Study, there were no differences between employed and nonemployed women in blood pressure levels, obesity, and smoking. However, significant differences were observed in cholesterol and triglyceride levels, with the pattern of differences favoring employed women over the nonemployed (Kangilaski 1983).

Positive health outcomes may be inherent in the benefits derived from employment (Kessler and McRae 1982). Nye (1974) concluded that the adverse effects of dual role responsibilities must be mitigated by the psychological, social, and economic benefits of employment. The social support available through employment is particularly beneficial to women lacking other social ties, such as the unmarried (Thoits 1984; Nathanson 1980). Epstein (1983) suggests that role diversification is essential to mental health; greater autonomy and integration result from the social supports available through work outside the home. If housework is indeed the frustrating and menial role that some propose (Bernard 1972; Gove and Tudor 1973), it follows that release from that role through employment outside the home would foster health and well-being. The mental health advantages of employment are further described by Kessler and McRae (1981). Although women typically have had higher rates of mental illness than men, the relationship between sex and mental illness has been declining in the last two decades. They find that this decline is associated with women's increasing labor force participation, and conclude that employment outside the home provides women with rewards not available to homemakers.

Marriage and parenthood are additional roles that may promote health. Although the health benefits of marriage are stronger for men than women (Berkman and Syme 1979; Verbrugge 1979), married women tend to have lower age-adjusted mortality and morbidity rates than do single women (Retherford 1975; Nathanson 1975). While healthy people may be disproportionately selected into marriage compared to less healthy persons, marriage also may protect men and women from stressors in the environment (Nathanson and Lorenz 1982; Kobrin and Hendershot 1977) and contribute to feelings of success and life satisfaction (Mortimer et al. 1982). In addition, marriage may provide important social

ties that deter risk-taking and promote self-protection
(Berkman and Syme 1979). Woods (1978) found that multiple-
role commitments had deleterious consequences for mental
health only among women who negatively evaluated their role
performance and lacked social support from significant
others. Married persons may be more resilient in the face
of employment stressors, given the potency of the confiding
intimate relationship as a coping resource (Kessler and
Essex 1982). However, there is evidence that the positive
health effects of employment are most marked among those
lacking alternative sources of social support (Nathanson
1980; Findlay-Jones and Burvill 1977).

The spouse provides some women with assistance with
childcare and household responsibilities, as well as social
support for their job endeavors. While wives generally
spend more time performing household and childcare tasks
than husbands (Pleck and Rustad 1980), Kessler and McRae
(1982) report that women's mental health is enhanced when
husbands contribute to childcare. Similarly, Ross et al.
(1983) report that women are less depressed when their husbands contribute to housework. Epstein (1983) suggests that
for professional women, husbands' support and interest in
their wives' careers may be even more important in coping
with dual responsibilities than their assistance with family
chores.

Children represent another source of role expansion.
The presence of children in the home has been associated
with lower death rates for men and women (Kobrin and
Hendershot 1977) and for women, fewer or less severe meno-
pausal symptoms (Van Keep and Kellerhals 1974; Crawford and
Hooper 1973), and decreased likelihood of taking the sick
role (Nathanson 1980; Marcus and Seeman 1981; Geersten and
Gray 1970; Verbrugge 1983). Women with no children at home
experience more illness symptoms than women with children
(Marcus and Seeman 1981). Gore and Mangione (1983) report
that married working women were less impacted by the
stresses of childbearing than were housewives, and that
working actually played a protective role for mothers.
Blood pressure levels have been inversely correlated with
family size among both men and women (Miall 1959; Humerfelt
and Wedervang 1957), and sudden death from arteriosclerotic
heart death has been reported to be more common among
unmarried women and women with fewer children (Talbott
et al. 1977). These findings suggest that a positive impact
of the presence of children may supersede the negative

effects of increased workload.

As is clear from the discussion of these first three models, findings on the relationship between women's work and their health are far from conclusive. Differing methodologies and alternative definitions both of health and of employment experiences make for a complex picture. In the final model to be discussed, an additional variable is considered: individual differences among workers. The person-environment fit model suggests that health benefits are derived when a good fit is found between worker needs and abilities and the job itself.

The Person-Environment Fit Model

The model of person-environment fit suggests that workers' job distress or satisfaction is the consequence of the "fit" or congruence between individual needs, abilities, and values and the demands and requirements of the job. According to this model, job stressors may include: (1) pressures, which are produced by a discrepancy between interpersonal or performance demands of the job and the workers' abilities, and (2) deprivations, which result when job rewards do not meet the workers' needs or expectations (House 1980). A misfit between the worker and the job is likely to lead to distress, dissatisfaction, and ill health. In contrast, a good fit enhances the worker's sense of competence, self-worth, and efficacy, thus contributing to physical and mental well-being (Morse 1975; Van Harrison 1978). Verbrugge (1985) reports that persons who dislike their roles are more vulnerable to illness and more likely to take curative actions for their health problems than happier people.

Clearly, there are individual variations in expectations, values, and needs that are likely to evoke different responses to stressors and rewards among workers (Mortimer 1979). For example, compared to men, women place greater importance on their interpersonal relationships at work and on factors that make their jobs compatible with their home responsibilities, such as travel time and hours away from home (Quinn et al. 1974). However, workers often adjust their needs and expectations over time to match what is available to them in their jobs, thus diminishing incongruence and resulting job dissatisfaction (Mortimer and Lorence 1979a).

Lack of fit between the worker and the job can foster strain (Van Harrison 1978), manifested in psychological responses (such as anxiety or restlessness) and physiological strains (such as high blood pressure). Behavioral symptoms may include increased smoking or seeking of medical help. Prolonged misfit may lead to an accumulation of such symptoms of strain, causing decrements in mental health (such as depression) or physical health, including peptic ulcer or heart disease.

Among women, health is likely to be influenced by the fit between individual needs, values, and preferences and employment status or job experiences. For example, women's commitment or desire to work outside the home conditions the relationship between employment status and psychological well-being (Ross et al. 1983). Women whose social, psychological, and financial needs are met in the absence of employment may not benefit from having a job (Warr and Parry 1982). The proportion of American women preferring full-time homemaking over combining housework and paid employment is decreasing (Townsend and Gurin 1981). Nonetheless, several studies suggest that housewives who do not desire employment outside the home express greater satisfaction with their lives, and report better mental and physical health than do housewives who would prefer employment (Townsend and Gurin 1981). Similarly, Hauenstein et al. (1977) found that job dissatisfaction and poor job performance were associated with high blood pressure levels among "reluctant" women workers, but not among those working "by choice." Housewives' dissatisfaction and generally poorer physical health in comparison to employed women may actually be restricted to the career-oriented housewife.

Similarly, the impact of family roles on health may vary according to the quality of the person-environment fit. In an analysis of changing trends in the sex differential in rates of mental illness, Kessler and McRae (1981) found that men's and women's rates were becoming increasingly similar regardless of marital status and childrearing experiences. They concluded that women in a wide variety of roles were adapting well to their role choices. It may be that an increasing "fit" between women's needs and preferences and their family roles contributes to the improvement in their mental health.

This evidence thus appears to support the model of person-environment fit. However, the question remains as to the relative importance of individual needs and values for

job stress and health decrements through the life span. In
Chapter 5 of this volume, Mortimer et al. argue that the
distinctive outlooks, values, and needs of men and women of
different age could generate varying reactions to work.
They find some support for this application of the fit
hypothesis, in that work autonomy was a much more powerful
determinant of job satisfaction among the youngest male
workers in the panel (ages 16-29) than in the other groups.
It is probable that the fit hypothesis is also relevant to
understanding the interrelations of age, work, and health,
given workers' changing capacities and needs as they grow
older. While Schwalbe and Gecas (Chapter 8, this volume)
examine some relevant evidence in the context of disability,
the application of the "fit" paradigm to an understanding of
the health consequences of work for women, as well as men,
of different ages remains a potentially fruitful direction
for further research.

CONCLUSION

Assertions that women's increasing participation in the
labor force will have detrimental effects on their health,
in view of their continuingly demanding family responsibilities, rely on only a partial view of the currently
available evidence. Moreover, treatment of employment as an
all-or-none issue ignores the varied effects that are likely
to result from the diverse combinations of women's occupational experiences and family roles through the life course.
Work may contribute to a wide variety of health outcomes,
ranging from physical and mental ill health due to prolonged
exposure to stressors on the job and in the home, to the
health benefits associated with jobs that provide opportunites for self-direction and social support, and foster a
sense of coherence and job satisfaction. Also, the task of
juggling home and job responsibilities is not always stressful; many women appear to be very resourceful in coping with
these potentially conflicting demands. Indeed, according to
the role expansion model, the multiple roles of mother,
wife, and worker actually may benefit health by providing
alternative sources of satisfaction, self-esteem, and personal identity.

The diverse conclusions of this body of literature
indicate important directions for future research.
Longitudinal studies are needed to examine the possibility

that selection factors account for health differences between employed and non-employed women, among women in different types of jobs, and among women with different work and family statuses. Studies also are needed to elaborate the health benefits resulting from women's varied job experiences, and from the fit (or lack of fit) between job conditions and women's values, preferences, and needs.

It is evident from our review of the growing literature on this subject that more attention needs to be directed to the changing interrelations of work roles (including both paid employment and unpaid family work) and health as women move through the life span. The empirical evidence supporting each of the four models shows that each one has merit. What remains to be determined are the conditions under which each paradigm is most applicable. With respect to the "stress model" and the "health benefits model," researchers have already begun to identify the features of work and family roles that are conducive to health and those that are health-threatening. In considering the relevant evidence with respect to these models, it appeared that the stressors of work and family roles were more pronounced in early adulthood; some health enhancing factors, such as work autonomy and job satisfaction, were more prevalent among middle-aged and older women.

Researchers should now address, more directly, the health effects of the particular combinations of work and family roles that are encountered as women go through the life cycle. Just as work experiences have varying effects on job satisfaction, depending on age, so too may the constellations of work and family responsibilities, pressures, and opportunities have differing implications for the health of women in different phases of their lives. Future studies should thus examine whether position in the life course—as defined by age, tenure in the labor force, or stage in the family life cycle—interacts with the characteristics of work and family roles in influencing health outcomes. For example, with respect to the role expansion model, it would be of interest to determine whether the simultaneous occupancy of multiple role positions has the same beneficial outcomes for women of different ages. It is plausible to assume that women are increasingly able to reap the health benefits of their employment and family roles, as they acquire greater tenure in the labor force and experience in juggling conflicting work and family demands.

A life course perspective (Elder 1985) sensitizes the researcher to the possibility that the particular consequences of experiences and events in the context of one role trajectory (e.g., the work career) will importantly depend on what is happening in other trajectories (e.g., the family life cycle). For example, unemployment may be expected to have more serious psychological and health-related consequences for a woman who is the sole support of her family than for one who is supplementing her husband's income. Similarly, as noted earlier, social support at work may be a more crucial determinant of health for women in the stages of the life cycle in which there is less likely to be an intimate, ongoing set of family relationships (e.g., among the single, divorced, or widowed).

To address concerns about the health effects of the jobs they occupy as they go through their lives, women must be offered greater access to positions that benefit their health--jobs that provide opportunities for self-direction and autonomy; that will enhance their sense of coherence, self-esteem, and efficacy; that provide social support; and that enhance job satisfaction. Comparable pay for equal work performed by men and women is necessary to reduce the stressors associated with financial need. To enable women to meet the demands at home and on the job, greater flexibility in work scheduling and broader availability of high quality day care for those with young children is necessary. By enhancing the conditions of work, employment may actually contribute to the health of the growing number of women who are entering and remaining in the labor force for much of their adult lives.

NOTES

    1. This work was supported in part by Grant No. 2 T32 HL07328 of the National Heart, Lung, and Blood Institute.

    2. The age-specific rates of labor force participation are derived from McLaughlin et al. (1985:Appendix Table D.1), who compiled them from U.S. Bureau of the Census (1975, 1984) and U.S. Bureau of Labor Statistics (1983) tables.

184

REFERENCES

Andrisani, P., and G. Nestel. 1976. "Internal-External
    Control as Contributor to and Outcome of Work
    Experience." Journal of Applied Psychology 61(2):
    156-165.
Antonovsky, A. 1979. Health, Stress, and Coping.
    San Francisco: Jossey-Bass.
Barrett, N. 1979. "Women in the Job Market: Occupations,
    Earnings, and Career Opportunities" and "Women in the
    Job Market: Unemployment and Work Schedules."
    Pp. 31-98 in R. Smith (ed.), The Subtle Revolution:
    Women at Work. Washington, D.C.: Urban Institute.
Bart, P. 1970. "Mother Portnoy's Complaints." Trans-
    action 9 (November-December):69-74.
Baruch G., R. Barnett, and C. Rwers. 1983. Lifeprints:
    New Patterns of Love and Work for Today's Women. New
    York: McGraw-Hill.
Beller, A. M. 1985. "Changes in the Sex Composition of
    U.S. Occupations, 1960-1981." The Journal of Human
    Resources 20(2):236-250.
Bengtsson, C., T. Hallstrom, and G. Tibblin. 1973.
    "Social Factors, Stress Experience, and Personality
    Traits in Women with Ischaemic Heart Disease, Compared
    to a Sample of Women." Acta Medica Scandinavica 549
    (Supplement):82-92.
Berkman, L.F., and L. Syme. 1979. "Social Networks, Host
    Resistance, and Mortality: A Nine-Year Follow-up Study
    of Alameda County Residents." American Journal of
    Epidemiology 109:186-204.
Berkman, P. L. 1969. "Spouseless Motherhood, Psychological
    Stress, and Physical Morbidity." Journal of Health
    and Social Behavior 10(4):323-334.
Bernard, J. 1972. The Future of Marriage. New York:
    World Book.
Bishop, G. D. 1984. "Gender, Role, and Illness Behavior in
    a Military Population." Health Psychology 3(6):
    519-534.

Bronfenbrenner, U., and A. C. Crouter. 1981. "Work and Family Through Time and Space: Report Prepared for the Panel on Work, Family and Community." Committee on Child Development and Research and Public Policy. National Academy of Sciences, National Research Council.

Brown, G., and T. Harris. 1978. Social Origins of Depression. New York: Free Press.

Burke, R. J., and T. Weir. 1976. "Relationship of Wives' Employment Status to Husband, Wife, and Pair Satisfaction and Performance." Journal of Marriage and the Family (May):279-287.

Caplan, R. D., S. Cobb, and J. R. P. French, Jr. 1975. "Relationship of Cessation of Smoking with Job Stress, Personality, and Social Support." Journal of Applied Psychology 60:211-219.

Cassel, J. 1976. "The Contribution of the Social Environment to Host Resistance." American Journal of Epidemiology 104(2):107-123.

Cleary, P. D., and D. Mechanic. 1983. "Sex Differences in Psychological Distress Among Married People." Journal of Health and Social Behavior 24(2):111-121.

Coburn, D. 1978. "Work and General Psychological and Physical Well-Being." International Journal of Health Services 8(3):415-435.

Corcoran, M., G. J. Duncan, and M. S. Hill. 1984. "The Economic Fortunes of Women and Children: Lessons from the Panel Study of Income Dynamics." Signs 10(2): 232-248.

Crawford, M. P., and D. Hooper. 1973. "Menopause, Aging, and Family." Social Science and Medicine 7 (June): 469-482.

Dubin, R., J. E. Champoux, and L. W. Porter. 1975. "Central Life Interests and Organizational Commitment of Blue-Collar and Clerical Workers." Administrative Science Quarterly 20 (September): 411-421.

Elder, Glen H., Jr. 1985. "Perspectives on the Life Course." Pp. 23-49 in Glen H. Elder, Jr. (ed.), Life Course Dynamics, Trajectories, and Transitions, 1968-1980. Ithaca, N.Y.: Cornell University Press.

186

Engel, G. H., and A. H. Schmale. 1972. "Conservation-Withdrawal: A Primary Regulatory Process for Organismic Homeostatsis." In Ciba Foundation, Physiology, Emotion, and Psychosomatic Illness. Symposium 8. Amsterdam: Elsevier.

Epstein, C. F. 1983. "The New Total Woman." Working Woman (April).

Featherman, D. L., and R. M. Hauser. 1976. "Sexual Inequalities and Socioeconomic Achievement in the U.S., 1962-1973." American Sociological Review 41 (June): 462-483.

Feld, S. 1963. "Feelings of Adjustment." In F. I. Nye, and L. W. Hoffman, (eds.), The Employed Mother in America. Chicago: Rand McNally.

Feree, M. M. 1976. "Working Class Jobs: Housework and Paid Work as Sources of Satisfaction." Social Problems 23 (April):431-441.

Findlay-Jones, R. A., and P. W. Burvill. 1977. "The Prevalence of Minor Psychiatric Morbidity in the Community." Psychological Medicine 7:475-489.

Finseth, K., J. Dallal, L. Brynjes, et al. 1975. "Health Problems of Employed Women Enrolled in an HMO." Presented at the Annual Meeting of the American Public Health Association. November.

Fowlkes, M. R. 1980. Behind Every Successful Man: Wives of Medicine and Academe. New York: Columbia University Press.

Frankenhaeuser, M. 1977. "Job Demands, Health, and Well-Being." Journal of Psychosomatic Research 21: 313-321.

Garbus, S. B., and S. B. Garbus. 1980. "Will Improvement in the Socio-economic Status of Women Increase their Cardiovascular Morbidity and Mortality?" Journal of the American Medical Women's Association 35 (November): 257-261.

Geersten, H. R., and R. M. Gray. 1970. "Familistic Orientation and Inclination Toward Adopting the Sick Role." Journal of Marriage and the Family 32 (November):638-646.

Gore, S. 1978. "The Effect of Social Support in Moderating the Health Consequences of Unemployment." Journal of Health and Social Behavior 19 (June):157-165.

Gore, S., and T. W. Mangione. 1983. "Social Roles, Sex Roles, and Psychological Distress: Additive and Interactive Models of Sex Differences." Journal of Health and Social Behavior 24(4):300-312.

Gove, W. R., and M. R. Geerken. 1977. "The Effect of Children and Employment on the Mental Health of Married Men and Women." Social Forces 56:66-76.

Gove, W. R., and M. Hughes. 1979. "Possible Causes of the Apparent Sex Differences in Physical Health: An Empirical Investigation." American Sociological Review 44 (February):126-146.

Gove, W. R., M. Hughes, and C. B. Style. 1983. "Does Marriage Have Positive Effects on the Psychological Well-Being of the Individual?" Journal of Health and Social Behavior 24(2):122-131.

Gove, W., and J. Tudor. 1973. "Adult Sex Roles and Mental Illness." American Journal of Sociology 78:812-815.

Hauenstein, L., S. Kasl, and E. Harburg. 1977. "Work Status, Work Satisfaction, and Blood Pressure Among Married Black and White Women." Psychology of Women Quarterly:334-49.

Haw, M. A. 1982. "Women, Work, and Stress: A Review and Agenda for the Future." Journal of Health and Social Behavior 23 (June):132-144.

Haynes, S., and M. Feinleib. 1980. "Women, Work and Coronary Heart Disease: Prospective Findings from the Framingham Heart Study." American Journal of Public Health 70(2):133-141.

Hepworth, S. J. 1980. "Moderating Factors of the Psychological Impact of Unemployment." Journal of Occupational Psychology 53:139-145.

Herold, J., and I. Waldron. 1985. "Part-Time Employment and Women's Health." Journal of Occupational Medicine 27(6):405-412.

Hochschild, A. R. 1975. "Inside the Clockwork of the Male Career." Pp. 47-80 in F. Howe (ed.), Women and the Power to Change. New York: McGraw-Hill.

House, J. S. 1974. "Occupational Stress and Coronary Heart Disease: A Review and Theoretical Integration." Journal of Health and Social Behavior 15:12-27.

House, J. 1980. Occupational Stress and the Mental and Physical Health of Factory Workers. Ann Arbor, Mich.: University of Michigan, Institute for Social Research, Research Report Series.

188

House, J., and J. Wells. 1978. "Occupational Stress, Social Support, and Health." Pp. 8-29 in A. McLean (ed.), Reducing Occupational Stress. Washington, D.C.: U.S. Department of Health, Education, and Welfare, Public Health Service.

Hughes, D. 1979. "Role Stress Reported by Directors of Nurses in Skilled Nursing Homes." Presented at the 43rd Annual Meeting of the Midwest Sociological Society.

Humerfelt, S., and A. Wedervang. 1957. "A Study of the Influence upon Blood Pressure of Marital Status, Number of Children, and Occupation," Acta Medica Scandinavia 159:489-497.

Jacobson, D. 1974. "Rejection of the Retiree Role: A Study of Female Industrial Workers in Their 50s." Human Relations 27:477-492.

Jenkins, C. D. 1971. "Psychologic and Social Precursors of Coronary Disease." New England Journal of Medicine 284 (February 4, February 11):244-255, 307-317.

Jenkins, C. D., R. H. Rosenman, and M. Friedman. 1966. "Components of the Coronary Prone Behavior Pattern: Their Relation to Silent Myocardial Infarction and Blood Lipids." Journal of Chronic Diseases 19:599-609.

Jennings, S., C. Mazaik, and S. McKinlay. 1984. "Women and Work: An Investigation of the Association between Health and Employment Status in Middle-Aged Women." Social Science and Medicine 19(4):423-431.

Johnson, C. L., and F. A. Johnson. 1977. "Attitudes Toward Parenting in Dual Career Families." American Journal of Psychiatry 134:391-395.

Kahn, Robert. 1981. Work and Health. New York: John Wiley.

Kahn, R.L., D. Wolfe, R. Quinn, J. Snoek, and R. Rosenthal. 1964. Organizational Stress: Studies in Role Conflict and Ambiguity. New York: Wiley.

Kangilaski, J. 1983. "Wives Who Work Increase Their HDL Levels." Medical News, Journal of the American Medical Association, February 11.

Kanter, R. 1977a. Work and Family in the U.S.: A Critical Review and Agenda for Research and Policy. New York: Russell Sage.

Kanter, R. 1977b. Men and Women of the Corporation. New York: Basic Books.

Karasek, R. A. 1979. "Job Demands, Job Decision Latitude, and Mental Strain: Implications for Job Redesign." Administrative Science Quarterly 24:285-307.

Karasek, R., D. Baker, F. Marxer, A. Ahlbom, and T. Theorell. 1981. "Job Decision Latitude, Job Demands, and Cardiovascular Disease: A Prospective Study of Swedish Men." American Journal of Public Health 71(7):694-705.

Kasl, S. 1978. "Epidemiological Contributions to the Study of Work Stress." Pp. 30-50 in C. Cooper, and R. Payne (eds.), Stress at Work. New York: John Wiley.

Kessler, R. C., and M. Essex. 1982. "Marital Status and Depression: The Importance of Coping Resources." Social Forces 61(2):484-507.

Kessler, R. C., and J. A. McRae, Jr. 1981. "Trends in the Relationship Between Sex and Mental Illness: 1957-1976." American Sociological Review 46:443-52.

Kessler, R. C., and J. A. McRae, Jr. 1982. "The Effect of Wives' Employment." American Sociological Review 47(2):216-226.

Kobasa, S. C., R. R. J. Hilker, and S. R. Maddi. 1979. "Who Stays Healthy Under Stress?" Journal of Occupational Medicine 21(9):595-598.

Kobrin, F. E., and G. E. Hendershot. 1977. "Do Family Ties Reduce Mortality? Evidence from the United States, 1966-1968." Journal of Marriage and the Family 39(November):737-745.

Kohn, M. L., and C. Schooler. 1982. "Job Conditions and Personality: A Longitudinal Assessment of Their Reciprocal Effects." American Journal of Sociology 87(6):1257-1286.

Kreps, J., and R. Clark. 1975. Sex, Age, and Work: The Changing Composition of the Labor Force. Baltimore: Johns Hopkins University Press.

Lewis, C., and M. Lewis. 1977. "The Potential Impact of Sexual Equality on Health." New England Journal of Medicine 297:863-869.

Locke, E. 1976. "The Nature and Causes of Job Satisfaction." Pp. 1297-1349 in M. Dunnette (ed.), Handbook of Industrial and Organizational Psychology. Chicago: Rand McNally College.

Lopata, H. 1971. Occupation: Housewife. New York: Oxford University Press.

Manuso, J. 1977. "Coping with Job Abolishment." Journal
of Occupational Medicine 19(9):598-602.

Marcus, A., and T. Seeman. 1981. "Sex Differences in
Reports of Illness and Disability: A Preliminary Test
of the 'Fixed Role Obligations' Hypothesis." Journal
of Health and Social Behavior 22:174-182.

Matthews, K. A., and F. E. Saal. 1978. "Relationship of the
Type A Coronary Prone Behavior Pattern to Achievement,
Power, and Affiliation Motives." Psychosomatic
Medicine 40:631-637.

McLaughlin, S. D., J. O. G. Billy, T. R. Johnson,
B. D. Melber, L. D. Winges, and D. M. Zimmerle. 1985.
The Cosmopolitan Report on the Changing Life Course of
American Women. Seattle: Battelle Human Affairs
Research Centers.

McMichael, A. 1976. "Standardized Mortality Ratios and the
'Healthy Worker Effect': Scratching Beneath the
Surface." Journal of Occupational Medicine 18(3):
165-168.

Medalie, J. H., M. Snyder, J. J. Groen, N. H. Neufeld,
U. Goldbourt, and E. Riss. 1973. "Angina Pectoris
Among 10,000 Men." American Journal of Medicine 55:
583-594.

Miall, W. E. 1959. "Follow-Up Study of Arterial Pressure
in the Population of a Welsh Mining Valley." British
Medical Journal (December 5):1204-1210.

Miller, J. 1980. "Individual and Occupational Determinants
of Job Satisfaction." Sociology of Work and
Occupations 7(3):337-366.

Miller, J., C. Schooler, M. Kohn, and K. Miller. 1979.
"Women and Work: The Psychological Effects of
Occupational Conditions." American Journal of
Sociology 85(1):66-94.

Moen, Phyllis. 1985. "Continuities and Discontinuities in
Women's Labor Force Activity." Pp. 113-155 in Glen H.
Elder, Jr. (ed.), Life Course Dynamics, Trajectories,
and Transitions: 1968-1980. Ithaca, N.Y.: Cornell
University Press.

Morse, J. J. 1975. "Person-Job Congruence and Individual
Adjustment and Development." Human Relations 28:
841-861.

Mortimer, J. 1979. Highlights of the Literature: Changing
Attitudes Toward Work. Scarsdale, N.Y.: Work in
America Institute, Inc.

Mortimer, J. T. 1980. "Occupation-Family Linkages as Perceived by Men in the Early Stages of Professional and Managerial Careers." Pp. 99-117 in Research in the Interweave of Social Roles: Women and Men, Vol. 1. Greenwich, Conn.: JAI Press.

Mortimer, J. T., and M. D. Finch. 1986. "Self-Esteem in the Early Work Career." Work and Occupations 13: 217-39.

Mortimer, J. T., R. Hall, and R. Hill. 1978. "Husbands' Occupational Attributes as Constraints on Wives' Employment." Sociology of Work and Occupations 5: 285-313.

Mortimer, J., and J. Lorence. 1979a. "Work Experience and Occupational Value Socialization: A Longitudinal Study." American Journal of Sociology 84(6):1361-1385.

Mortimer, J., and J. Lorence. 1979b. "Work Experience and the Self-Concept: A Longitudinal Study. Social Psychology Quarterly 42 (December):307-323.

Mortimer, J., J. Lorence, and D. Kumka. 1982. "Work and Family Linkages in the Transition to Adulthood: A Panel Study of Highly Educated Men." Western Sociological Review 13(1):50-68.

Mortimer, J. T., and G. Sorensen. 1984. "Men, Women, Work, and Family." Pp. 139-167 in D. Quarm, K. Borman, and S. Gideonse (eds.), Women in the Workplace: The Effects on Families. Norwood, N.J.: Ablex Publishing Corporation.

Nathanson, C. A. 1975. "Illness and the Feminine Role: A Theoretical Review." Social Science and Medicine 9: 57-62.

Nathanson, C. A. 1980. "Social Roles and Health Status Among Women: The Significance of Employment." Social Science Medicine 14A:463-471.

Nathanson, C. A., and G. Lorenz. 1982. "Women and Health: The Social Dimensions of Biomedical Data." Pp. 37-87 (Chap. 2) in J. Z. Giel (ed.), Women in the Middle Years: Current Knowledge and Directions for Research and Policy. New York: Wiley Interscience.

National Commission on Working Women. 1979. National Survey of Working Women: Perceptions, Problems, and Prospects. Washington, D.C.: Center for Women and Work, National Manpower Institute.

192

National Commission on Working Women. 1982a. "A Few Facts
About Working Women; Prime Concerns of Women in the
80 Percent," Fact Sheets in Women at Work. Washington,
D.C.: Center for Women and Work.
National Commission on Working Women. 1982b. "An Overview
of Women in the Work Force." Fact Sheet. Washington,
D.C.: Center for Women and Work.
Newberry, P., M. M. Weissman, and J.K. Meyers. 1979.
"Working Wives and Housewives: Do They Differ in
Mental Status and Social Adjustment?" American Journal
of Orthopsychiatry 49:282-291.
Nye, F. I. 1974. "Effects on Mother." Pp. 207-225 in
L. W. Hoffman and F. I. Nye (eds.), Working Mothers.
San Francisco: Jossey-Bass.
Oppenheimer, V. K. 1975. "The Sex-Labeling of Jobs."
Pp. 307-325 in M. T. S. Mednick, S. S. Tangri, and
L. W. Hoffman (eds.), Women and Achievement,
Washington, D.C.: Hemisphere Publishing.
Palmore, E. B. 1969. "Physical, Mental, and Social Factors
in Predicting Longevity." Gerontologist 9(2: Part I):
103-108.
Papanek, H. 1973. "Men, Women, and Work: Reflections on
the Two-Person Career." American Journal of Sociology
78(January):852-872.
Patterson, M., and L. Engelberg. 1978. "Women in Male
Dominated Professions." Pp. 266-292 in A. Stromberg
and S. Harkness (eds.), Women Working: Theories and
Facts in Perspective. Palo Alto, Calif.: Mayfield
Publishing.
Pearlin, L. I., and J. S. Johnson. 1977. "Marital Status,
Life Strains, and Depression." American Sociological
Review 42:704-715.
Pleck, J. 1977. "The Work-Family Role System." Social
Problems 24:417-427.
Pleck, J., and M. Rustad. 1980. "Husbands' and Wives' Time
in Family Work and Paid Work in 1975-76 Study of Time
Use." Unpublished paper. Wellesley College Center for
Research on Women. March.
Pope, C., and M. McCabe. 1975. "The Employment Status of
Women and Their Health and Well-Being." Presented at
the Annual Meeting of the American Public Health
Association. November.

Quinn, R. P., G. L. Staines, and M. R. McCullough. 1974. "Job Satisfaction: Is There a Trend?" Manpower Research Monograph No. 30. Washington, D.C.: U.S. Department of Labor, Manpower Administration.

Radloff, L. 1975. "Sex Differences in Depression: The Effects of Occupation and Marital Status." Sex Roles 1(3):249-265.

Regan, M. C., and H. E. Roland. 1982. "University Students: A Change in Expectations and Aspirations over the Decade." Sociology of Education 55(October): 223-228.

Renne, K. S. 1971. "Health and Marital Experience in an Urban Population." Journal of Marriage and the Family 33:338-350.

Reskin, B. F., and S. Coverman. 1980. "Sex Differences in Psychological Distress: The Roles of Marriage, Childrearing, and Employment." Unpublished paper. Earlier version presented to the 1978 Annual Meetings of the American Sociological Association, San Francisco.

Retherford, R. D. 1975. The Changing Sex Differential in Mortality. Westport, Conn.: Greenwood Press.

Rhodes, S. R. 1983. "Age-Related Differences in Work Attitudes and Behavior: A Review and Conceptual Synthesis." Psychological Bulletin 93(2):328-367.

Roberts, C. R., R. E. Roberts, and J. M. Stevenson. 1982. "Women, Work, Social Support, and Psychiatric Morbidity." Social Psychiatry 17:167-173.

Roberts, R. E., and S. J. O'Keefe. 1981. "Sex Differences in Depression Reexamined." Journal of Health and Social Behavior 22(December):394-400.

Ross, C. E., J. Mirowsky, and J. Huber. 1983. "Dividing Work, Sharing Work, and In-Between: Marriage Patterns and Depression." American Sociological Review 48(6): 809-823.

Rubin, L. 1979. Women of a Certain Age: The Midlife Search for Self. New York: Harper Colophon Books.

Sales, S. M., and J. House. 1971. "Job Dissatisfaction as a Possible Risk Factor in Coronary Heart Disease." Journal of Chronic Diseases 23(May):861-873.

Schooler, C., M. Kohn, K. Miller, and J. Miller. 1983.
"Housework as Work." Pp. 242-260 in Work and
Personality: An Inquiry into the Impact of Social
Stratification, M. Kohn and C. Schooler with the colla-
boration of J. Miller, K. Miller, C. Schoenbach, and
R. Schoenberg. Norwood, N.J.: Ablex Publishing
Corporation.

Seeman, M., and J. W. Evans. 1962. "Alienation and
Learning in a Hospital Setting." American Sociological
Review 27:772-783.

Seeman, M., and T. E. Seeman. 1983. "Health Behavior and
Personal Autonomy: A Longitudinal Study of the Sense
of Control in Illness." Journal of Health and Social
Behavior 24(2):144-159.

Seligman, M. E. P. 1975. Helplessness. San Francisco:
W. H. Freeman.

Sexton, P. C. 1977. Women and Work. Washington, D.C.:
U.S. Department of Labor, Employment and Training
Administration.

Shaw, L. B. 1985. "Determinants of the Increasing Work
Attachment of Married Women." Work and Occupation
12(1):41-57.

Smith, R. 1979. "The Movement of Women into the Labor
Force." Pp. 1-29 in R. Smith (ed.), The Subtle
Revolution: Women at Work. Washington, D.C.: Urban
Institute.

Sorensen, G., P. Pirie, A. Folsom, D. Jacobs, and R. Gillum.
1985. "Sex Differences in the Relationship Between
Work and Health: The Minnesota Heart Survey."
Journal of Health and Social Behavior 26:379-394.

Stafford, E. M., P. R. Jackson, and M. H. Banks. 1980.
"Employment, Work Involvement, and Mental Health in
Less-Qualified Young People." Journal of Occupational
Psychology 53:291-304.

Stevenson, M. H. 1978. "Wage Differences Between Men and
Women: Economic Theories." Pp. 89-107 in A. H.
Stromberg and S. Harkness (eds.), Women Working:
Theories and Facts in Perspective. Palo Alto, Calif.:
Mayfield Publishing.

Syme, S. L., M. M. Hyman, and P. E. Enterline. 1964. "Some
Social and Cultural Factors Associated with the
Occurrence of Coronary Heart Disease." Journal of
Chronic Diseases 17:277-289.

Talbott, E., L. H. Kuller, K. Detre, and J. Perper. 1977.
"Biologic and Psychosocial Risk Factors of Sudden Death
from Coronary Disease in White Women." American
Journal of Cardiology 39:858-864.

Thoits, P. A. 1984. "Multiple Identities: Explaining
Gender and Marital Status Differences in Distress."
Presented at the Self and Identity Conference, Cardiff,
Wales, July 9-13.

Thompson, M. K., and J. S. Brown. 1980. "Feminine Roles
and Variations in Women's Illness Behaviors." Pacific
Sociological Review 23(October):405-422.

Townsend, A., and P. Gurin. 1981. "Re-examining the
Frustrated Homemaker Hypothesis: Role Fit, Personal
Dissatisfaction, and Collective Discontent."
Sociology of Work and Occupations 8(4):464-488.

Treiman, D., and K. Terrell. 1975. "Sex and the Process of
Status Attainment: A Comparison of Working Women and
Men." American Sociological Review 40(April):174-200.

U.S. Bureau of the Census. 1975. Historical Statistics of
the United States, Colonial Times to 1970, Bicentennial
Edition, Part 1, pp. 131-132. Washington, D.C.: U.S.
Government Printing Office.

U.S. Bureau of the Census. 1984. Statistical Abstract of
the United States. Washington, D.C.: U.S. Government
Printing Office.

U.S. Bureau of Labor Statistics. 1983. Handbook of Labor
Statistics, Bulletin 2175. Washington, D.C.: U.S.
Government Printing Office.

U.S. Department of Commerce. 1984. National Data Book and
Guide to Sources: Statistical Abstract of the United
States, 104th edition. Washington, D.C.: U.S. Bureau
of the Census.

U.S. Department of Labor. 1980a. "Employment and
Unemployment During 1979." Special Labor Force Report
234, Monthly Labor Review, 1980b.

U.S. Department of Labor. 1980b. Perspectives on Working
Women: A Databook, Bulletin 2080. Washington, D.C:
U.S. Government Printing Office.

U.S. Department of Labor, Bureau of Labor Statistics (BLS).
1982. Tables of Working Life: The Increment-
Decrement Model, Bulletin 2135. Washington, D.C.:
U.S. Government Printing Office.

Van Harrison, R. 1978. "Person-Environment Fit and Job
Stress." Pp. 175-208 in C. L. Cooper and R. Payne
(eds.), Stress at Work, Toronto: John Wiley.

Van Keep, P. A., and J. M. Kellerhals. 1974. "The Impact of Socio-Cultural Factors on Symptom Formation: Some Results of a Study of Aging Women in Switzerland," Psychotherapy and Psychosomatics 23 (Annual): 251-163.

Vanek, J. 1978. "Housewives as Workers." In A. Stromberg and S. Harkness (eds.), Women Working: Theories and Facts in Perspective. Palo Alto, Calif.: Mayfield Publishing.

Vanfossen, B. E. 1981. "Sex Differences in the Mental Health Effects of Spouse Support and Equity." Journal of Health and Social Behavior 22:130-143.

Verbrugge, L. 1979. "Female Illness Rates and Illness Behavior: Testing Hypotheses About Sex Differences in Health." Women and Health 4(1):51-78.

Verbrugge, L. M. 1982. "Work Satisfaction and Physical Health." Journal of Community Health 7(4-Summer): 262-283.

Verbrugge, L. 1983. "Multiple Roles and Physical Health of Women and Men." Journal of Health and Social Behavior 24(1):16-29.

Verbrugge, L. M. 1985. "Gender and Health: An Update on Hypotheses and Evidence." Journal of Health and Social Behavior 26:156-82.

Verbrugge, L. M. In press. "Role Burdens and Physical Health of Women and Men." In F. Crosby (ed.), Modern Woman: Managing the Dual Roles. New Haven, Conn.: Yale University Press.

Waldron, I., J. Herold, D. Dunn, R. Staum. 1982. "Reciprocal Effects of Health and Labor Participation Among Women—Evidence from Two Longitudinal Studies." Journal of Occupational Medicine 24:126-132.

Warr, P. 1982. "Psychological Aspects of Employment and Unemployment." Psychological Medicine 12:7-11.

Warr, P., and G. Parry. 1982. "Paid Employment and Women's Psychological Well-Being." Psychological Bulletin 91(3):498-516.

Welch, S., and A. Booth. 1977. "Employment and Health Among Married Women." Sex Roles 3(August):385-396.

Woods, N. F. 1978. "Women's Roles, Mental Ill Health, and Illness Behavior." Unpublished doctoral thesis. Chapel Hill, N.C.: University of North Carolina.

Woods, N. F., and B. S. Hulka. 1979. "Symptom Reports and Illness Behavior among Employed Women and Homemakers." Journal of Community Health 5:36-45.

Wright, J. D. 1978. "Are Working Women Really More
    Satisfied? Evidence from Several National Surveys."
    Journal of Marriage and the Family (May):301-313.
Zalokar, J. B. 1960. "Marital Status and Major Causes of
    Death in Women." Journal of Chronic Disease II:50-60.

Part 3

Midcareer and Older Workers

Shirley M. Clark, Mary Corcoran

7. Vitality of Midcareer and Older Professionals: Problems and Prospects

BACKGROUND

Concerns with issues of vitality, obsolescence, and productivity in the work force abound in our society, as the median age is gradually rising. The observed and expected increase in the average worker's age is viewed almost exclusively as a problem, with numerous negative consequences and few positive aspects. This chapter will focus on the vitality problems of professional workers, and within that broad occupational category, of faculty members especially. Although the contemporary scholarly literature has paid particular attention to vitality issues in higher education, science, and engineering, we are not unaware of the fact that these areas represent only a part of the total of professionally oriented fields.

Over a decade ago, it was recognized that the exponential growth of science could not continue indefinitely and, in fact, had tapered off (Zuckerman and Merton 1972). Predictions related to this trend included: an increase in the median age of scientists, fewer new research installations and new departments in new universities, and diminished productivity of the older research groups. More recently, and as a result of the slowed expansion of the higher education system, the oversupply of trained and talented doctorates from many disciplines for whom there are few faculty positions, and the reduction of resources that might be used to maintain individual vitality, analysts have warned of dire outcomes of faculty aging (c.f. Hansen 1985; Blackburn and Lawrence 1985). While this change may be somewhat less dramatic than popularly supposed--an increase of about 10 percent of the faculty in senior rank and tenured from 1969 to 1979, according to data provided by Finkelstein (1984)--a number of position papers and books have now considered issues of faculty and institutional vitality with this new reality in mind (National Science Foundation Advisory Council 1978; Carnegie Council on Policy Studies in Higher Education 1980; Austin and Gamson 1983; Clark and Lewis 1985). Briefly put, the institutional scenario includes deterioration in the conditions of academic work brought about by declines in enrollment and associated financial support, changes in the character of student bodies, shifts in demands for fields of study, declines in research sponsorship, and increasing average age of the faculty. The individual scenario includes "graying" faculty members who are declining in productivity and morale, and unable to respond to new demands and adapt to the changes. In addition, the age and opportunity structures of science and academe may be unable to accommodate the forward thrust of new groups such as women and minorities.

PERCEPTIONS OF THE PROBLEM

The vitality problem arises in life as we pass from youth to the point where we come to realize that there are increasing limits to our physical capabilities and to our abilities to tackle challenges. As Sarason says, it is a matter of "growing up and running down" (1977:257). The trajectory of life is metaphorically upward, with the value of growth expressed in continuing and higher educational attainments and organized personal growth experiences (e.g., personal growth seminars and contracts, self-actualization, exploiting one's human potential). Emphasizing growth may be the antithesis of a deliberate concern with aging and death. According to Sarason, emerging values since World War II have emphasized personal growth and new experience. "Personal growth as a value is a litmus test by which all major areas of living (work, sex, friendship, marriage, parenthood) are tested" (1977:261). These values were reflected in the significance attached to education when the theme of

lifelong education as liberation from various problems
began to emerge and receive social and political support.
    As we look around us, we see everywhere--in the arts,
in science, in politics--individuals who, like Pablo
Picasso, Margaret Mead, Barbara McClintock, Jessie
Bernard, Robert Havighurst, Ronald Reagan, and Deng
Xiaoping, go on in their seventies and eighties to new
challenges of body and mind. In a purely physiological
sense, there are typically gradual declines in
capabilities, but these are relatively limited in their
meaning for most lives until the decade of the seventies.
More serious and limiting is the sense people develop that
they lack the possibility of tackling something new, that
it may be beyond them, that in some sense the world is
passing them by. As we look into these feelings, we begin
to see that the problem of vitality in midlife and beyond
is not and need not be an inevitable one. For some
people, it is in no way an issue, and for others, it may
be a problem of social forces and powerful cultural
expectancies as much as of individual conditions.
    The argument of this chapter is that the problem of
individual vitality is the sense of declining ability to
live and work effectively; it is a problem for society as
well as for the individual. It follows that the best
prospects for preventing vitality problems and alleviating
those that do occur lie in changes in the ways in which
key social institutions--family, schools, work place,
professions, health services--view older people and relate
to them. As is true of most problems, prevention is a
better course of action than remediation after the problem
becomes acute. But prevention requires understanding, as
well as a desire for action. The main thrust of this
chapter is therefore an examination of the nature of the
problems of vitality of midcareer and older professionals
in their work lives, recognizing that an underlying issue
for many is the sense that the biological clock is running
down. Drawing on this analysis, approaches to preventing
career vitality problems from becoming critical and
remedies for some forms of such vitality problems will be
suggested.
    How is the career vitality problem perceived?
Several alternative perspectives come to mind. One
widespread perspective incorporates a linear assumption
about aging and productivity, especially in the more
codified sciences. The imagery of science as the

territory of the young (e.g., "Science is a young man's game") is linked to the fact that formal education is typically confined to the early decades of life and, at any given time, older people are generally disadvantaged, with respect to the knowledge transmitted, relative to younger ones. Science is a special case of rapidly changing content of formal preparation, a situation which may produce problems of career obsolescence for scientists as they move through their careers (Zuckerman and Merton 1972). It is believed that the age structure of scientific groups affects their productivity, but little good data are available on this point. This belief also appears to be generally held with respect to the "seniorization" of the professoriate, and concomitant declines in productivity regardless of the paradigmatic natures of their many disciplines.

Another perspective on career vitality problems draws attention to employment policies that effectively screen out new applicants in their fifties and sixties for new employment positions. Although this is less of an issue for some professionals than others, it seems to be the case that the mid-career professional (faculty member or engineer, for example) who is not in private practice finds relocation increasingly difficult as he or she gets older. Assumptions on the one hand that they may not be as well trained, productive, adaptable, and flexible as younger professional cohorts, and, on the other, that they are more expensive seem to account for the loss of mobility.

A third perspective highlights the widespread stereotyping and cultural devaluing of older people (Levine 1980). The image of the Yuppie on the fast track (e.g., the ambitious young person who invests exclusively in self-development and career advancement) as a cultural ideal is part of the more general idealization of well-educated, newly skilled youth in a post-industrial society. In contrast is a somewhat less valued but more balanced picture of a mid-career worker whose life is organized around occupational and family roles, and whose goals have been re-evaluated in the light of the work situation, his/her own experiences, and a self-assessment (Clausen 1972).

A fourth perspective is the notion of "stuckness" in mid-career that was presented by Kanter in Men and Women of the Corporation (1977) and in a paper, "The Shape of

Work in Academe" (1979), specifically addressed to persons in higher education. "Stuck" people have low ceilings in their jobs, or are blocked from promotion in a system where vertical hierarchical movement spells success. We have learned that "stuckness" is not an unusual experience for faculty members at some point in their lives. How and how well the problem is resolved is a useful indicator of the self-renewal capabilities of the individual, an important aspect of vitality (Corcoran and Clark 1985). More will be said of this later.

A final perspective on vitality is Sarason's "one life-one career imperative" for professionals (1977). According to this imperative, the developmental task of the individual is to decide on a single career. The force of culture leaves unquestioned in the individual's mind that no matter how dysfunctional this choice may seem to be later on, the individual should remain committed to the occupation. The immutability of the choice is reinforced by the investment in extended training, by aspects of the occupational socialization process, and by occupational identity and lifestyle. If catastrophe strikes, it may be very difficult for the individual affected by this potent imperative to contemplate a career change. Faculty members and scientists are good examples of the imperative, and they generally exit their professions through death or reluctant retirement.

Underlying these several perspectives on the vitality problem, whether viewed as a potential national crisis or as a problem of individual career stagnation, are assumptions about the ability of individuals to perform effectively in a professional environment of changing expectations. They reflect a value system which idealizes youth and devalues older people. For individuals themselves, there may be problems of declining productivity, such as an inability to keep up with output expectations (patients treated, cases handled, publications produced, etc.), or with demands brought about by changes in the profession (greater usage of computers in every field, technical advances in medicine, etc.). A sense of obsolescence may develop, colored by a feeling that the basic values of the profession which had been its attraction in the beginning have been undermined. For example, Sarason (1977) writes of mid-life physicians who entered medicine after World War II, picturing a future of autonomy, service, and satisfaction, only to find themselves "dethroned" by armies of new professionals, changing governmental regulations, and self doubts about the quality of their work. From the standpoint of the employer, there may be dissatisfaction with the professional leading to removal from positions of power rather than outright dismissal. There may also be a loss of respect from colleagues and associates, inevitably leading to loss of a personal sense of status and esteem.

The circular effects of these experiences, the loss of status fostering still further declines in energetic and active involvement in work, present a sorry picture for those coming up the professional ladder, as they encounter the inevitable problems of the middle and later stages of the career. This rather depressing picture presents the worst face on the mid-career and older professional worker's situation. It is not the typical situation, and need not be the normative one. But as is often the case, inquiries tend to be focussed on the problems. Our analysis thus begins with further delineation of the conceptualizations of vitality and obsolescence, and an attempt to assess the seriousness of professional career vitality problems. After that, we will examine the relationship between vitality and aging. Then, drawing from a study of faculty career vitality in a major research university, we will explore a specific vitality problem, that of career blockage or "stuckness," and how individuals and institutions respond to it. Finally, policy implications and possible strategies for dealing with vitality issues will be discussed from an institutional or corporate perspective on human resource development.

CONCEPTUALIZATIONS OF OBSOLESCENCE AND VITALITY

Obsolescence

The idea of obsolescence as an indicator of vitality has been with us for some time. According to Miller,

Human obsolescence was first identified
when the onrush of technological change
outstripped the education of engineers and
scientists. Thus it was seen as "knowledge
obsolescence." In some cases, it
represented a failure to add new knowledge.
In this era, we discovered the so-called
half-life of an engineering education. We
discovered that the content of an
undergraduate education was changing by 50
percent in about seven years. Change rate
caused the problem. At the core of the
problem also was our concept of careers.
It was believed that preparation for a
career took place early in life and would
last for life (1979:29).

The professional's expert knowledge, originally
obtained during formal educational preparation, is
strengthened and extended in the performance of the
professional work role. However, the professional whose
expertise is based on scientific or technical knowledge is
continually confronted with knowledge obsolescence (Taylor
1968). Perucci and Rothman (1969) have conceptualized
obsolescence as a dual process involving both
deterioration or depreciation of knowledge and the
professional's failure to acquire new knowledge in the
field.

Rapid obsolescence of professional competence is a
phenomenon of our times (Lindsay, Morrison, and Kelley
1974). The accelerating pace of information generation,
rapid advances in technology, and changes in various
societal institutions have made it difficult for
professionals (indeed, for all) to keep abreast of
developments. Among professionals, engineers have been
especially concerned with conditions thought to be
obsolescence-inducing. Kaufman (1979) has identified four
broad factors, and studied their effects on several
hundred engineers in a major high technology organization:
rapid environmental change such as advances in technical
knowledge, the organizational climate and reward system in
which engineers work, the nature of technical work to
which engineers are assigned, and individual
characteristics (cognitive, motivational, and personality)
of the engineer. Interestingly, no evidence was found to

support the widespread belief that older engineers are more obsolete than young ones; obsolescence was determined to be a consequence of organizational practices and policies, including the nature of the work assigned.

The relationship between the process of obsolescence and the career patterns of engineers was examined by Rothman and Perucci (1970). Four career options of four cohorts of engineers were selected for study: breadth of technical complexity and responsibility, technical vs. administrative involvement, research and development, and stable vs. dynamic industries. Their findings lent support to the contention that technical obsolescence and career patterns are interrelated. Conducive to weakening of professional expertise were positions involving narrow technical activities, extensive administrative responsibilities, application rather than research, and organizational situations involving stable technologies. The authors speculated that these positions neither required nor stimulated the maintenance of expertise. These positions also offered the less knowledgeable an acceptable career adaptation to pressures produced by obsolescence.

The rate of obsolescence or depreciation of knowledge may also be affected by the paradigmatic status of the field. Zuckerman and Merton reviewed characteristics of highly codified "hard" fields and less codified "soft" fields, suggesting that the more highly codified fields tend to "obliterate the original versions of past contributions by incorporating their essentials into newer formulations" (1972:303). Evidence from a study of career interruptions of academic women supports the idea that obsolescence is field related (McDowell 1982). Choice of field significantly affected the consequences of career interruption, with more negative effects upon careers in fields with less durable knowledge (physical sciences) than in those with more durable knowledge (humanities).

Vitality

Vitality is an even more primitive, imprecise concept than obsolescence. As far as can be determined from reviewing the literature, there is no "theory" of professional career vitality, at least not in any strict sense of the term. Nor have many attempted to define vitality (or related terms such as renewal, revitalization, or productivity). Contemporary writers may assume agreement with respect to the concept, an assumption open to question.

Vitality, as a heuristic concept, may be useful for describing a complex phenomenon in the professions, including higher education. Although it is difficult to say just what vitality is, what we can do is ask two questions: First, to what phenomena does the concept of vitality sensitize us? And second, what more concrete phenomena or ideas can we attempt to specify or measure that are derived from the concept of vitality?

Several writers who have pondered the meaning of vitality as it applies to late 20th-century higher education credit John W. Gardner with stimulating their thinking (Peterson and Loye 1967; Maher 1982; Centra 1985; Clark, Boyer, and Corcoran 1985). In two of his popular works, Gardner presents the reader with several kinds of theoretical statements or hypotheses about the capacities of individuals, institutions, and societies for adaptation and change. For example, in Self-Renewal (1963), the following ideas emerge:

> ...Continuous renewal depends upon conditions that encourage fulfillment of the individual...(p. 2)
> Too often in the past we have designed systems to meet all kinds of exacting requirements except the requirement that they contribute to the fulfillment and growth of the participants....It is essential that in the years ahead we undertake intensive analysis of the impact of the organization on the individual (pp. 63-64).

In a later book, Morale (1978), Gardner provides some synonyms for vitality, and some further statements of meaning:

> "regeneration" (p. 13)
> "physical drive and durability" (p. 59)
> "enthusiasm"..."zest"..."sense of curiosity"..."care about things"..."reach out"..."enjoy"..."risk failure" (p. 62)

"A society concerned for its own continued
vitality will be interested in the growth
and fulfillment of individual human
beings--the release of human
potentialities" (p. 73)

In his introduction to Conversations Toward a
Definition of Institutional Vitality, Peterson
acknowledges the creative stimulation provided by
Gardner's ideas to the development of an inventory for
measuring institutional functioning (Peterson and Loye
1967). Peterson and his colleagues struggled to define
both institutional vitality and an idealized institution
of higher learning. Discussants suggested that the
definitions should be multidimensional, should include the
idea that the vitality of institutions comes from the
vitality of the people in it, should not be elitist but
open to a diversity of institutional types, and should
allow for the notion of dynamic vitality.

This early work by scholars at the Educational
Testing Service predated the systematic attempts in the
1970s to undertake curricular reviews and reforms, to
initiate and institutionalize faculty development, to
improve and evaluate instruction, and to experiment with
organizational and administrative development activities.
However, conditions and issues in academe continued to
change throughout the 1970s, and while they seem to have
intensified concern for faculty and institutional
vitality, they also have added to the complexity of the
matter. A more recent statement of institutional vitality
by Maher (1982) reflects this:

In essence, then, the quest for vitality
might be said to focus on the capacity of
the college or university to create and
sustain the organizational strategies that
support the continuing investment of energy
by faculty both in their own career and in
the realization of the institution's
mission (p. 7).

The intertwining or interaction of institutional and faculty vitality is an important theme. Ideal types of faculty will differ according to institutional type and mission. Thus, for example, at a large, land-grant, research-oriented institution such as the University of Minnesota where the mission is tripartite (i.e., teaching, research, and service), a draft position paper on planning strategies contains the following definition of faculty vitality:

> A faculty is vital if it exhibits sustained productivity in its teaching, its research, and its service activities....if it is continually creating important, new knowledge and expanding our understanding of the world in which we live....if the instructional programs of the University are continually being monitored and developed....if it is responding to the needs of the state, the nation, and the world for new knowledge. Perhaps most important a faculty is vital if its members find their work stimulating, enjoyable, and satisfying (Planning Council, University of Minnesota, 11 February 1980:4).

It is well known that a division of labor exists between "teaching" and "research" institutions in higher education. Even within these kinds of institutions, value-laden definitions of faculty vitality will differ in their emphases for, say, two-year community colleges, liberal arts colleges, and universities with greater or lesser research orientation. As suggested by Fulton and Trow (1974), ideal types of academic roles include the expectation of continuing research activity in some universities and colleges, but not in others; in yet other institutions, teaching is emphasized and research is not a normal expectation. Prevailing ideal types of faculty roles affect patterns of recruitment and socialization for faculty members. Reflected and reaffirmed in the reward structures, these ideal types may be linked with personal preferences, social origins, and other variables about which relatively little is known.

In sum, notions of faculty vitality seem to have a contextual dimension that makes defining the concept difficult at best without taking into account institutional type and mission. Doing so leads one to consider institutions as the settings in which faculty members pursue careers as scholars, teachers, and researchers, and as organizations that shape these careers.

VITALITY AND AGING ISSUES

     In earlier sections of this chapter, we characterized vitality problems of midcareer and older professionals as not unlikely but highly variable in their effects upon individuals and institutional concerns. In the preceding section, it became apparent that individual career obsolescence or vitality, in the case of faculty members and some other professionals, is related to organizational structures, expectations, practices, and policies. In this section, we wish to deal more directly with the widespread belief that age represents a reasonably good proxy variable for work productivity.

     This belief almost always conveys directionality; increased age is associated with lower productivity. As expressed by Blackburn and Lawrence in the case of the professoriate, "Indeed, the observed and predicted increase in the average faculty age is viewed almost exclusively as a problem, that is, an event which has numerous negative consequences and few, if any, positive outcomes" (1985:2-3). The list of believed deficiencies of older faculty is long; it includes: less productivity, less creativity, less adaptability to changed conditions, less effectiveness as teacher and researcher, and many more. Furthermore, older faculty members cost more in higher salaries. Specific assumptions about obsolescence are sometimes comingled with beliefs about the declining productivity of older faculty. For example, Shin and Putnam assert that "Older scientists tend to lose touch with the developing heart of their discipline, their knowledge becomes obsolete, and they are less likely to achieve the innovative theory or influential breakthrough than younger colleagues" (1982:222). With such beliefs and perceptions commonplace, it is important to determine whether a basis exists for a tight coupling between age and age-related factors on the one hand, and professional worker performance, on the other.

There are many theories of aging and work, most of
which can be classified as biological/physiological,
psychological, or sociological. From each of these
theoretical streams, central research findings will be
drawn regarding performance and aging. The focus of
biological/physiological theories of aging is on losses of
responsiveness, sight, hearing, coordination, taste,
smell, and other physiological functioning which
accompanies aging. However, age seems to be a poor proxy
for physical, mental, or emotional status. Comprehensive
surveys of medical and psychological evidence dating from
the past 40 years and cited in the gerontological
literature on a wide variety of occupations (Butler 1975;
Levine 1980; Meier and Kerr 1976) conclude that the
competence and work performance of older workers are, by
any general measures, at least equal to those of younger
workers. The evidence clearly establishes the continued
productivity of workers who are 65 years of age or older.
Furthermore, Meier and Kerr (1976) have concluded that the
physical demands of most jobs today are well below the
capabilities of healthy aging personnel. Properly placed,
older workers function effectively, steadily, and loyally.

As for findings in this domain, one would not expect
to find any significant reduction in professional workers'
ability to perform up to the age of retirement. (This
overall finding would need to be modified for those
professionals, such as surgeons, whose work would be
affected by slowed reaction time or decreased physical
strength.) While the official age of retirement for
faculty members is now set at 70 years, some faculty
members--and certainly many physicians and
lawyers--continue to work at professional tasks well into
their seventh and eighth decades. Studies by Havighurst
(1980, 1985) of male social scientist faculty and academic
administrators support the continuity principle. That is,
"there is continuity or stability of life-style from
middle age through the age period from 60-75, with little
or no change caused by retirement, mandatory or voluntary"
(1985:106). High and low publishers among the social
scientists continued their principal concerns. Of the
four definable sub-groups among administrators, only one,
consisting of people who radically changed their
lifestyles, was sharply discontinuous from previously
established roles. Work time may be lost due to health,
but "reduced mental acuity and physical performance are

not 'normal' aging consequences" (Blackburn and Lawrence 1985:5).

Psychological approaches to aging include attention to intelligence, learning, and memory, and to adult development stages. There is a variety of opinion and thought on relations between age and creativity (discoveries, path-breaking work) in the various academic disciplines (Reskin 1985). Suffice it to say that different disciplines show different patterns possibly related to the paradigmatic nature of fields. Two broad categories of intellectual performance studied by Horn and Cattell (1967) in relation to aging are categorized as crystallized and fluid intelligence. Crystallized intelligence is the collective societal intelligence (word meanings, mechanical knowledge, fluency of ideas, general information, arithmetic ability). Fluid intelligence (inductive reasoning, figure matching, perceptual speed) is thought to be more directly dependent upon the physiological structure of the organism. It is therefore more subject to decline after middle age than is crystallized intelligence, although many older adults compensate by taking more time with certain tasks. In sum, crystallized intelligence continues to grow slowly during the adult years, and even after age 60 if the person is intellectually active. Fluid intelligence declines slowly with age, but compensations are possible and even typical.

As for the life-span psychological theories which serve as underpinnings of adult and career development frameworks and of the faculty development movement, Dannefer (1984) has argued that these theories are ontogenetic and deterministic. Instead of positing a fixed universal sequence of life/career stages, Dannefer prefers a more sociogenic paradigm that includes greater attention to environmental effects on humans who are malleable throughout their lives. Like the findings from biological theories, the general principle drawn from psychological evidence is that while there are some losses with aging, they are rather minor when compensatory behaviors are taken into consideration. With good health and exercizing of psychological functions, there is little basis for positing loss over the normal worklife span.

Sociological theories of aging include concerns with age stratification, age stereotyping, intergenerational rivalry, cultural devaluing, role disengagement, and organizational demography. Sociologists of science, in particular, have long been interested in the relationship between aging and scientific productivity, the quality and quantity of discoveries and contributions. Reskin (1985) presents a summary and a methodological critique of recent major studies of scientists serving as faculty members in academic departments. She reviewed several models of the relationship between age and the research productivity of faculty members. These models included: linear or cumulative growth; declining rate of increase, which reflects the notion that performance tapers off over time; leveling out or plateauing function due to aging; obsolescence function, a parabolic function in which performance rises and then declines; spurt function, a bimodal distribution that combines the expected effects of the academic reward system and the effects of aging to produce two peaks--one early in the career and the second about a decade or so later; and finally, a spurt-obsolescence function bimodal distribution, in which the second peak is followed by a performance decline. Reskin then applied these models to several fields on which age and productivity data are available, including physics, astronomy, mathematics, chemistry, chemical engineering, biochemistry, biology, earth sciences, geology, psychology, economics, and sociology. Her conclusions are that some regularities do occur across disciplines; first, in no case did research productivity show a simple, negative relationship with age. Generally, a simple linear model of cumulative growth was inadequate too. Second, the results by discipline suggest that linear models are inadequate and spurt-obsolescence models are generally better; market, generational, and selective attrition effects seem to be overlaid with any effects of aging. Third, any simple effects of aging seem to be small.

Blackburn (1985) has used faculty productivity data plotted against career age from major studies as evidence in his search for a theory of career development. He examined some existing relevant theories, such as the Levinson adult development stage theory, demographic theory, and socialization theory, and overlaid the age and productivity grids on the theoretical career stages, events, activities, and processes. In this confrontation of evidence with theory, Blackburn found that psychological stage theory did not fit the productivity

evidence particularly well. A better fit was obtained
when a career events (degrees and professorial ranks
earned) line was added to the grid.

With respect to teaching and aging, the data are even
more inadequate. Methodologically, there are several
problems: the studies are cross-sectional, and with
regard to assessments of effectiveness of teaching, the
assessment measure is effectiveness as judged by students.
Institutions neither collect longitudinal data on the
effectiveness of the same teachers, nor is there
consistency in the instruments across the institutions or
through time (Blackburn and Lawrence 1985). There is some
evidence that interest in teaching increases with age
(Fulton and Trow 1974), although it may not be the case
that more attention is devoted to it. Several studies
over a 30-year period find low-order positive correlations
between teaching effectiveness and academic rank, but
since the rank of full professor covers roughly the age
span of 40-to-70-year-olds, one must be careful in
inferring a positive relationship with aging (Blackburn
and Lawrence 1985). Centra and Zinn's cross-sectional
study of aging and teaching performance found lower
ratings for older faculty (1976). As Blackburn summarized
the situation, "The conclusion from direct evidence, then,
is that there are not career phases in the motivation to
teach. On the other hand, in the absence of a purposeful
test of this proposition, one is reluctant to close the
books" (1982:96).

In summary, each of the three major approaches sheds
some light on the relationships between working and aging.
There is little basis for decline in professional
performance in middle and later years due to the biology
and physiology of the aging process. Psychologically, the
same conclusion is supported, although the expectancies
created by assumptions of a fixed sequence of adult
development stages could affect individuals' behaviors and
the social response to them, as in the example of the
"mid-life crisis." Sociological theories suggest that
midcareer and older workers must be considered in the
general context of roles in social institutions and
organizations, in culture and society. The specific
contexts of workers must also be considered, as different
disciplines or fields involve particular socialization
processes, expectations, and rewards that structure and
give meaning to aging as the individual moves through the
work career.

"STUCKNESS": A VITALITY PROBLEM

Several years ago, we recognized that universities
had begun to face serious problems in academic personnel
planning. But we were not at all sure that what was being
identified as a problem of faculty vitality and what was
being proposed to solve it matched very well with the
conditions of faculty life. We were also concerned that
recommendations for faculty development were typically
designed to change the individual, but ignored the
organizational and institutional contexts that shape and
structure careers. We saw evidence of overgeneralization.
Problems of obsolescence particular to engineering and the
sciences are assumed to apply to faculties at large,
despite different rates of change in various fields, and
quite different responsibilities of faculties in
undergraduate and graduate institutions.

As part of a study that aimed to identify individual
and organizational conditions that support effective,
productive, and creative faculty work, we interviewed 147
faculty members at the University of Minnesota from four
fields: the biological sciences, the physical sciences
and mathematics, the social sciences and, the humanities.
Respondents were categorized into three sample groups: a
representative group, a highly active group, and a delayed
promotion group. The study as a whole is discussed
elsewhere (c.f. Corcoran and Clark 1984; Clark and
Corcoran 1985). The focus here is on illustration of the
career blockage experience or "stuckness," and its
resolution as a critical incident and indicator of faculty
vitality.

The notion of "stuckness" is one that has received
particular attention because of Rosabeth Moss Kanter's
much quoted works (1977, 1979). Kanter uses the term
"stuckness" primarily to refer to individuals who reach a
dead end in opportunity in industry. These are people who
have "low ceilings in their jobs," who are blocked from
movement, and lack opportunity in a system where mobility
above all means success. In this context, awareness of
stuckness involves a low promotion rate, a ceiling on
one's opportunities for promotion, and getting old in
one's job. Although it is clear that academics do not
necessarily view promotion in the administrative hierarchy
as opportunity, they certainly look at rank promotion as

significant. Kanter's ideas with respect to the
experiences and reactions of "stuck" individuals are
reflected in our attention to a delayed promotion group in
our study. They also informed our analysis of
"successful" faculty who view themselves as good but not
at the "top of the ladder." As she notes, the most vital
and active individuals may well be those who feel most
dissatisfied with their jobs because of their sense of
frustration in realizing their career goals.

Nature of the "Stuck" Experience

Although the characteristic pattern which emerged
from the interviews was suggestive of a collectively vital
faculty, career blocks are not unusual. About two out of
five (38%) of the representative faculty group reported
having had such an experience, as did the same proportion
of the highly active group. Not surprisingly, the
proportion of the delayed promotion group so reporting was
higher, almost three out of five or 57 percent. Given the
fact that at least one-third of the groups interviewed had
not yet reached their mid-forties, often the critical
period for career assessment, it might be said that most
faculty members will at some time in their careers feel
that they are in some sense "stuck" or blocked from moving
ahead in their work.

Most faculty members in reporting career blocks,
spoke about blocks in their research or scholarly work.
These blocks took several forms:

1. Consistently productive researchers who
   thought they were on a plateau.
2. Faculty whose research was set aside for
   administrative work at some point and found
   it hard to resume this aspect of their
   career.
3. Faculty who prefer a line of research that
   is "out of favor" with funding agencies.
4. Some faculty who saw their research
   interests as lacking value in the eyes of
   colleagues (e.g., because it is not
   experimental in an experimentally dominated
   area, or because it deals with the pedagogy
   of the field).

5. Faculty whose line of research is exceptionally costly in time and travel, or for other reasons is unusually difficult to bring to maturity.

6. Cases where the shift from the first line of work to another is particularly problematic (e.g., the case of the second book in history, the first book being based on the dissertation).

These situations are representative rather than exhaustive, but indicate the dominant inclination to attribute blockage to situational circumstances, including those related to funding, lack of collegial support, lack of graduate student interest, lack of career mobility opportunity, and a general sense that opportunities for advancement are tightening up.

But there were also some faculty members, particularly among the delayed promotion group, for whom blockage involves a difference in expectations between the faculty member and colleagues. In some instances, there was disenchantment and disagreement with what is judged to be the values governing the "system." Illustrative of the latter was one scientist whose career was shaped, as he saw it, by an earlier and more humane model of academe which he now feels has been taken over by a ruthless group of "grantsmen."

For others, the problem seems related to change in job since time of appointment, either because the individual was hired to fill a particular role in a department that no longer exists, or because the level of expectations with respect to faculty productivity has changed since the time they received tenure.

Personal factors were noted by a few, notably marital problems, or the economic stress of providing for children's education (e.g., taking on summer or evening teaching overloads). Almost all of the women interviewed pointed to some career barrier at early stages in their careers, such as lack of encouragement from advisors and diversion into inferior placement (Clark and Corcoran 1986).

For some, there was a sense of a mid-life crisis in terms of their ability to further their research. As one quite successful biologist said, "I think I've reached that point now. In fact, I think I reached it five years

ago... when I realized that when you approach my age, it
is going to become very difficult to move, to better
yourself." He recognized, as do others, that he had some
options such as serving as department head, but they were
not attractive to him.

Resolution of Career Blocks

As we have seen, faculty career blockage experiences
vary in their scope: Some focus on one highly salient
career function, research, while others are broadly
pervasive, involving a total career outlook. They also
vary in attribution. Some involve an inward orientation
to individual life circumstances, while others are
oriented outward toward contemporary conditions of
academic life. These variations in specificity and
attribution are reflected in the approaches faculty
members use in addressing blockage experiences. Quite a
number were successful in shifting to a new research area.
This was, in fact, the most frequent resolution reported.
Some contemplated—and a rare few were in process of
making—a career change to a non-university position, such
as a move to an industrial laboratory or a different
profession such as law. Others seemed to be still trying
to come to terms with a life stage with which they were
unprepared to deal. A few appeared to be resigned to
living out their careers by satisfying minimal teaching
requirements and seeking satisfactions elsewhere.

As we looked at these varying responses and, in
particular, as we compared those reported by the highly
active and delayed promotion groups, we were struck by two
findings. First, although most faculty members see
themselves as primarily responsible for their careers,
they do think colleagues could be more helpful, not so
much to themselves as to others facing critical career
points. Very few report receiving any specific help from
department chairs, deans, or from other institutional
sources. The major exception is that for not a few, a key
intervention has been the availability of a sabbatical
leave.

Second, the highly active group tended to take a more
active, problem-solving approach, rooted in a realistic
understanding of the circumstances of academic life. Some
also showed a maturing concern for helping younger

colleagues and graduate students in shaping their careers, expressing a concern for "generative" responsibilities and for serving appropriately in mentor relationships. One highly active faculty member emphasized problem solving as a response to career blockage: "Our whole job is to find solutions where none existed before and so...you should view a career block as but another problem to be solved."

By contrast, the delayed promotion group appeared to be less resourceful in seizing on opportunities and in finding ways to create opportunities. The less adequate career socialization of this group and their tendency to be less well-informed about and prepared for their role as faculty members has been reported in earlier papers (Clark and Corcoran 1983; Corcoran and Clark 1984).

The delayed promotion group also tended to talk about more diffuse problems and less often about their own attempts at resolution. When they did speak of their own efforts to resolve the problem, they tended to be less specific. For example,

> Now that I perceive that that will be a thing of the past, I'm sort of optimistic that newer interests of mine will emerge. I will expand into new areas. And I am willing to take advantage of these various opportunities to renew interests and to branch out into other interests.

However, we did find an occasional instance of seeming revitalization in this group. As one man said, "I was really overwhelmed by work and didn't know how to get out of it. I was very ineffective at getting out from under." But as he says, he changed and his circumstances changed. "I have much less of a teaching load now and I am also not drinking alcohol." He also reported that he is now much better at delegating, at picking out priorities and setting realistic limits. "People who have known me both in earlier years and now say, 'God, you've finally learned!'"

For some, intervention by a department chair at an appropriate time was reported to have helped considerably. "The department head told me that he thought I was getting into something of a rut." It is interesting that as he reflects on the incident which occurred five or six years ago, he concludes that it was he himself that had to accomplish the change. "So I think really it was just a matter of my being told that something had happened or was happening, or I wasn't performing as I should be, then essentially my pulling myself together and doing things differently."

Among the conclusions drawn from study of the vitality of faculty groups is that stuckness or blockage is not an unusual experience. It is likely to happen at some point during a career lifetime. While some blockages are related to "mid-life crises," others occur earlier or later. Blockages are contextual or situational in origin. Faculty who are experiencing delays in promotion are more likely to report stuckness or problems. Finally, most often, faculty resolve their own blockages with little help forthcoming from colleagues or institutional sources. Their career socialization, maturity, and problem solving orientation contribute to effective problem resolution.

POLICY IMPLICATIONS

In this chapter, we have considered how the problem of the vitality of midcareer and older professionals, especially faculty members, is perceived, how obsolescence and vitality are conceptualized, how individual career vitality and organizational vitality are interrelated, and how simplistic assumptions about the effects of aging on work do not describe the experience of professionals adequately or accurately. Further, drawing from a study of faculty career vitality at a major research university, we have illustrated the career blockage experience of "stuckness" as a vitality issue thought to be associated with mid-career or older professional workers. To keep faculty or older professionals among the "moving" rather than the "stuck" will require the development and maintenance of an opportunity and power structure that opens career paths, provides developmental activities, facilitates lateral or vertical movement to assure stimulation, involves people in organizational decision-making processes, deliberately builds sponsorship ("old hand-newcomer") relationships within the organization, and recognizes good performance in a variety of ways. Thus, in addressing needs of professionals who may vary on vitality indicators, we favor an expanded and differentiated institutional or corporate perspective on human resource development.

Human resource development perspectives reflect the idea that individual and institutional vitality are interrelated and interactive. Miller (1979) asks, "What is a human resources strategy and how can it impact vitality and overcome obsolescence?" (p. 30). The organization which invests in training, retraining and education, and advances its own employees is operating with a strategy that humans are enhanceable. The strategy

> supports and enhances vitality because
> individuals sense the security necessary for
> taking risks of individual growth. It also
> supports vitality because it provides for job
> changes which stimulate both productivity and
> personal development. Lastly, it supports
> vitality because employees sense that the
> organization puts a high value on its human
> resources (p. 30).

Institutional or corporate perspectives on human resource development are being bolstered and enriched by the studies of organizational cultures and climates and their effects on the behavior of managers and workers in a wide variety of organizations, including colleges and universities (Masland 1985). However, to date, little of a systematic nature has been developed to assist policy-making and personnel management in the matter of vitality enhancement.

When human obsolescence was first identified as knowledge obsolescence in the era of rapid technological change which resulted in the so-called half-life of professional/technical education, the first solutions to the problem were continuing education and reeducation. These solutions continue in favor; however, the extent to which education offsets obsolescence and maintains vitality is not clear and has not been demonstrated empirically. Historically, adult learning has been voluntary, and many are concerned that "mandated" adult education in the form of continuing education is coercive and not really a guarantee of permanent adequacy. According to Cross (1981), 45 states now require continuing education for optometrists, and 42 have continuing education requirements for nursing home administrators. In Iowa, in the late seventies, the

legislature passed a bill requiring all 23 professional
licensing boards in the state to establish continuing
education requirements for relicensure. Many other states
have mandatory continuing education required of certain
groups. Adult educators are divided on the issue of the
efficacy or the wisdom of mandatory requirements, and they
are aware that professional associations desire to protect
the integrity of their fields themselves through
monitoring, and through didactic and informal educational
activities. Without a doubt, this policy area will
continue to be filled with jurisdictional conflicts,
tensions, and developments (Houle 1980).

Traditional approaches to encouraging
"anti-obsolescence" in professionals, especially in highly
technical fields, have included self-assessment
(introspective evaluation and soul-searching), seminars,
workshops, courses, and self-study (Kaufman 1979; Sonner
1983). Many professionals are learning effective use of
the microcomputer via a combination of these methods.
Another way of keeping up to date is to move from
positions concentrating on theory and research to those
focussing on practice and application and back again.
(This could work in the reverse direction as well.)
Illustrative of this approach is faculty consulting work,
summer or part-time employment in applied fields related
to professional and disciplinary expertise (Boyer and
Lewis 1985).

Earlier we had remarked that the general condition of
academe in terms of projected institutional and faculty
vitality is mixed, and long-term solutions to problems
appear to be limited. Institutions, of course, can
attempt to alter the rate and composition of new faculty
entering their employ, or alter the rate and composition
of faculty leaving academe in order to achieve a more
optimal age structure. Much has been written about these
two strategies in recent years. Possibly the best known
of the proposals to increase the number of new young
faculty members ("fresh blood") involves petitioning of
federal agencies or philanthropic foundations for support
of young doctorates in regular institutional positions to
the point of tenure, when the institutions themselves take
over fiscal responsibilities for their support (Radner and
Kuh 1978). Costs of these programs have been high, and
the number of them funded to the present is undoubtedly
low.

The second strategy for changing the faculty age distribution involves altering the rate and composition of faculty leaving academe. At least in part, this strategy is predicated on conventional notions of aging and productivity that we have argued are open to question. However, a substantial minority of faculty members may not be happy with their careers; they may feel blocked, stuck, demoralized, or highly dissatisfied with intrinsic and extrinsic rewards (Carnegie Foundation for the Advancement of Teaching 1985; Schuster and Bowen 1985). Under favorable circumstances, some of these individuals have shown themselves willing to consider voluntary midcareer options, or phased or early retirement. Patton and Palmer (1985), Hansen (1985) and Holden (1985) have analyzed these options and the conditions under which they seem to work best. Cautionary reminders are given with the variability of individual and institutional needs in mind. For example, age composition differs greatly from institution to institution; early retirement incentives are very costly, and phased retirement programs may have the unanticipated consequence of later retirements than might have been the case otherwise, or more productive people may opt for phased or early retirement in order to pursue other options; only a one-time effect on the institution's demography is obtained.

While these strategies may result in a modest degree of change in the near future, it is a certainty that most regular faculty members, as other professional employees, will stay put for the rest of their careers. The question remains: "What might be done to enhance the vitality of existing faculty in whom resources have been invested and to whom institutional commitments have been made?" (Clark, Corcoran, and Lewis 1986). We believe strategies that are premised on shared individual and organizational responsibility for vitality enhancement are the most realistic, feasible, and compatible with the professional ethos. There is some urgency attending analysis of these issues and the formulation of policies to enhance vitality, and some have asserted that organizations haven't given sufficient attention to the human needs of their staffs. As Schuster and Bowen (1985) state, on the basis of their recent 38 institution study,

Alas, educational leaders must also ask
themselves what can be done now when

> resources are scarce and may become
> scarcer....One thing they could do is to
> improve the quality of interpersonal
> relations between administrators and
> faculty and among faculty members. It is
> our contention that an unfortunate paradox
> exists: on the one hand, our colleges and
> universities are unquestionably the leading
> repositories of knowledge about enlightened
> human relations. Yet we find that many
> colleges and universities do a relatively
> poor job in paying attention to the human
> needs of their instructional staff (p. 21).

A relatively recent response to human resource development needs in higher education is faculty development programs. But these have focussed almost exclusively on improving instructional competence, have not been targeted to faculty whose needs for assistance even in that domain are greatest, and have been reduced with retrenchments even while the higher education literature is arguing their importance. It appears that fewer sabbaticals are being awarded (and many eligibles feel that they cannot afford to take them because income is reduced), research funds are scarce and more competitive, and less money is available to support participation in conferences of professional associations which provide opportunities for anti-obsolescence activities and networking. These commonplace observations seem to be related to faculty malaise, immobilization, reduced opportunity and perceptions of "stuckness" which we have discussed earlier.

From an institutional perspective with concern for fostering long-term vitality of existing faculty, particularly those productive and engaged faculty who are not potential candidates for the early exit strategies, several suggestive substrategies have emerged from consultation with faculty members themselves (Clark, Corcoran, and Lewis 1986). The first is the importance of administrative leadership behavior and attitudes which reflect scholarly professional concerns, which recognize the full range of accomplishments, and which encourage the development of an intellectually stimulating group of colleagues who have a psychological sense of community. The second policy strategy focuses on supporting,

functionally and symbolically, important professional
values of the faculty: freedom of inquiry; interest in
scholarly research activities and adequate, concentrated
time in which to do their work; provision of "seed" money
to initiate new studies and new instructional activities;
and of course, adequate facilities for the work to be
done. For faculty members in research-oriented
institutions, concerns about quality of, and support for,
graduate students also enters this policy substrategy.
The third area includes targeted assistance to meet the
vitality needs of individual faculty, such as those whose
research interests have run dry, those whose research is
not currently attractive to the programmatic orientations
of funding agencies, those whose teaching areas are weak
in student and programmatic demand, those who experience
discontinuities between role and performance expectations
and the reward system, and those who confront the high
productivity standards now set for probationary faculty in
a time of uncertain rewards.

Regardless of the human resource principles and
policies of an organization, and of the enlightened and
informed quality of the administrative leaders/managers,
individual vitality is also a personal responsibility.
Problem solving is an important part of the occupational
role socialization of faculty members, physicians,
engineers, lawyers, and others. We expect to define and,
in the main, to be the key actors in solving our own
problems. With organizational resources, a supportive
climate, and facilitative strategies available to us, we
can do it. Professionals would have it no other way.

228

REFERENCES

Austin, A. and Z. Gamson. 1983. Academic Workplace: New
Demands, Heightened Tensions. ASHE-ERIC Higher
Education Research Report 10. Washingon, D.C.:
Association for the Study of Higher Education.
Blackburn, R. T. 1982. "Career Phases and Their Influence
on Faculty Motivation." Pp. 95-98 in J. Bess (ed.) New
Directions for Teaching and Learning: Motivating
Professors to Teach Effectively. San Francisco:
Jossey-Bass.
_____. 1985. "Faculty Career Development: Theory and
Practice." Pp. 55-58 in S. Clark and D. Lewis (eds.),
Faculty Vitality and Institutional Productivity:
Critical Perspectives for Higher Education. New York:
Teachers College Press.
Blackburn, R. T., and J. Lawrence. 1985. "Aging and
Faculty Job Performance." Paper presented at the annual
meeting of the American Educational Research
Association, Chicago.
Boyer, C., and D. Lewis. 1985. And on the Seventh Day:
Faculty Consulting and Supplemental Income. ASHE-ERIC
Higher Education Research Report 3. Washington, D.C.:
Association for the Study of Higher Education.
Butler, R. 1975. Why Survive? Being Old in America. New
York: Harper and Row.
Carnegie Council on Policy Studies in Higher Education.
1980. Three Thousand Futures: The Next Twenty Years
for Higher Education. San Francisco: Jossey-Bass.
Carnegie Foundation for the Advancement of Teaching. 1985.
"The Faculty: Deeply Troubled." Change 17:31-34.
Centra, J. 1985. "Maintaining Faculty Vitality Through
Faculty Development." Pp. 141-156 in S. Clark and D.
Lweis (eds.), Faculty Vitality and Institutional
Productivity: Critical Perspectives for Higher
Education. New York: Teachers College Press.
Centra, J., and R. I. Zinn. 1976. "Student Points of View
in Ratings of College Instruction." Educational and
Psychological Measurement 36:693-703.
Clark, S., C. Boyer, and M. Corcoran. 1985. "Faculty and
Institutional Vitality in Higher Education." Pp. 3-24
in S. Clark and D. Lewis (eds.), Faculty Vitality and
Institutional Productivity: Critical Perspectives for
Higher Education. New York: Teachers College Press.

Clark, S., and M. Corcoran. 1983. "Professional
Socialization and Faculty Career Vitality." Paper
presented at the annual meeting of the American
Educational Research Association, Montreal.
_____. 1985. "Individual and Organizational
Contributions to Faculty Vitality: An Institutional
Case Study." Pp. 112-138 in S. Clark and D. Lewis
(eds.), Faculty Vitality and Institutional Productivity:
Critical Perspectives for Higher Education. New York:
Teachers College Press.
_____. 1986. "Perspectives on the Professional
Socialization of Women Faculty: A Case of Accumulative
Disadvantage?" Journal of Higher Education 57:20-43.
Clark, S., M. Corcoran, and D. Lewis. 1986. "The Case for
an Institutional Perspective on Faculty Development."
Journal of Higher Education 57:176-195.
Clark, S., and D. Lewis (eds.). 1985. Faculty Vitality
and Institutional Productivity: Critical Perspectives
for Higher Education. New York: Teachers College
Press.
Clausen, J. 1972. "The Life Course of Individuals." Pp.
457-514 in M. W. Riley, M. Johnson, and A. Foner (eds.),
Aging and Society. Volume Three: A Sociology of Age
Stratification. New York: Russell Sage Foundation.
Corcoran, M., and S. Clark. 1984. "Professional
Socialization and Contemporary Career Attitudes of Three
Faculty Generations." Research in Higher Education
20:131-153.
_____. 1985. "The 'Stuck' Professor: Insights Into an
Aspect of the Faculty Vitality Issue." Pp. 57-81 in C.
Watson (ed.), The Professoriate: Occupation in Crisis.
Toronto: Ontario Institute for Studies in Higher
Education.
Cross, K. P. 1981. Adults as Learners. San Francisco:
Jossey-Bass.
Dannefer, D. 1984. "Adult Development and Social Theory:
A Paradigmatic Reappraisal." American Sociological
Review 49:100-116.
Finkelstein, M. J. 1984. The American Academic
Profession. Columbus: Ohio State University Press.
Fulton, O., and M. Trow. 1974. "Research Activity in
American Higher Education." Sociology of Education
47:29-73.
Gardner, J. 1963. Self-Renewal. New York: Harper and
Row.

230

_____. 1978. Morale. New York: Norton.

Hansen, W. L. 1985. "Changing Demography of Faculty in Higher Education." Pp. 25-54 in S. Clark and D. Lewis (eds.), Faculty Vitality and Institutional Productivity: Critical Perspectives for Higher Education. New York: Teachers College Press.

Havighurst, R. 1980. "The Life Course of College Professors and Administrators." Pp. 79-95 in K. W. Back (ed.), Life Course: Integrative Theories and Exemplary Populations. Boulder, Colorado: Westview Press.

Havighurst, R. 1985. "Aging and Productivity: The Case of Older Faculty." Pp. 98-111 in S. Clark and D. Lewis (eds.), Faculty Vitality and Institutional Productivity: Critical Perspectives for Higher Education. New York: Teachers College Press.

Holden, K. 1985. "Maintaining Faculty Vitality Through Early Retirement Options." Pp. 177-197 in S. Clark and D. Lewis (eds.), Faculty Vitality and Institutional Productivity: Critical Perspectives for Higher Education. New York: Teachers College Press.

Horn, J. L., and R. B. Cattell. 1967. "Age Differences in Fluid and Crystallized Intelligence." Acta Psychologica 26:107-129.

Houle, C. 1980. Continuing Learning in the Professions. San Francisco: Jossey-Bass.

Kanter, R. 1977. Men and Women of the Corporation. New York: Basic Books.

_____. 1979. "Changing the Shape of Work: Reform in Academe." Current Issues in Higher Education 1:3-9.

Kaufman, H. G. 1979. "Technical Obsolescence: Work and Organizations Are the Key." Engineering Education 69:826-830.

Levine, M. 1980. "Four Models for Age/Work Policy Research." The Gerontologist 20:561-574.

Lindsay, C., J. Morrison, and E. J. Kelley. 1974. "Professional Obsolescence: Implications for Continuing Professional Education." Adult Education 25:3-22.

Maher, J. 1982. "Institutional Vitality in Higher Education." AAHE Bulletin 34: no. 10.

Masland, A. 1985. "Organizational Culture in the Study of Higher Education." Review of Higher Education 8:157-168.

McDowell, J. 1982. "Obsolescence of Knowledge and Career Publication Profiles: Some Evidence of Differences Among Fields in Costs of Interrupted Careers." American Economic Review 72:752-768.

Meier, E., and E. Kerr. 1976. "Capabilities of Middle-Aged and Older Workers: A Survey of the Literature." Industrial Gerontology 3:147-156.

Miller, D. 1979. "Counteracting Obsolescence in Employees and Organizations." Professional Engineer 49:29-31.

National Science Foundation Advisory Council. 1978. Report of Task Group #1: Continued Viability of Universities as Centers for Basic Research. Washington, D.C.: National Science Foundation.

Patton, C., and D. Palmer. 1985. "Maintaining Faculty Vitality Through Midcareer Change Options." Pp. 157-176 in S. Clark and D. Lewis (eds.), Faculty Vitality and Institutional Productivity: Critical Perspectives for Higher Education. New York: Teachers College Press.

Perrucci, R., and R. Rothman. 1969. "Obsolescence of Knowledge and the Professional Career." Pp. 247-275 in R. Perrucci and J. Gerstl (eds.), The Engineers and the Social System.

Peterson, R., and D. Loye. 1967. Conversations Toward a Definition of Institutional Vitality. Princeton, N. J.: Educational Testing Service.

Planning Council. 1980. "A Proposal for a Study on 'The Future Vitality of the Faculties of the University.'" Memorandum to President C. Peter Magrath, University of Minnesota, Minneapolis.

Radner, T., and C. Kuh. 1978. "Preserving a Lost Generation: Policies to Assure a Steady Flow of Young Scholars Until the Year 2000." A report and recommendation to the Carnegie Council on Policy Studies in Higher Education.

Reskin, B. 1985. "Aging and Productivity: Careers and Results." Pp. 86-87 in S. Clark and D. Lewis (eds.), Faculty Vitality and Institutional Productivity: Critical Perspectives for Higher Education. New York: Teachers College Press.

Rothman, R., and R. Perrucci. 1970. "Organizational Careers and Professional Expertise." Administrative Science Quarterly 15:282-293.

232

Sarason, S. B. 1977. Work, Aging, and Social Change: Professionals and the One Life-One Career Imperative. New York: Free Press.

Schuster, J., and H. Bowen. 1985. "The Faculty at Risk." Change 17:13-21.

Shin, K., and R. Putnam. 1982. "Age and Academic-Professional Honors." Journal of Gerontology 37:220-229.

Sonner, J. 1983. "Combating Technical Obsolescence in ET Faculty." Engineering Education 73:803-804.

Taylor, L. 1968. Occupational Sociology. New York: Oxford.

Zuckerman, H., and R. Merton. 1972. "Age, Aging and Age Structure in Science." Pp. 292-356 in M. W. Riley, M. Johnson, and A. Foner (eds.), Aging and Society, Volume Three: A Sociology of Age Stratification. New York: Russell Sage Foundation.

Michael L. Schwalbe, Viktor Gecas

8. Social Psychological Dimensions of Job-Related Disability

SCOPE OF THE PROBLEM

The statistics on occupational injury and disease in the United States are gruesome. In the early 1970s, the National Institute for Occupational Safety and Health estimated that 100,000 people died annually from job-related diseases, and another 390,000 became seriously ill. National Safety Council estimates at that time put the number of yearly deaths due to accidents on the job at 14,000 and the number of disabling injuries at 2.2 million. According to Ashford's (1976) benchmark study, Crisis in the Workplace, the true figure for disabling injuries was closer to 11 million.

By the early 1980s, after a decade of underenforcement of the Occupational Safety and Health Act, not much had changed. The National Safety Council estimated that in 1981, workplace accidents claimed 12,300 lives, and produced 2.1 million disabling injuries. According to Derr et al. (1981), these figures, derived from industry-supplied data, again understated the problem; they estimated 75,000 job-induced deaths per year and 10 million injuries. Occupational diseases also continue to exact a brutal toll. According to the U.S. Department of Labor (1980), 2 million workers now suffer some degree of disability from a work-related disease, while 700,000 suffer long-term total disability. These figures too might well be low, when one considers that one in four American workers--about 25 million people--are potentially exposed to a major health hazard at work (Currie and Skolnick 1984; see also Berman 1979).

In light of these figures it is not surprising that 71% of a national sample of workers cited work injury or illness as a very important problem for them (Wallick 1972; see also Shostak 1980). Such fears hardly seem exaggerated. Davis (1977, 1979) estimates that 15% of the black workforce and 10% of the white workforce cannot work because of a job-related disability. And while many of these estimates have been derived from studies of male workers, recent studies of female workers have revealed frighteningly similar patterns (see Chavkin 1984). The actual experiences of injury, illness, and disablement--and the stress induced by fear of them--are unfortunately common aspects of many people's working lives. Disability remains, as Krause (1976) put it, one of the chief products of the workplace. This "product," however, is not equally distributed across age and social class groups.

Because of inconsistencies in record keeping, indus-try tendencies toward denial and under-reporting, and the extended latency periods for many occupational diseases, it is difficult to get a clear picture of the population experiencing disability due to occupational injury and disease. We can, however, get a clear picture of the population currently (1980) experiencing some type of work disability by relying on census data (U.S. Department of Commerce 1985). Age and social class appear to be the most important variables affecting prevalence of work disability.

Age shows a positive association with prevalence of work disability. Among men, 5% of those 18-34, 9.8% of those 35-54, and 23.5% of those 55-64 years old suffer from some type of work disability. Among women, 3.6% of those 18-34, 9.2% of those 35-54, and 20.5% of those 55-64 suffer from some type of work disability. This relation-ship probably reflects a number of things: the appearance of job-related diseases in later life, the cumulative effects of job-related physiological damage over the work career, and diminished recuperative powers with advancing age.

These same data also show social class (in terms of education and income) to have a significant effect on job-related disability. In general, as one goes down the social class ladder, the prevalence of work disability goes up. In large part, this seems to be a consequence of the greater risk of occupational injury and disease in low-skilled and low-paying jobs. We must also point out, however, that since these data derive from a census classification of "work disabled," some of the association between work disability and social class simply reflects the greater physical demands often associated with lower-status jobs; the result is that an injury that might cause a manual laborer to be classified as disabled would not have the same consequence for, say, an engineer or a supervisor. Nonetheless, the general relationship between the likelihood of occupational injury and disease and social class contains the potential for devastating psychological damage, since, as we will argue later, those most at risk tend also to possess the fewest resources for coping with job-related disabilities.

While the physical damage done by dangerous working conditions can be readily comprehended, the psychological damage is often more insidious and less easily grasped. It is, however, no less painful, debilitating, or worthy of therapeutic response. Dealing effectively with the psychological consequences attendant to disabling occupational injuries and disease requires, of course, an understanding of how these consequences arise. In this chapter, we develop a theoretical framework for understanding how job-related disabilities produce various psychological consequences, and how psychological factors figure in recovery and rehabilitation. Before presenting our analysis, we must first delimit the range of our concerns, and then justify the social-psychological approach we take to addressing them.

Despite a vast literature on disability (see Self 1984), much contention remains as to just how it should be defined (Duckworth 1982; Badley and Bury 1982). Krause (1972), for example, draws out three kinds of definitions of disability that tend to be confused in the literature: biopsychological--as determined by the judgments of physicians and other professionals supposedly qualified to assess physical and mental functioning according to generally accepted standards; social role--determined relative to the social role demands of a particular individual; and legal--determined with reference to medical, psychological, and social criteria that have the force of law. The kind of definition used in any case reflects the particular dimensions of the problem being addressed. For our purposes, we need a working definition useful for addressing the social-psychological dimensions of the problem.

The following indicates, in general terms, the range of our concerns. All kinds of physical injuries and diseases occurring or originating in the workplace are potentially relevant. More specifically, however, we are concerned with those injuries or diseases that singly, or in combination with other factors, disrupt a person's normal patterns of action and interaction such that significant psychological adaptation is necessary. This implies that job-related disabilities are, as we conceive them, a function of the relationship between a person's capacities, his or her needs and wants, and the obstacles a given environment presents to satisfying those needs and wants.

From this, it should be apparent that we intend to construct a theoretical framework that treats disability in general terms. Specific patterns of disability and adaptation can then be interpreted within this framework. Thus we will not dwell on specific types of biomechanical disabilities (as is more commonly done in the disability literature), but will speak in general terms of major and minor, long- and short-term, immediate and delayed disruptions in normal patterns of action and interaction. We will speak similarly of the adaptations these disruptions demand. Our strategy is therefore to analyze the phenomenon of job-related disability and its psychological consequences in broad social-psychological terms, rather than in the more specialized and narrow terms of the disability literature.

We have taken this approach for three reasons. First, we think it is essential to understand the individual, whether disabled or modally functioning, as a social product.[1] Many analyses of the psychological consequences of disability have failed to fully appreciate the socially shaped nature of the individual and his or her responses to disability. Our focus on the self-concept, which is a special kind of social product, as the motivational basis for individual responses to disability tries to counter this reductionist tendency. We will attempt to show, in other words, why the psychological aspects of disability must always be understood in social-psychological terms.

Second, we also think it is essential to understand the network of social relations within which problems of disability arise. The individual cannot properly be seen as having an individual problem of disability; inasmuch as this problem is a function of the person-environment relationship, it must be conceived and dealt with as a social problem (cf. Vance 1973). Brief consideration of matters such as the labeling of the disabled, the social support that influences coping, and the formal organizations that process the disabled should suffice to make this point. The psychological consequences of disability are thus as much consequences of the social arrangements within which disability occurs as they are of people's personalities and coping abilities.

Finally, we think it is essential to understand the connections between individual experiences of disability, the immediate contexts within which these experiences arise, and the broader social-structural system within which all this occurs. This is to say that the problem of understanding the psychological consequences of job-related disabilities is analogous to the problem of understanding social structure and personality. It is impossible, in other words, to fully understand why job-related disabilities are so common, why individuals and organizations respond to them as they do, and why certain adaptations are possible or not, without taking broader social structures into account. While we cannot pursue such an expansive analysis here (cf. Albrecht 1976), we do pursue a distinctly sociological social-psychological analysis of the problem. Our interest is in developing a more comprehensive theoretical analysis of the psychological consequences of job-related disabilities by drawing on recent work in the social psychology of the self-concept. Our goal, then, is to further understanding of the social-psychological dimensions of the problem and thereby contribute to the creation of more effective solutions.

This chapter contains five sections. The immediately following section sets forth our general perspective on work, disability, and psychological well-being. The next section explores the role of the self-concept in health and injury, setting forth in more specific terms our social-psychological perspective. The next section develops a parallel analysis of the role of the self-concept in recovery and rehabilitation. The next-to-last section focuses on the organizational contexts within which recovery and rehabilitation occur, and on their implications for the self-concept. The final section draws out some policy implications of our analysis.

WORK, DISABILITY, AND PSYCHOLOGICAL WELL-BEING

Work creates a double-bind situation for many people in our society. It is something they cannot live healthily with or without. Excessive work demands and dangerous working conditions can damage both mind and body. Yet work can be an important source of psychic rewards, without which both body and mind can deteriorate. Thus, it is not surprising that studies of the relationships between work and mental health have produced apparently inconsistent results (see Kasl 1977; and Sorensen and Mortimer, Chapter 6 in this volume). These results can be understood, however, given an appropriate interpretive framework.

We propose, first, to view psychological well-being as dependent on the ability to access and mobilize the resources necessary to cope with environmental demands without experiencing severe psychological distress. This means that psychological well-being is a function of the relationships between environmental demands, individual coping abilities, and the availability of coping resources. The psychological distress that constitutes, in metaphorical terms, mental illness, may involve intense anxiety, paralyzing helplessness and despair, emotional volatility, extreme confusion, and low self-esteem. Positively defined, then, psychological well-being is that orientation to self, world, and others characterized by sociability, security, happiness, mastery, a sense of coherence, high self-esteem, and emotional stability.

We are thus not especially concerned with whether psychological distress is manifested in deviant behavior that leads to formally labeling a person "mentally ill." What we are concerned with are a person's adaptive abilities and psychic comfort at any point in time. Our preference, in fact, is not to speak of mental health and illness at all, but rather of a person's location on a continuum of psychological ill-being/well-being (collapsing, for heuristic purposes, each of the dimensions into a single dimension). Work can then be viewed as one source of experiences that can push a person toward either end of the continuum (cf. Antonovsky 1979). To anticipate an argument we will develop later, it is the self-concept that provides a person's firmest anchor to any particular location on this continuum.

The implication arising from this view of the relationship between work and psychological well-being is that work experiences must be analyzed in terms of their positive and negative effects on well-being. This is also a useful way to think about the relationships between job-related disabilities and their psychological consequences, as we will argue later. To proceed, then, we shall first consider the positive contributions of work to psychological well-being, secondly, its negative contributions, and thirdly, in light of this, the

relationship   between   job-related   disability   and
psychological well-being.

Work can potentially contribute to psychological
well-being in at least eight ways:

1. by providing a context in which social support
    and community feeling are derived;
2. by providing a source of material rewards neces-
    sary for satisfying physical and social needs;
3. by providing a sense of mastery or
    self-efficacy;
4. by providing a sense of self-worth via occupa-
    tional prestige and fulfillment of a cultur-
    ally-valued 'breadwinner' role;
5. by providing a source of identity, a sense of
    our location in the social structure;
6. by providing a basis for making life predict-
    able;
7. by giving meaning to a person's life activity;
    and
8. by contributing to development of problem-
    solving abilities and general coping powers that
    increase the likelihood of successful adaptation
    to environmental demands arising outside of
    work.

Unfortunately, very little work in our capitalist,
bureaucratic, mechanized society actually provides all
these things (U.S. Department of Health, Education and
Welfare 1973; Braverman 1974). A large proportion of
wage-earners in our society derive little meaning,
efficacy, or self-worth from their paid labor. Others in
the managerial, professional, and technical ranks tend to
be more fortunate in these respects. Independent artisans
and craftsmen, pursuing in large part aesthetic ends, may
be more fortunate still. That the class structure of a
capitalist society generates an unequal distribution of
these psychic rewards through work does not, however,
obviate our basic point: work can be a source of these
rewards, even if it is seldom a source of all of them for
everyone (cf. Johada and Rush 1980).

Work can contribute to psychological ill-being in a
corresponding set of ways:

1. by overwhelming a person, thereby undermining a
    sense of mastery;
2. by demeaning a person, thereby undermining a
    sense of self-worth;

3. by "underloading" a person, thereby causing problem-solving abilities and coping powers to atrophy;

4. by demanding an obedience to authority and an amorality that undermine a person's sense of autonomous identity;

5. by exhausting a person to the extent that psychic rewards may be impossible to pursue outside of work;

6. by demanding devotion to performance of inherently meaningless tasks, thereby generating cynicism and alienation;

7. by engendering excessive competitiveness and hostility toward others; and

8. by providing only a subsistence level of material rewards, generating chronic economic strain.

The preceding discussion is not intended merely to note the dark side of work in complex, industrial society. It is intended, rather, to identify the undeniably common work experiences that can push a person toward psychological ill-being (see also Elliot and Eisdorfer 1982:81-146). Again, these experiences are no more equally distributed than the positive ones identified earlier. Our concern at the moment, however, is with their combined effects on the individuals confronting them more so than with their structurally-based distribution across class positions. At a social-psychological level, we are concerned with the relative importance attached to each of these positive or negative experiences, and with their additive, multiplicative, and countervailing effects.

We have found this a useful framework for thinking about how work experience can potentially affect psychological well-being. We believe it is also useful for thinking about how job-related disabilities can affect psychological well-being. In this regard we now shift our concerns to:

1. how a particular disability might preclude certain positive experiences;

2. how it might generate or amplify certain negative ones;

3. how it might alter the importance of certain positive or negative experiences;

4. how it might diminish abilities to cope with negative experiences or to derive the greatest benefit from positive ones; and

5. how it might tip the balance of these experiences in one direction or the other, pushing the
individual toward psychological ill-being or
well-being.

Some types of disability (job-related or otherwise)
might, for example, take a person entirely out of a context that normally provides a wide range of positive experiences. The most obvious case is the loss of a valued
job because of injury or other illness. In turn, this
might have the consequences of undermining social support,
material rewards, mastery, self-worth, identity, environmental predictability, and meaningfulness. On the other
hand, it could offer an ultimately beneficial escape from
a psychologically damaging work environment (see also
Safilios-Rothschild 1970 on the "secondary gains" of
disability). Clearly, however, work is not the only context in which the positive or negative experiences that
affect psychological well-being arise. Other contexts in
which the person acts and interacts must be taken into
account. The same logic can nonetheless be applied to
understanding how experiences within diverse contexts--or
the lack of those experiences--can give rise to psychological consequences.

This logic dictates that we look first at the concrete actions and interactions that are either precluded
or made inevitable by a particular disability in a particular environment. But secondly, and perhaps more
important, we must look at the meanings attached to these
actions and interactions, and at how a particular disability may alter these meanings. The psychological consequences of some change in these patterns of action and
interaction may be substantial or negligible, depending on
the meanings given to the activities actually affected.
Given these meanings, we must also consider how a particular disability may affect a person's abilities to cope
with negative experiences and derive benefit from positive
ones. To put it another way, it is essential to understand the perspective of the individual in order to understand the effects of any change in environment or self
upon him or her (Roessler and Bolton 1978).

Implicit here is a 'continuity model' of the relationship between normality, disability, and psychological
well-being. In other words, we do not distinguish between
normality and disability with regard to the processes
operating to produce psychological ill-being or well-being
in either case (cf. Mechanic 1969). The same generic factors must be considered whether we are concerned with the

modally functioning person or the disabled person. Severe disabilities may indeed produce severe psychological consequences. But the processes through which this occurs are not fundamentally altered because some sort of disability is involved.

Our framework can thus be readily extended beyond the matter of work and its psychological effects to considering the effects of job loss, job-related disability, and physical impairment in general. In any particular case we will always want to know about the positive or negative experiences a person confronts because of his or her position in a social system, the coping skills the person possesses, the coping resources (both material and social) the person can mobilize, the balance that is maintained between environmental demands and coping responses, and the thrust toward psychological ill-being or well-being that thus arises (cf. Shontz 1975).

At this point it is necessary to correct the impression of individual passivity we may have created. The individual not only copes with and responds to environmental demands, but sometimes actively seeks to change the environment and him or her self along with it. In other words, the individual is not held in place on the ill-being/well-being continuum by inertia alone. As we suggested earlier, it is the self-concept that provides not only an anchor, but sometimes a motive force for determining a person's location on this continuum. It is the self-concept, as a relatively stable, organized set of beliefs about the self, that forms the core of personality around which behavior and cognition revolve (Rokeach 1979; Gecas 1982).

As the core of the person, the self-concept is implicated in our analysis of the psychological consequences of job-related disabilities in three basic ways. First, we see behavior, in the modally functioning and disabled person alike, as a product of substantive self-conceptions and of attempts to maintain or enhance self-esteem. Second, we see the interpretations people give to their experiences as significantly influenced by their self-conceptions. And third, we see the most serious consequences of disability arising because of its implications for the self-concept and self-esteem (see also Wright 1960; Safilios-Rothschild 1970; Roessler and Bolton 1978; Vash 1981). These views will be elaborated on later as we consider the relationships between self-conceptions, health, injury, rehabilitation, and recovery.

THE SELF-CONCEPT IN HEALTH AND INJURY

It is increasingly apparent that how we think about ourselves is very much affected by our conditions of health, illness, or injury. Before elaborating on this relationship, a few conceptual matters require discussion. The "self" is that aspect of personality which is reflexive, that is, both subject and object (Mead 1934; James 1890). The product of this reflexive or reflective activity is the self-concept (Gecas 1982; Rosenberg 1979), which Rosenberg defines broadly as "the totality of the individual's thoughts and feelings having reference to himself as an object" (1979:7). As such, the self-concept is a multidimensional phenomenon encompassing a broad range of psychological elements in terms of which people define themselves, such as attitudes, beliefs, values, experiences, accomplishments, productions, along with their evaluative and affective components (Gecas and Mortimer 1986).

An elementary--and particularly relevant (for our purposes)--focus of self-referent thoughts and feelings is one's body, which we will refer to as one's "body image." Body image refers to the perception and evaluation we have of our bodies, in whole or in part, regarding their structure, functioning, appearance, and sensations (such as pleasure and pain). One's "body sense," or conception of self as a physical body, is a fundamental aspect of the self-concept, developing very early in life--from an initial sense of one's physical being to an increasingly differentiated and evaluated "body image."

As with many aspects of the self-concept, we are most acutely conscious of and focused on our bodies when something goes wrong or changes. To be sure, a body sense is there in our awareness even when things are right. For example, people may be quite self-conscious of their beauty, strength, speed, coordination, stamina, grace, or robust health, and exalt in these positive self-appraisals. But it is more likely the case that the body becomes a focus of attention when something goes wrong. This notion is in keeping with the pragmatist conception of the development of mind and self. Mead (1934) and James (1890) stressed that mind and self arise and develop in the context of problematic situations, and are both mechanisms for dealing with such situations.

The most obvious consequence of work-related (and other) injury for the self-concept is a change in body image, in the broad sense of the term. But the effects of injury on the self-concept vary considerably, depending on such things as the nature and severity of the injury, the extent to which functioning is impaired, the visibility of the injury, the prognosis for recovery, etc. Injuries resulting in permanent disabilities, extensive impairment, and visible disability typically have more pronounced and extensive consequences for the self-conception of the injured worker. All three processes of self-concept formation (see Rosenberg 1979; Gecas 1982) enter into the redefinition of self: self-attributions, social comparisons, and reflected appraisals.

Self-attribution, the process by which we develop a conception of self from observations of our behavior (Bem 1972), is central to post-injury stock-taking. Particularly with traumatic injuries, such as those involving amputation or paralysis, the individual tries to assess the extent of damage and impairment of function. This is done mainly by observing one's own behavior and the making of inferences or attributions about one's capabilities and worth.

Social comparison and reflected appraisals are also important processes in self-concept formation and reassessment. Social comparison is the process by which people assess their own abilities and virtues by comparing them to those of others. This process involves the use of a reference group, or reference others, as yardsticks against which individuals measure themselves on some attribute. The injured worker may compare self with non-injured co-workers, or with the pre-injured self. In either case the comparisons are likely to be unfavorable, having negative consequences for the self-concept.[2] Reflected appraisals, under circumstances of injury, can also be hard on the injured workers self-concept. These are appraisals that we perceive others to be making of us. To the extent that the injured worker perceives that significant others see him or her as diminished (in competence, value, or appearance) by the injury, the self-concept will suffer (Safilios-Rothschild 1976, equates the condition of disabled persons with that of other minorities subject to discrimination and stigmatization).[3] All three processes enter into the reformation of the worker's body image and body sense after injury.

The potentially negative consequences of these processes for the injured worker's self-concept can be mitigated by the reorganization of the self-concept with regard to its salience hierarchy. Rosenberg's (1979) concept of "psychological centrality" and Stryker's (1980) concept of "identity salience" suggest that the various elements of the self-concept are organized in a hierarchy of importance. Following serious injury, a reorganization in a person's hierarchy of values and identities is one way of protecting self-esteem (see Kerr 1961, and DeLoach and Greer 1981). For example, the loss of beauty by a disfiguring injury might result in the person's downgrading the importance of beauty and elevating other qualities in importance.

Body image, however, is not the only, nor even the most important, aspect of self-concept affected by injury. Two evaluative aspects of self-concept are particularly important in health and injury: self-efficacy and self-worth. Both contribute to one's overall self-esteem, the degree of positive or negative attitude about oneself. Self-efficacy and self-worth are the most important bases of self-esteem (Gecas 1971; Rokeach 1979). Self-efficacy refers to one's sense of effectiveness and mastery in dealing with the environment. It is the degree to which individuals see themselves as being in control of forces that affect their lives, and as being competent individuals. Self-worth refers to the moral aspect of self-evaluation: the extent to which people see themselves as being moral and as having value. Self-efficacy and self-worth are important dimensions of self, not only because they are experienced in strongly positive and negative terms, but especially because of their motivational significance. People are motivated to maintain and enhance their self-efficacy, self-worth, and their overall self-esteem, which is reflected in the association of these two self-dimensions with a wide range of behavioral and psychological consequences (a theme which we treat more fully later).

As might be expected, injury and the concomitant stress associated with it have a negative effect on self-esteem. It is easy to see how negative self-attributions and reflected appraisals, as well as unfavorable social comparisons associated with actual or perceived diminished capacity would diminish one's self-efficacy and self-worth. This is particularly likely if the injury results in job disruption and economic strain--not uncommon consequences of work-related injury. For example, Pearlin et al. (1981) found, in their analysis of the stress process, that increases in economic strain associated with disruptive job events have a substantial negative effect on self-esteem (B = -.56) and (what they call) sense of mastery (B = -.70). Although the Pearlin study focused on job disruption and not on injury per se, the two conditions are clearly related. Job disruption due to injury may be that much worse, since the worker may be in a physically as well as a psychologically weakened condition to cope with the problem. Not surprisingly, Pearlin et al. also found job disruptions to be associated with depression via their effect on self-mastery and self-esteem. Low self-efficacy and self-esteem have frequently been associated with depression (see Seligman 1975; Wells and Marwell 1976), and especially under conditions of physical disability (see, for example, Albrecht 1976; and Turner et al. 1985).

Several other aspects of self-concept are relevant to a consideration of work-related injury. These fall mostly in the identity dimension of self-concept (i.e., the designation of what or who one is). The importance of identities is that they give meaning, purpose, structure, and direction to our lives. Identities not only give personal meaning to people's lives, but they also connect individuals to systems of social relationships. In particular, "role-identities" are typically lodged in networks of social relationships, which in effect constitute a "role-set." For example, a worker identity, such as "factory foremen," involves relationships with line workers, upper management, foremen in other units of the company, etc. Loss or disruption of this identity means the loss or disruption of the whole system of relationships entailed by the identity. The loss of significant identities due to injury or disease can thus undermine the social rootedness of the person (see, for example, Charmaz 1983).

The self-concept can be viewed as an organization of identities and their evaluations (Stryker 1980), with some identities more salient or important than others. Some of the most important identities in our culture can be affected by serious injury: "worker," "provider," "colleague," "able-bodied adult," and maybe even one's sex-role and family identities (e.g., "man," "woman," "husband/father," "wife/mother").

Let us consider the identity implications of a work-related injury that leads to unemployment (temporary or permanent). For most workers in our society, the status of "employed" is a positive one. It has connotations of responsibility, dependability, independence, respectability. As a result, those adults who become "unemployed" may lose status and respect in their own eyes and in the eyes of others. This is reflected in the marginally lower self-esteem and self-efficacy of the unemployed (Kasl 1977). Furthermore, loss of the identity of "worker" has implications for social relationships beyond the work setting. For example, this change is quite likely to affect family identities and family relationships as well. To the extent that the worker is also the provider or "breadwinner" in the family, loss of employment undermines these family identities; unemployment thus may lead to loss of status within the family, and to alterations of the division of labor and power in the home.[4] In the process, the identities of husband/father or wife/mother would be negatively affected, with a further loss of self-esteem and self-efficacy for the injured, unemployed worker. Albrecht (1976) observes that disabled husband-fathers seem to place more stress on the family than do disabled wife-mothers, perhaps because the provider role and its associated identities are more central to men's self-conceptions.

Rosenberg and McCullough's (1981) concept of "mattering" is also relevant here. "Mattering" refers to the importance of being a significant other to someone; of being consequential or important to others. A decrease in mattering, as Rosenberg has found, has negative consequences for mental health--it is associated with depression, listlessness, and feelings of alienation. If central family identities (such as "provider," "husband," "father") are diminished through injury and unemployment, a person may come to feel that he or she matters less to important others than before, thus exacerbating depression and despair.

Sex-role identities may also be affected by injury and job disruption. In our society, adequacy in the traditional married male role is premised on the ability to provide for the family. Unemployment may thus have negative consequences for some men's sex-role identities. The same principle would apply to unemployed women whose sense of adequacy in the mother role was tied to the ability to provide for their families. Furthermore, changes in body image due to injury may spill over into sex-role identities. If a man's masculinity is staked largely on his physical prowess, serious injury may have pronounced consequences for his conception of himself as a man. Similarly, a woman whose sense of femininity is based largely on appearance may be shaken in her sex-role identity by a disfiguring injury or ailment.

We must remember, however, that social identities and other aspects of self-concept are maintained or transformed in the context of interpersonal relationships. The responses and reactions of others to the injured worker will therefore substantially affect the extent of the psychological damage associated with injury. In general, supportive family members, friends, and co-workers will tend to buffer the negative consequences. There are other important qualifiers as well: the type of injury; whether the injury results in permanent disability; age of the injured worker (younger workers may be able to recover or retrain faster than older workers); and the type of occupation involved (physical injury would be more consequential in jobs requiring strength, stamina, coordination, etc.). The negative consequences of injury for the self-concepts of injured workers need to be tempered and qualified by a number of conditional factors. In general, however, the consequences of disability for self-conceptions are pervasive, substantial, and often devastating.

Self-Concept and the Recovery Process

In discussing the consequences of work-related disabilities for the worker's self-concept, it is easy to give the misleading impression that the influence is unidirectional, when, in fact, the relationship is highly reciprocal. The self-concept is not a passive object of environmental influence. In this section, we consider how the self is active in affecting the course of disablement and recovery.

The view of the self-concept as having an effect on its environment is most evident in the operation of three self-motives: self-esteem, self-efficacy,[5] and self-coherence (see Rosenberg 1979; and Gecas 1982, for an elaboration). Briefly, people are motivated to maintain or enhance their self-esteem; to perceive themselves as being efficacious and as having control over their circumstances; and to perceive themselves and their worlds as meaningful. Because of the operation of these self-motives, individuals go to great lengths to structure their environments and themselves in order to enhance their self-esteem, self-efficacy, and self-coherence (see, for example, Rosenberg's [1979:Chapter 11] discussion of the use of selectivity in the service of the self-esteem motive; and Greenwald's [1980] discussion of "cognitive conservation"--the active reconstruction of memories and knowledge structures--in the service of the self-coherence motive). Further evidence for the motivational significance of self-concept is found in research on the negative consequences that arise when these self-motives are frustrated: low self-esteem has been generally associated with depression and unhappiness (Wells and Marwell 1976); low self-efficacy has been associated with learned helplessness (Seligman 1975); and the inhibition or disruption of self-coherence may lead to such existential malaise as a sense of meaninglessness, anomie, and alienation (Frankl 1939). In summary, the self-concept is the locus of motivations in the individual's dealings with the environment (see Gecas [1986] for a development of this view). If the individual is unsuccessful in satisfying these self-motives, negative consequences usually ensue.

What effect does all this have on the process of re-covery from illness or injury? We think it is these self-motives, with their positive and negative psychologi-cal implications, which make the self-concept an important factor in the process of recovery from injury or disa-bility. On the basis of existing research, the strongest case can be made for the self-efficacy motive. The indi-vidual's sense of control has appeared in the health lit-erature under various labels: self-efficacy (the label we use, along with Bandura 1977); helplessness (Seligman 1975); loss of freedom (Wortman and Brehm 1975); power-lessness (Seeman 1972); and internal locus of control (Rotter 1966). Whatever the label, this aspect of the self-concept focuses on the individual's self-definitions in terms of control and efficacy in dealing with the physical and social environments.

In general, high self-efficacy has been found to have salutary and therapeutic consequences for the individual, and low self-efficacy is associated with poor coping abilities and negative health outcomes. For example, Seeman and Seeman (1983), in a recent longitudinal study, found individuals with low self-efficacy to

1. be less likely to initiate preventive care;
2. be less optimistic about the effectiveness of early treatment;
3. rate their health as poorer; and
4. have more illness episodes, more bed confine-ment, and greater dependence on the physician.

Langer and Rodin (1975) demonstrated the positive health consequences of increased opportunity for decision making in a study of the institutionalized aged. Seeman and Evans (1962) found "internals" (i.e., those high on self-efficacy) to be more attuned to mastery-relevant information than were "externals," and thus better able to deal with their disease. Taylor (1985) reported impressive findings on the therapeutic effect of perceived "cardiac efficacy" (i.e., the belief that one's heart is working well) in postcoronary recovery and rehabilitation. In a more personal vein, Cousins (1979) eloquently described his battle with a serious, and usually fatal, disease. He recounted the course of his experiences during this illness, from the initial feelings of helplessness and passivity (when the disease was getting progressively worse), to his decision to reject the passive role of patient and insist on being an active participant in planning his own therapy--which apparently was a turning point in his illness, leading to recovery. The accumulating evidence suggests that attitudes of self-efficacy make a difference in the course of illness and recovery. Since loss of self-efficacy is one of the most significant consequences of injury and illness, it is important that individuals try to regain it in order to facilitate the process of recovery.

The direct effect of self-esteem on the recovery process is less evident than is the effect of self-efficacy, even though these two components of self-concept are related (Gecas and Schwalbe 1983). However, self-esteem certainly has an indirect effect. It is a central aspect of one's overall sense of well-being, and is related to such cognitive states as depression and joy. It also seems to be a central aspect of the self-concept in the stress process (Pearlin et al. 1981), with high self-esteem alleviating feelings of stress, and low self-esteem increasing stress. This may be one of the most important means by which self-esteem affects physical well-being (Antonucci and Jackson 1983), since stress tends to be associated with negative physical consequences.

The motivation for "self-coherence," used here as the motivation to seek or impute coherent meanings to self and surroundings, to make sense of oneself and one's world, also has mainly an indirect influence on the course of recovery. This aspect of self-concept has been relatively neglected, compared to self-esteem and self-efficacy. It is nonetheless an important aspect of psychological well-being, as it forms the basis for effective and satisfying interactions with others and with the physical world.

A common observation is that after a crisis or trauma occurs--such as being struck by a serious injury or

illness--the "victims" of such misfortune seem compelled
to make sense out of their experiences (Bulman and Wortman
1977; Chodoff et al. 1964; Parkes 1972, 1975). Traumas
caused by serious injury and disability often shatter people's views that they are living in an orderly, under-
standable, and meaningful world (Silver and Wortman 1980).
A new order or understanding needs to be created if the
severely traumatized are to carry on with life (Jaffe
1985). The search for meaning helps them come to terms
with the crisis. For example, Andreasen and Norris (1972)
found that a number of the severly burned patients they
interviewed saw their experience as "a trial by fire or a
purgatory through which they have passed, having proved
themselves and improved themselves by surviving"
(1972:359). Apparently, by placing their misfortune
within the context of a broader meaning system--this is
"God's will" and is ultimately for the best; the trauma
has made me a stronger person; it has brought our family
closer together; my misfortune may help others avoid similar injuries; etc.--individuals are able to come to terms
with the experience, and are better able to cope with the
consequences (Weisman and Worden 1976).

Self-efficacy, self-esteem, and self-coherence as
sources of motivation seem to have a bearing on the course
of recovery, or at least on the ability of the individual
to cope with his or her disability. There may also be
other aspects of the self relevant to this process, such
as the individual's self-conception as courageous, persistent, determined to overcome this obstacle, optimistic,
resourceful, etc. What is evident from this brief consideration of the self as an agent in its environment, creating its own conditions, is that the progress of recovery
from physical injury is a function of a highly reciprocal
process between self and circumstance, each affecting the
other and the course of recovery.

We must also remember that the individual is typically not alone in this process, but is embedded in systems of social relationships--family, work, legal,
medical, and other institutions and groups. The injured
worker's relationships with these people and these organizations, and their responses to him or her, are also
relevant to the recovery process. We consider this in the
next section.

THE INSTITUTIONAL CONTEXTS OF RECOVERY AND REHABILITATION

Our analysis suggests that the key psychological dimension of recovery and rehabilitation is the restoration
of a sense of self-efficacy (cf. Roessler and Bolton 1978;
Safilios-Rothschild 1976; Jaffe 1985). While the self-
directing individual contributes to this process through
autonomous action, much of the process occurs in institutional settings in direct interaction with others. By institutional settings we mean all culturally persisting
social groups, both primary and secondary, that the recovering person is likely to encounter. It is important,
we believe, to take into account the therapeutic resources
these groups provide, the experiences they permit or preclude, and the people in them, as they affect the recovering person's feelings of self-efficacy. The institutions
we will consider here are the family, the compensation
bureaucracy, the medical bureaucracy, the rehabilitation
bureaucracy, and the workplace. In each case we will discuss their positive and negative contributions to restoring a damaged self-concept.

First, it will be useful to identify the basic features of these institutions that are most likely to affect
self-efficacy. We propose there are five such features,
each describable in bipolar terms. There is, first, the
matter of impersonality vs. validation of self-worth. By
this we mean the extent to which action and interaction in
the particular institution tend either to deny the individuality and moral worth of the recovering person or to
reaffirm these things. Where individuality and moral
worth are not upheld, reestablishing self-efficacy, and
self-esteem in general, will be difficult. In turn, recovery and rehabilitation may be impeded.

Second, there is the matter of mystification vs.
openness. By this we mean the degree to which the reasons
underlying others' actions toward the recovering person
are revealed and clearly communicated. Knowledge of
medical prognoses, of reasons for particular therapeutic
practices, and of others' attitudes are important for the
recovering person to maintain a sense of coherence
throughout the rehabilitation process. In general, a
sense of coherence (i.e., a perception that the world is
well-ordered and predictable) is essential to anyone's
sense of efficacy; effective action in the social world
presupposes being able to make some sense of its motive
forces and patterns of operations. Attempts at rehabilitation that obscure such forces and patterns can

undermine the reestablishment of self-efficacy. Openness would seem to have the greater therapeutic value, as it makes the world of the recovering person more predictable and subject to control.

Third, there is, following from the principle just suggested, the matter of control vs. autonomy. Here, we are referring to the degree to which attempts are made to limit the independent, self-directed action of the recovering person. Restricting autonomy, in our view, also serves to undermine the sense of personal agency essential to self-efficacy. If the recovering person feels he or she cannot freely pursue self-determined ends, self-efficacy will be compromised. There is obviously, however, a potential contradiction between the real need for help and the need for autonomy. Help must be available as needed, but if it is perceived as constraining, if it fosters dependency instead of autonomy, it can be counterproductive. We will say more about this in our discussion of the family.

A fourth feature concerns encouraged passivity vs. activity. This differs from the preceding in that passivity or activity (on the part of the recovering person) can only be encouraged or discouraged, while control and autonomy can be limited objectively by physical capacities, legal and bureaucratic rules, standard medical practices, and material resources. Clearly the passivity/activity and control/autonomy dimensions are likely to covary. But what we are distinguishing here are orientations to life that people in institutional settings subtly or overtly urge the recovering person to embrace or reject, within the constraints imposed by physiology, bureaucracy, and economies. In our view the active orientation is to be preferred; a passive orientation to the world cannot engender self-efficacy. The paradox that necessary help, if it encourages passivity, can hinder recovery appears again here.

Finally, the degree to which an institutional setting reaffirms a valued identity vs. proferring a relatively devalued "disabled identity" is also important to self-efficacy and recovery. The recovering person, we have suggested, is in part struggling to reestablish a positively valued identity along with a sense of self-efficacy. This does not imply denial of the real limitations imposed by disability. What it implies is the greatest possible effort to create meanings for the self that reaffirm a person's capacities for meaningful action and interaction. To realistically accept one's physical limitations is one thing, to premise an identity on those limitations is another. The latter can be maladaptive. Institutions that intentionally or inadvertently foster such identities can impede recovery and rehabilitation by undermining feelings of efficacy predicated on valued identities (cf. Friedson 1965).

Not all of these features are equally salient in all of the institutional settings confronting the recovering person. Some are more salient in the secondary-group settings, such as the aforementioned bureaucracies and the workplace. Others are more salient in the primary-group setting of the family. The following will consider the family, workplace, and various bureaucracies in terms of the obstacles and aids they create to restoring feelings of self-efficacy. We will begin with the family because of its distinction as a primary-group setting.

The family is unique in its power both to simulate and stall recovery via restoration of self-efficacy (Litman 1972; Cogswell 1976; Power and Dell Orto 1980). Validation of self-worth by significant others in the family is perhaps the family's most important contribution to recovery. The security and predictability the family environment provides can foster a sense of agency and control more effectively than any secondary-group institution. Moreover, the family can foster restoration of self-efficacy indirectly, because of its needs for economic support; that is, the family may motivate a more intense struggle on the part of an injured worker to recover and resume a highly valued provider role.

Despite the social support, security, and motivation the family can provide, it can also impede recovery under certain circumstances. It is possible, for example, for the support and security the family offers to foster dependency rather than autonomy and control (McMichael 1971; Dean 1961; Mailick 1984). It is also possible for the pressures it creates to resume the provider role to become overwhelming. If so, it may reinforce feelings of failure and despair rather than efficacy and hope. Further, family members' attempts to overcome the denial of disability on the part of the injured person may actually reinforce a devalued "disabled identity" (cf. Litman 1972).

What actually occurs in the family is not, of course, solely a matter of what family members do to the recovering person. The recovering person is not a passive object in this process (cf. McDaniel 1969). The psychological consequences that arise in the family are always an interactive product of the recovering person's esteem-protecting strategies and family members' support (or, possibly, degradation) strategies. Recognizing this, the psychological outcomes of family actions are difficult to predict. Certain forms of social support may be appropriate and therapeutic with some recovering persons in some families, while those same forms of support might be destructive under other circumstances (see Thoits 1983). In some cases family members might wisely seek to limit the autonomy of persons who cannot realistically accept their new physical limitations. In still other cases family members may be more prone to denial than the injured person him or her self. If so, they may be unable to provide the real help the recovering person needs; they may also be unable to reinforce the valued identities that can help sustain a sense of self-efficacy. The point, in brief, is that the intensity of family relationships and their significance for self-conceptions make the family extremely important, but also potentially equivocal in its effects on self-efficacy.

The three bureaucratic institutions noted earlier-- the medical, compensation, and rehabilitation--are similar in the obstacles they create to restoring self-efficacy. These are, chiefly, impersonality, mystification, restricted autonomy, and encouraged passivity (Krause 1976; Sussman 1969; White 1983). Perhaps the most notorious in these respects is the compensation bureaucracy. Here, the injured worker is confronted by a multi-layered organizational apparatus, complex rules and procedures, cryptic legal codes, and unfamiliar people. The injured worker is also, naturally enough, likely to be treated as a case rather than a person. And in this arena of professional domination, passivity is subtly or overtly encouraged--the bewildered worker is urged to let others steer his or her course through the bureaucracy. Indeed, there is often little choice. In this institution the recovering person thus enjoys little opportunity for autonomous action. None of this enhances a sense of coherence, self-worth, or efficacy. Much like an asylum can create more psychological distress than it alleviates, the compensation bureaucracy can do the same (see Hodgins 1977; Kerr 1977).

It is difficult to make a case for the positive psychological effects of experience with the compensation bureaucracy. For a lucky few (indeed, a very few: less than 10% of all injured workers ever receive workmen's compensation; White 1983), successfully dealing with the compensation bureaucracy might provide some basis for enhanced self-efficacy.

The medical bureaucracy is likely to be somewhat less damaging in these respects, although professional domination and mystification remain serious problems (Friedson 1970). Medical professionals, most notably physicians, tend to treat rehabilitants as poor judges of what is best for them. Prognoses and rationales for treatment are often less than fully communicated. This is especially problematic considering the large status differences that typically exist between physicians and injured workers (Nagi 1969; Page and O'Brien 1973). Conflicting medical opinions in cases where compensation claims are disputed can also contribute to the confusion generated in this institutional setting. The recovering person is thus often left in the dark about his or her own physical condition and chances for full recovery. Because of extreme professional domination in the medical sphere, and the mystification that tends to accompany it, the autonomy of the recovering person is quite restricted (Albrecht 1976). The recovering person is forced to put his or her fate in the hands of the physician. Such hands are likely to be impersonal, and of little positive consequence for reaffirming a sense of self-worth or a valued identity. This problem may be further exacerbated by the fact that recovering workers are often dealing with specialists rather than their own more familiar general practitioners.

To the extent it facilitates physical recovery, the medical bureaucracy can, of course, contribute to restoring self-efficacy. But this is only to grant credit for its (hoped for) product, not the experiences-in-process it typically creates for injured workers.

The rehabilitation bureaucracy is perhaps the least prone to mystification, impersonality, restricting autonomy, and encouraging passivity, although these problems are still present. Professional domination often prevails here, too (Sussman 1969; Roth and Eddy 1967). Injured workers must again face unfamiliar people, endure impersonal treatment, take instructions from those who deign to know what is best for them, and, to facilitate interaction in this setting, adopt a disabled identity. It is encouraging, however, that rehabilitation professionals have been conscious of the potentially anti-therapeutic consequences of these tendencies. If practices have not always kept pace with theory, there has been movement toward more openness in explaining therapeutic procedures, toward more rehabilitant participation in devising therapeutic plans, and away from applying labels of "disabled" in the supposed interest of realism (see Friedson 1965).

Obviously, it is one goal of the rehabilitation bureaucracy and the professionals in it to restore a sense of self-efficacy. As argued, however, the nature of bureaucracy itself, cultural tendencies toward professional domination, and the complex, interactive psychology of rehabilitation, can generate counterproductive forces despite benevolent intentions. But to the extent that rehabilitation efforts succeed in restoring a person's powers to the fullest possible degree, they will contribute to restoring self-efficacy. In fact, physical and psychological rehabilitation, as we have implied throughout, are inseparable; they are mutually interdependent and reciprocally amplifying.

Like the family, the workplace represents an institution both powerful and potentially contradictory in its effects on self-efficacy. Returning to work and resuming the provider role can heal a damaged sense of efficacy as perhaps no other experiences can. Yet there are at least two major problems this institution presents to the recovering person. First, there is always the possibility that the challenge of returning to full productive activity cannot be met. If so, and if this underscores a recovering person's anxieties about his or her productive abilities, efficacy may in fact be diminished. There is also the problem of labeling and reinforcement of devalued identities; that is, if post-injury employment is premised on the limited capacities attributable to injury, it may not reaffirm a positively valued identity, but instead serve as an inescapable reminder of a devalued one.

The issue must also be raised of how much autonomy and control--and thereby contributions to self-efficacy--a job provides even under the best of circumstances (see Staples, et al. 1984; Schwalbe 1985). As pointed out earlier, work can be a source of efficacy and opportunities to expand one's productive powers. Often, though, it is not, especially for those workers most likely to be seriously injured on the job. Upon returning to the workplace, then, what potentials for enhancing self-efficacy can be realized? It is possible that post-injury potentials of this sort--presuming reemployment in a position of equal prestige and pay--will be slightly diminished relative to those of the pre-injury situation. Thus while the initial return to work and productivity can tremendously boost self-efficacy, the long-run effect may be quite limited.[6]

All five of these institutional settings thus contain contradictory tendencies with regard to restoring self-efficacy. Each poses problems the solution of which can contribute to restoring self-efficacy. But only if such problems are surmountable in ways that affirm self-worth, yield a sense of personal agency, and reinforce valued identities, will efficacy be enhanced. The dangers are that many of the problems these institutions, especially the bureaucratic ones, create for recovering persons are not surmountable in ways that support self-efficacy. Problems of professional domination, impersonality, labeling, restricted autonomy, and subtly encouraged passivity can undermine efforts to restore self-efficacy.

This is our social-psychological analysis of how social structures impinge on the self-conceptions of recovering workers and, therefore, on their chances for regaining physical and mental health. We refer the interested reader to other sources for more detailed treatment of the experiences of the disabled in these contexts (see Boswell and Wingrove 1974; Brechin, Liddiard, and Swain 1981; Carver and Rodda 1978; Katz 1981; Thomas 1982).

POLICY IMPLICATIONS

Four themes have run throughout our analysis of the psychological consequences of job-related disabilities. First, there is the importance of control and self-efficacy on the part of the disabled worker. The experience of disablement can, as shown, undermine both control and self-efficacy, thereby creating a host of secondary psychological problems and obstacles to recovery. Second, there is the importance of understanding problems of disability in terms of the person-environment relationship. We must always consider how an individual's coping abilities are matched to the demands of a particular environment. This in turn leads us to look at how environments can be modified and coping abilities enhanced to bring the person and the environment into more functional alignment. Third, there is the importance of considering self-esteem enhancing resources of all kinds within the environment of the disabled or recovering person. By doing so it becomes possible to identify potential alternative esteem-enhancing resources when disability precludes reliance on usual resources. And finally, we have emphasized the importance of understanding the psychological functioning of the individual within both the immediate organizational environment and the larger sociocultural environment. Only in this way can the psychological consequences of job-related disabilities be understood sociologically. The policy implications discussed later extend these themes.

Our concerns are with prevention, minimizing the psychological distress and damage that result from job-related disabilities, and expediting recovery and rehabilitation. Given these concerns, we will draw out the implications of our analysis for action on the part of government, unions, employers, medical and other rehabilitation professionals, and disabled workers themselves. In some cases our recommendations simply echo and amplify current progressive trends. Such progress, however, remains spotty. To lessen the tremendous psychological damage done by occupational injury and disease, it is necessary to more concertedly and forcibly move in the directions suggested by the social scientific research reviewed here.

Much of what can potentially be done to solve the problems of job-related disabilities can be done by state and federal governments. In the current political climate, however, it seems unlikely that much will be done without intense lobbying pressure. Presuming such pressure could be generated, we recommend it be directed at seeking five broad governmental measures:

1. direct financing of advocacy and support groups organized by disabled workers themselves;
2. full disability insurance for all workers, covering occupational injury and disease, paid for in part by taxes on firms levied according to how much injury and disease they produce;
3. full subsidies for retraining and re-educating disabled workers;
4. a vast streamlining of the compensation process; and
5. stronger and better enforced occupational safety and health laws.

These recommendations for government action are intended to enhance the control disabled workers can maintain over their own lives, to create opportunities for deriving self-esteem from alternative sources, to minimize

the degradation associated with the cumbersome compensation system, and to eliminate the debilitating economic
strain that typically accompanies disablement. While only
government commands the legal and economic resources
needed to make these things happen, government action
alone cannot solve all of the problems arising from
job-related disability. There are, of course, other important actors who must both use government and act independently.

We thus further propose that unions and other
employee organizations work, both singly and collectively,
to

1. lobby for the policies and programs proposed;
2. get new national health and safety legislation
    passed modeled on Swedish laws that give
    employee-run safety committees the power to shut
    down workplaces where unsafe conditions exist
    and to veto the introduction of unsafe chemical
    or mechanical technologies; and
3. provide technical, legal, and financial support
    for disabled workers' organizations. Without
    strong union backing, such organizations will
    struggle to survive; and without strong union
    pushing, legislators will not move as far or as
    fast as necessary.

Change is also needed at the level of the individual
firm. Our initial recommendations were directed to those
groups who might be expected to represent and act on the
interests of workers. Nonetheless, we do propose that employers consider three strategies to help prevent and deal
with job-related disabilities—strategies that may well be
in their best long-run economic interests. In this regard
we recommend that employers

1. try to enhance employee commitment to the firm
    by **guaranteeing** reemployment or alternative
    placement in wage- or salary-equivalent posi-
    tions following the recovery from job-related
    disability;
2. guarantee support for retraining or formal edu-
    cation as necessary to make use of disabled
    workers' capacities; and
3. pressure insurance companies to reduce rates for
    firms making extensive safety efforts, which
    must include cooperation with employee-run
    safety committees.

Researchers, physicians, and other rehabilitation
professionals also have roles to play in this reform

process. In very broad terms, we propose some shifts in the perspectives that tend to guide the work of professionals in this area. Specifically, we encourage

1. a shift from therapeutic models that reinforce professional domination and client passivity to models that diminish professional domination and reinforce client control and self-efficacy;

2. a shift from professional training that mystifies "expert knowledge"--and thereby disempowers clients--to training that emphasizes empowering clients through sharing knowledge and skills;

3. a shift from psychologically-oriented research focusing on the disabled person in isolation to sociologically-oriented research that focuses on the disabled person as affected by his or her membership in multiple social networks; and

4. a shift from research oriented to filling gaps in the literature to applied research that begins with the concrete problems of disabled workers themselves.

As we acknowledged earlier, these shifts are already evident in some quarters. Nonetheless, the social forces that perpetuate professional domination, psychological reductionism, and largely self-serving academic research are powerful. Inasmuch as they still operate to limit our effectiveness in solving the problems of job-related disabilities, they warrant continued criticism. In light of the analysis developed here, these, then, are the directions we feel will lead to new knowledge and more effective practices for dealing with the psychological consequences of job-related disabilities.

Finally, in keeping with our theme of control and self-efficacy, we recommend that disabled workers themselves expand and intensify their collective efforts to overcome the problems they face. Specifically, we recommend

1. establishing more support groups through extension and outreach efforts by existing groups;

2. establishing a national network of disabled workers' groups to more effectively lobby for legislative reform; and

3. developing educational programs for disabled workers that emphasize self-understanding of psychological problems and understanding of the sociocultural conditions out of which they arise.

The latter recommendation is, in other words, for an in-house, worker-controlled therapeutic education program. Control is what disabled workers are typically denied and suffer for the lack of; collective action and self-education are important avenues to regaining control and health.

Although it may seem that some of our recommendations go beyond the bounds of what social-psychological analysis can support, we do not think this is really so. We have been concerned throughout with the social conditions responsible for creating job-related disabilities and the psychological problems they bring with them. The psychological, as implied throughout our analysis, is inseparable from the sociological. It makes no sense, in our view, to focus on the psychological troubles of the individual as if they were not linked to the social structural conditions under which they arise. We have thus not limited ourselves to suggesting how damaged self-conceptions can be patched-up. We have taken the next socio-logical step and suggested what can be done to keep those self-conceptions intact in the first place. Beyond this--reluctantly accepting the inevitability of some job-related disabilities--we have also proposed what can be done to minimize the psychological damage caused by disability, to encourage both physical and psychological healing, and to respect the dignity and integrity of the individual throughout this extremely difficult process.

NOTES

1.   Although it is common to think of people as "disabled or not," disability is hardly a dichotomous variable. In the real world, people are only more-or-less able to meet prevailing norms for engaging in various physical and social activities. Such norms are of course highly variable across groups, over time, and from one situation to the next. We thus counterpose "being disabled" to "being modally functional" to acknowledge the cultural, historical, and situational relativity of disablement.

2.   Injured workers may also make more favorable comparisons with those who are perceived as worse off physically or mentally. These more favorable comparisons are more likely to occur later as the injured worker copes with and adjusts to his or her condition.

3.   There is, however, frequent incongruity between the actual and perceived appraisals of others, as research (Felson 1980) and everyday experience suggest. Usually, it is the perceived appraisals of others that are more consequential for our self-concepts than the actual appraisals (Shrauger and Schoeneman 1979).

4.   Much of the research on conjugal power suggests that the power relationship between husbands and wives is largely affected by the employment status and relative economic resources of husbands and wives (Blood and Wolfe, 1960; Rodman, 1972).

5.   Even though self-efficacy is one of the major bases of self-esteem, its importance for self-concept goes beyond this association with self-esteem. This is particularly evident when we consider self-efficacy as a self-motive in its own right.

6.   Our point is that without any significant change in either a person's job or orientation to the job, the self-efficacy benefits of returning to work are likely to be shortlived. This is not to say that injury always diminishes self-efficacy in the long run. Indeed, it seems that in some cases traumatic injury and subsequent recovery can produce a renewed, enhanced sense of efficacy (see Jaffe, 1985; DeLoach and Greer, 1981).

REFERENCES

Albrecht, G. L. 1976. "Socialization and the Disability Process." Pp. 3-38 in The Sociology of Physical Disability and Rehabilitation. Pittsburgh: University of Pittsburgh Press.

Andreason, N. J., and A. S. Norris. 1972. "Long-term Adjustment and Adaptation Mechanisms in Severely Burned Adults." Journal of Nervous and Mental Disease 154:352-362.

Antonovsky, A. 1979. Health, Stress, and Coping. San Francisco: Jossey-Bass.

Antonucci, T. C., and J. S. Jackson. 1983. "Physical Health and Self-esteem." Family and Community Health 6:1-9.

Ashford, N. A. 1976. Crisis in the Workplace: Occupational Disease and Injury. Cambridge, Mass.: MIT Press.

Badley, E. M., and M. R. Bury. 1982. "The Identification and Assessment of Disability." Pp. 27-34 in W. T. Singleton and L. M. Debney (eds.), Occupational Disability. Lancaster, U.K.: MTP Press Ltd.

Bandura, A. 1977. "Self-efficacy: Toward a Unifying Theory of Behavioral Change." Psychological Review 84:191-215.

Bem, D. J. 1972. "Self-perception Theory." In L. Berkowitz (ed)., Advances in Experimental Social Psychology, Vol. 6. New York: Academic Press.

Berman, D. 1979. Death on the Job. New York: Monthly Review.

Blood, R. O., and D. M. Wolfe. 1960. Husbands and Wives: The Dynamics of Married Living. Glencoe, Ill.: Free Press.

Boswell, D., and J. M. Wingrove (eds.). 1974. The Handicapped Person in the Community. London: Tavistock.

Braverman, H. 1974. Labor and Monopoly Capital. New York: Monthly Review Press.

Brechin, A., P. Liddiard, and J. Swain (eds.). 1981. Handicap in a Social World. Kent, U.K.: Hodder and Stoughton.

Bulman, R. J., and C. B. Wortman. 1977. "Attributions of Blame and Coping in the 'Real World': Severe Accident Victims React to Their Lot." Journal of Personality and Social Psychology 35:351-363.

Bury, M. R., and E. M. Badley. 1982. "Social Aspects of Disablement." Pp. 37-44 in W. T. Singleton and L. M. Debney (eds.), Occupational Disability. Lancaster, U.K.: MTP Press Ltd.

Carver, V., and M. Rodda. 1978. Disability and the Environment. New York: Schocken.

Charmaz, K. 1983. "Loss of Self: A Fundamental Form of Suffering in the Chronically Ill." Sociology of Health and Illness 5 (2):168-195.

Chavkin, W. (ed.). 1984. Double Exposure: Women's Health Hazards on the Job and at Home. New York: Monthly Review.

Chodoff, P., S. B. Friedman, and D. A. Hamburg. 1964. "Stress, Defenses, and Coping Behavior: Observations in Parents of Children with Malignant Disease." American Journal of Psychiatry 120:743-49.

Cogswell, B. E. 1976. "Conceptual Model of Family as a Group: Family Response to Disability." Pp. 139-168 in G. L. Albrecht (ed.), The Sociology of Physical Disability and Rehabilitation. Pittsburgh: University of Pittsburgh Press.

Cousins, N. 1979. Anatomy of an Illness. New York: Norton.

Currie, E., and J. H. Skolnick. 1984. America's Problems; Social Issues and Public Policy. Boston: Little, Brown and Co.

Davis, M. 1977. "Occupational Hazards and Black Workers." Urban Health 6:16-18.

_____. 1979 "Black Workers' Hazards." Labor Occupational Health Monitor 7: 7-9.

Dean, D. G. 1961. "Alienation: Its Meaning and Measurement." American Sociological Review 26:753-759.

DeLoach, C., and B. G. Greer. 1981. Adjustment to Severe Physical Disability: A Metamorphosis. New York: McGraw-Hill.

Derr, P., R. Goble, R. E. Kasperson, and R. W. Kates. 1981. "Worker/Public Protection: The Double Standard." Environment (September):6-15, 31-36.

Duckworth, D. 1982. "Terminology in Relation to Disablement." Pp. 17-26 in W. T. Singleton and L. M. Debney (eds.), Occupational Disability. Lancaster, U.K.: MTP Press Ltd.

Elliot, G. R., and C. Eisdorfer (eds.). 1982. Stress and Human Health. New York: Springer.

Felson, R. B. 1980. "Communication Barriers and the Reflected Appraisal Process." Social Psychology Quarterly 43:223-233.

Frank, J. D. 1975. "Mind-Body Relationships in Illness and Healing." Preventive Medicine 2:46-59.

Frankl, Victor E. 1939. Man's Search For Meaning. New York: Simon and Schuster edition, 1963.

Friedson, E. 1965. "Disability as Social Deviance." Pp. 71-99 in M. Sussman (ed.), Sociology and Rehabilitation. Washington, D.C.: American Sociological Association.

_____. 1970. Professional Dominance. New York: Atherton.

Gecas, V. 1971. "Parental Behavior and Dimensions of Adolescent Self-Evaluation." Sociometry 34:466-82.

_____. 1982. "The Self-concept." In R. H. Turner and J. F. Short, Jr., (eds.), Annual Review of Sociology 8:1-33.

_____. 1986. "The Motivational Significance of Self-Concept for Socialization Theory." In E. J. Lawler (ed।), Advances in Group Processes: Theory and Research, Vol. 3. Greenwich, Conn.: JAI Press.

Gecas, V., and M. L. Schwalbe. 1983. "Beyond the Looking-glass Self: Social Structure and Efficacy-based Self-esteem." Social Psychology Quarterly 46 (2):77-88.

Gecas, V., and J. T. Mortimer. 1986. "Stability and Change in the Self-concept from Adolescence to Adulthood." In T. M. Honess and K. M. Yardley (eds.), Self and Identity. London: Routledge and Kegan Paul.

Greenwald, A. G. 1980. "The Totalitarian Ego: Fabrication and Revision of Personal History." American Psychologist 35: 603-18.

Hodgins, E. 1977. "Listen: The Patient." Pp. 37-45 in V. Stubbins (ed.), Social and Psychological Aspects of Disability. Baltimore: University Park.

Jaffe, D. T. 1985. "Self-renewal: Personal Transformation Following Extreme Trauma." Journal of Humanistic Psychology 25 (Fall):99-124.

James, W. 1890. Principles of Psychology. New York: Holt, Rinehart & Winston.

Johada, M., and Rush, H. 1980. "Work, Employment, and Unemployment: An Overview of Ideas and Research Results in the Social Science Literature." Science Policy Research Unit (U.K.), Occasional Paper Series No. 12.

Kasl, S. V. 1977. "Work and Mental Health: Contemporary Research Evidence." Pp. 85-110 in W. J. Heisler and V. W. Houck (eds.), A Matter of Dignity: Inquiries into the Humanization of Work. Notre Dame, Ind.: University of Notre Dame Press.

_____. 1979. "Changes in Mental Health Status Associated with Job Loss and Retirement." Pp. 179-200 in V. E. Barrett, R. M. Rosz, and G. L. Klerman (eds.), Stress and Mental Disorder. New York: Raven.

Katz, I. 1981. Stigma: A Social Psychological Analysis. Hillsdale, N.J.: Lawrence Erlbaum Associates.

Kerr, N. 1961. "Understanding the Process of Adjustment to Disability." Journal of Rehabilitation 27 (6):16-18.

_____. 1977. "Staff Expectations for Disabled Persons: Helpful or Harmful?" Pp. 47-54 in J. Stubbins (ed.), Social and Psychological Aspects of Disability. Baltimore: University Park Press.

Krause, E. 1972. "The Future of Rehabilitation Research." American Archives of Rehabilitation Therapy 20:19.

_____. 1976. "The Political Sociology of Rehabilitation." Pp. 201-221 in G. L. Albrecht (ed.), The Sociology of Physical Disability and Rehabilitation. Pittsburgh: University of Pittsburgh Press.

Kutner, B. 1969. "Professional Antitherapy." Journal of Rehabilitation 35:16-18.

Langer, E. J., and Rodin, J. 1975. "The Effects of Choice and Enhanced Personal Responsibility for the Aged: A Field Experiment in an Institutional Setting." Journal of Personality and Social Psychology 34:191-198.

Levi, L. 1981. Preventing Work Stress. Reading, Mass.: Addison-Wesley.

Litman, T. J. 1962. "Self-conception and Physical Rehabilitation." Pp. 565-566 in A. M. Rose (ed.), Human Behavior and Social Processes. Boston: Houghton Mifflin.

_____. 1972. "Physical Rehabilitation: A Social-Psychological Approach." Pp. 186-203 in E. G. Jaco (ed.), Patients, Physicians and Illness (2nd edition). New York: Free Press.

Mailick, M. 1984. "The Impact of Severe Illness on the Individual and Family: An Overview." Pp. 83-94 in E. Aronowitz and E. M. Bromberg (eds.), Mental Health and Long-Term Physical Illness. Canton, Mass.: Prodist.

McDaniel, J. W. 1969. Physical Disability and Human Behavior. New York: Pergamon.

McMichael, J. K. 1971. Handicap: A Study of Physically Handicapped Children and Their Families. Pittsburgh: University of Pittsburgh Press.

Mead, G. H. 1934. In Anselm Strauss (ed.), G. H. Mead on Social Psychology: Selected Papers. Chicago: University of Chicago Press, 1964.

Mechanic, D. 1969. Mental Health and Social Policy. Englewood Cliffs, NJ: Prentice Hall.

Michaels, D. 1982. "Minority Workers and Occupational Cancer: The Hidden Costs of Job Discrimination." Pp. 43-50 in D. L. Parron, F. Solomon, and C. D. Jenkins (eds.), Behavior, Health Risks, and Social Disadvantage. Washington, D.C.: National Academy Press.

Nagi, S. Z. 1969. Disability and Rehabilitation. Columbus: Ohio State University Press.

National Safety Council. 1983. Accident Facts. Chicago: National Safety Council.

Page, J. A., and M. O'Brien. 1973. Bitter Wages. Ralph Nader's Study Group Report on Disease and Injury on the Job. New York: Grossman.

Parkes, C. M. 1972. "Components of the Reaction to Loss of a Limb, Spouse or Home." Journal of Psychosomatic Research 16:343-349.

Parkes, C. M. 1975. "The Emotional Impact of Cancer on Patients and Their Families." Journal of Laryngology and Utology 89:1271-1279.

Pearlin, L. I., E. G. Menaghan, M. A. Lieberman, and J. T. Mullan. 1981. "The Stress Process." Journal of Health and Social Behavior 22:337-356.

Power, P. W., and A. E. Dell Orto (eds.). 1980. Role of the Family in the Rehabilitation of the Physically Disabled. Baltimore: University Park Press.

Rodman, H. 1972. "Marital Power and the Theory of Resources in Cultural Context." Journal of Comparative Family Studies 3:50-69.

Roessler, R., and B. Bolton. 1978. Psychosocial Adjustment to Disability. Baltimore: University Park Press.

Rokeach, M. 1979. "Some Unresolved Issues in Theories of Beliefs, Attitudes, and Values." Paper presented at the Nebraska Symposium on Motivation, March, Lincoln.

Rosenberg, M. 1979. Conceiving the Self. New York: Basic Books.

Rosenberg, M., and B. C. McCullough. 1981. "Mattering: Inferred Significance and Mental Health Among Adolescents." Research in Community and Mental Health, Vol. 2. Greenwich, Conn.: JAI Press, Inc.

Roth, J. A., and E. M. Eddy. 1967. Rehabilitation for the Unwanted. New York: Atherton.

Rotter, J. B. 1966. "Generalized Expectancies for Internal Versus External Control of Reinforcement." Psychological Monographs 80 (Whole No. 609).

Safilios-Rothschild, C. 1970. The Sociology and Social Psychology of Disability and Rehabilitation. New York: Random House.

_____. 1976. "Disabled Persons' Self-Definitions and Their Implications for Rehabilitation." Pp. 39-56 in G. L. Albrecht (ed.), The Sociology of Physical Disability and Rehabilitation. Pittsburgh: University of Pittsburgh Press.

Schlesinger, L. 1965. "Staff Authority and Patient Participation in Rehabilitation." Rehabilitation Literature 24:247-249.

Shontz, F. C. 1975. The Psychological Aspects of Physical Illness and Disability. New York: Macmillan Publishing Company.

Schwalbe, M. L. 1985. "Autonomy in Work and Self-esteem." The Sociological Quarterly 26 (4): 519-535.

Seeman, M. 1972. "Alienation and Engagement." In A. Campbell and P. E. Converse (eds.), The Human Meaning of Social Change. New York: Russell Sage.

Seeman, M., and J. W. Evans. 1962. "Alienation and Learning in a Hospital Setting." American Sociological Review 27:772-83.

Seeman, M., and T. E. Seeman. 1983. "Health Behavior and Personal Autonomy: A Longitudinal Study of the Sense of Control in Illness." Journal of Health and Social Behavior 24:144-160.

Self, P. C. 1984. Physical Disability: An Annotated Literature Guide. New York: Marcel Dekker.

Seligman, M.E.P. 1975. Helplessness: On Suppression, Development, and Death. San Francisco: Freeman.

Shostak, A. B. 1980. Blue-Collar Stress. Reading, Mass.: Addison-Wesley.

Shrauger, J. S., and T. J. Schoeneman. 1979. "Symbolic Interactionist View of Self-concept: Through the Looking Glass Darkly." Psychological Bulletin 86:549-573.

Silver, R. L., and Wortman, C. B. 1980. "Coping with Undesirable Life Events." In J. Garber and M. E. P. Seligman (eds.), Human Helplessness: Theory and Applications. New York: Academic Press.

Staples, C. L., M. L. Schwalbe, and V. Gecas. 1984. "Social Class, Occupational Conditions, and Efficacy-Based Self-Esteem." Sociological Perspectives 27 (1):85-109.

Stryker, S. 1980. Symbolic Interactionism: A Social Structural Version. Menlo Park, Calif.: Benjamin/ Cummings.

Sussman, M. B. 1969. "Readjustment and Rehabilitation of Patient." Pp. 244-264 in J. Kosa, A. Antonovsky, and I. K. Zola (eds.), Poverty and Health: A Sociological Analysis. Cambridge, Mass. Harvard University Press.

_____. 1976. "The Disabled and the Rehabilitation System." Pp. 223-246 in G. L. Albrecht (ed.), The Sociology of Physical Disability and Rehabilitation. Pittsburgh: University of Pittsburgh Press.

Taylor, C. B. 1985. "The Role of Perceived Cardiac Efficacy in Postcoronary Rehabilitation." Paper presented at the annual meeting of American Association for the Advancement of Science, Los Angeles.

Thoits, P. A. 1983. "Dimensions of Life Events That Influence Psychological Distress: An Evaluation and Synthesis of the Literature." Pp. 33-103 in H. B. Kaplan (ed.), Psychosocial Stress: Trends in Theory and Research. New York: Academic Press.

Thomas, D. 1982. The Experience of Handicap. London: Methuen.

Turner, R. J., S. Noh, and D. M. Levin. 1985. "Depression Across the Life Course: The Significance of Psychosocial Factors Among the Physically Disabled." In A. Dean (ed.), Depression in Multidisciplinary Perspective. New York: Bruner/Mazel.

U.S. Department of Commerce. 1985. Selected Characteristics of Persons with a Work Disability by State: 1980. Supplementary Report, PC80-S1-20, November (pp. 8-9). Washington, D.C.: U.S. Government Printing Office.

U.S. Department of Health, Education, and Welfare, 1973. Work in America. Cambridge: MIT Press.

U.S. Department of Labor. 1980. Interim Report to Congress on Occupational Diseases. Washington, D.C.: U.S. Government Printing Office, June.

Vance, E. T. 1973. "Social Disability." American Psychologist 28:498-511.

Vash, C. 1981. The Psychology of Disability. New York: Springer.

Wallick, F. 1972. The American Worker: An Endangered Species. New York: Ballantine.

Weisman, A. D., and J. W. Worden. 1976. "The Existential Plight in Cancer." International Journal of Psychiatry in Medicine 7:1-15.

Wells, L. E., and G. Marwell. 1976. Self-Esteem: Its Conceptualization and Measurement. Beverly Hills, Calif.: Sage.

Wertheim, E. S. 1975. "Person-Environment Interation: The Epigenesis of Autonomy and Competence." British Journal of Medical Psychology 48:1-8, 95-111, 237-256, 391-402.

White, L. 1983. Human Debris: The Injured Worker in America. New York: Seaview/Putnam.

Wortman, C. B., and J. W. Brehm. 1975. "Responses to Uncontrollable Outcomes: An Integration of Reactance Theory and the Learned Helplessness Model." In L. Berkowitz (ed.), Advances in Experimental Social Psychology, Vol. 8. New York: Academic Press.

Wright, B. A. 1960. Physical Disability--A Psychological Approach. New York: Harper and Row.

9. Policy Endnote

Two major policy-related issues crosscut the analyses made by virtually all the researchers whose work is included in this volume. The first relates broadly to stability and change in the psychological outcomes of work through the occupational career. The second concerns gender-related problems encountered primarily by working women who are juggling the competing demands of family and work. In this chapter, we will examine each of these issues as it is tied to the research evidence and as it extends to policy-related measures. We will first consider what we know on the basis of the work reported in this volume and its implications for workers. We can then address policy matters at several levels asking: Given what is known, what can we do to enhance the quality of work life as workers move through their careers? While we are not overly optimistic about the possibilities for implementing the various policy recommendations we make, given the current conservative political climate in the United States, we offer a number of suggestions for change to heighten the reader's awareness of the need for workplace reforms. Institutional and organizational changes are necessary to strengthen the position of workers throughout their engagement with the cycle of work.

Greenberger's study of part-time workers employed during high school suggests that they have little meaningful contact with adults in the workplace. The service jobs held by young, part-time workers segregate teenagers with their peers. Few adults are present to provide mentoring, an introduction to adult values, or knowledge about jobs with more complex tasks. Since most organizations employing these workers provide little room

for advancement to jobs requiring skilled performance,
there is little reason for adults to provide such
knowledge or training. Presumably, isolation from an age-
diverse set of co-workers is especially characteristic of
the experience of young part-time employees.
Greenberger's study also suggests some negative
consequences of part time work experience during high
school (e.g., depressed school grades), particularly when
work hours are excessive.

Borman describes a wider range of workplaces than
Greenberger, and a slightly older group of job holders
whose primary commitment, given their out-of-school
status, is to the labor market. Major developmental tasks
in the area of independence-seeking confront workers
during this period of their occupational development. The
experiences of these workers often do not contribute to
the formation of a stable attachment to a particular
employing organization.

On the basis of evidence drawn from these two studies,
it is clear that policies instituted at the local school
level and by the employer inadequately address the school-
to-work transition for the young. Although work-study
programs have long been a feature of training in
vocational education, there are few institutional supports
in place to ease the passage of young workers. Better
coordination between schools and employers and more
locally-sponsored school-business initiatives are in
order. It was noted in Borman's chapter that employers
infrequently seek out graduating seniors for their full-
time job openings. Moreover, young people are often more
effective in finding jobs through friends and relatives
than through the more formal channels. To remedy this
state of affairs, and to improve the job prospects of
those who lack informal connections capable of leading
them to jobs, new organizational arrangements are
necessary. Schools must become more responsive to
employer requests, when they do occur, for employment-
related information on students seeking jobs following
high school. For example, employee passports, used by
cooperating schools and workplaces participating in the
Boston Compact, provide the information most employers
consider of primary importance in making hiring decisions
(Hargroves 1986; Charner and Fraser 1984). The existence
and publicity surrounding such programs could make
employers more amenable to recruiting young job-seekers.

Businesses must also become more sensitive to their
young workers' training and socialization needs by

providing at least rudimentary mentoring or guidance from an adult; this should be someone at least five to seven years older than the novice. European countries-- specifically, Austria, Switzerland and West Germany--have institutionalized programs which foster the integration of recent secondary-school graduates into their first work roles. In these programs, the mentor or master is personally invested in the success of the novice, since the master's reputation at work is in part determined by the progress made by the trainee (Bishop 1985).

Although we are suggesting broad institutional provisions for the integration of the young worker into the job setting, we would also encourage more specific individual initiatives. Local businesses, for example, can address the special concerns of in-school youth by assuming more responsibility and concern in scheduling employee hours. The fact that those adolescents working the greatest number of hours have the poorest academic records, as reported by Greenberger, illustrates the negative outcomes that arise when employers exercise benign neglect.

The chapters on the adult worker focus on the work-related determinants of intellectual flexibility, job satisfaction, and health outcomes. Although Miller and her colleagues find that prior intellectual flexibility predicts the substantive complexity of work at later stages in the career, their central finding is that self-directed job conditions have a fairly uniform positive influence on cognitive flexibility for Polish and American workers of different ages. This chapter, as well as the research of Mortimer, et al., highlights the importance of self-directed and autonomous work for positive psychological outcomes throughout the work career. Mortimer et al. find that while autonomy has the most powerful effects on job satisfaction among younger workers, its impact remains significant for all age groups. Sorensen and Mortimer's "health benefits model" identifies the same constellation of work attributes as salutary for health.

These three chapters on work in adulthood point to the conclusion that efforts to widen the scope of worker decision-making and to increase the complexity and challenge of work activities should be encouraged. Further research is needed to monitor the effects of changes in job design (e.g., job expansion, rotation, worker participation) on the psychological development of workers. While these innovations are generally initiated to heighten productivity, and to reduce employee absenteeism, lateness, turnover, and other indications of poor morale, they may have substantial implications for workers' psychological functioning and behavior off the job (Kohn and Schooler and their collaborators, 1983:311-312; Crouter, 1984).

However, as is emphasized in Clark and Corcoran's discussion of mid-career and older professionals, the complexities and challenges of work may sometimes seem overwhelming. Highly educated workers in fields with a rapidly changing knowledge base sometimes experience declines in productivity, vitality, and morale, becoming increasingly less willing to tackle challenges. "Stuckness" appears to be rooted less in the decline of individual capacities than in the changing responsibilities assumed by maturing professionals, and in the rigidity of bureaucratic structures, especially in the university context. Many academicians, as well as professionals in other organizational settings, take on extensive administrative responsibilities as they age, and perceive few institutional supports, especially for their continuing research productivity, at this time. Also, those who have experienced delayed promotion and/or difficulties related to midlife alterations in their personal lives (as a result of divorce or separation) often report blocks and stoppages in their research and scholarly work.

Academic organizations are currently faced with an aging faculty population and little "room at the bottom" for newcomers. Given the difficulties stemming from the lack of available institutional services and supports for mid-career and older professionals in university and other organizational settings, human resource development should be a leading priority.

Finally, as workers age, job-related injuries, accidents, and disabilities become increasingly threatening. Schwalbe and Gecas carefully document the difficulties faced by mid-career and older workers in restoring a sense of self-worth and efficacy during the recovery from job-related injuries. These problems are exacerbated in the case of older and less affluent workers, both because they are the individuals most likely to suffer an occupationally-related health problem and because these workers are less likely to have sufficient resources to assist them during the period of recuperation. The bureaucratic structures whose purpose is to restore the health and administer the claims and accounts of injured workers--the medical, compensation, and rehabilitation industries--can present major obstacles to recovery. According to Schwalbe and Gecas, the injured person is confronted with a "multi-layered organizational apparatus, complex rules and procedures, cryptic legal codes, and unfamiliar actors."

Schwalbe and Gecas argue for a set of reforms to minimize the stress arising from job-related injuries and to assist in the worker's recovery. Their recommendations at the governmental level are sweeping and humane, and include such measures as disability insurance for workers (financed by industries according to fees set by the number of injuries occurring in their work places). Schwalbe and Gecas call for other activities at the union (and other employee collectivity) and firm levels. For example, employee organizations must lobby for a more stringent set of health and safety regulations, similar to those in place in Sweden, to allow workers more control of workplace safety conditions. Their recommendations also argue for increased client control of the process of recovery, rehabilitation, and retraining following a work-related injury. Firms must provide guarantees for rehiring and rehabilitating their injured workers, while also taking a stand against inflationary insurance premiums. Finally, researchers and social service advocates are charged with putting their own houses in order, making their activities more relevant to the needs of the aging worker.

Several researchers point to the greater difficulties confronted by women in the workplace. Borman's observational study reveals the problems faced by younger women in locating jobs. Women in her study relied on more formal and less effective job search strategies, frequently chasing more jobs less fruitfully than their male counterparts. Stress-promoting and health-benefiting aspects of work, coupled with competing family demands for women, are spread unevenly through the life cycle, according to Sorensen and Mortimer. Stress is heightened both at work and at home for women early in their careers if they elect to have children at this time. Because women's career mobility is often constrained by such structural characteristics as a sex-segregated labor market and concomitant restrictions on job advancement opportunities, they are disadvantaged in comparison to men with respect to income and other job rewards throughout their work careers (as demonstrated in the chapter by Mortimer and her colleagues). But despite these negative aspects of their work experiences, especially when these are compounded by family responsibilities, many women derive satisfaction from their work activities. Thus, it is important to consider the person-environment "fit" when analyzing the relationship between women's involvement in work and health-related outcomes, and when considering policy initiatives.

Finally, Clark and Corcoran's empirical study of the loss of vitality among highly educated professionals has gender-related implications. Although both men and women are likely to suffer "stuckness" in their career trajectories, the consequences for women are likely to be more severe. Because fewer women occupy the highest ranks of the professoriate, there are both fewer role models and fewer sources of social support and mentoring for female faculty. Women are more likely than their male colleagues to get stuck (given competing family demands) and stay stuck (given fewer resources).

The implications for reform are manifold. For example, to enable women workers to juggle competing child care and work responsibilities there is a pressing need for more high quality day care. The availability of child care facilities could be promoted by employers by the provision of on-site child care, by subsidies to designated facilities, or by the dissemination of child-care information. Far-reaching child care legislation at the federal level is an alternative strategy for change.

Employee-based initiatives, tailored to the unique problems facing women in a particular workplace, also have great potential. For example, advocacy groups such as the American Association of University Professors's Committee W or associations of women faculty can provide resources, support, and concerted political action for women in university settings, particularly at critical junctures in their careers. Senior women are in a position to provide important mentoring experiences for younger women on probationary tracks. While enumeration of the many policy options that would improve women's economic position and working conditions through the life span is beyond the scope of this chapter, it is clear that action is necessary on many diverse fronts (see Mortimer and Sorensen, 1984; Kamerman, 1980:Ch. 7; Voydanoff, 1984:Part Five; Borman et al., 1984).

In summary, the chapters in this volume indicate a wide range of concrete actions to foster positive psychological development in workers and minimize negative outcomes. Such actors include employers, managers and

administrators, unions, government, and workers
themselves. Understanding the implications of work for
psychological development through the life span suggests
directions for policy initiatives that could improve the
quality of working life for persons of all ages.

REFERENCES

Bishop, J. 1985. "Preparing Youth for Work." Columbus, Ohio: The National Center for Research in Vocational Education.

Borman, K.M., Quarm, D. and Gideonse, S. (eds.), 1984. Women in the Workplace: Effects on Families. Norwood, NJ: Ablex Publishing Corporation.

Charner, I., and B.S. Fraser. 1984. Fast Food Jobs. Washington, D.C.: National Institute for Work and Learning.

Crouter, A.C. 1984 "Participative Work as an Influence on Human Development." Journal of Applied Developmental Psychology 5(1): 71-90.

Hargroves, J. 1986. "The Boston Compact: A Systems Approach to School Dropouts." Paper presented at the annual meeting of the American Educational Research Association, San Francisco.

Kamerman, S.B. 1980. Parenting in an Unresponsive Society. New York: Free Press.

Kohn, M.L. and C. Schooler, with the collaboration of J. Miller, K.A. Miller, C. Schoenbach and R. Schoenberg. 1983. Work and Personality: An Inquiry into the Impact of Social Stratification. Norwood, New Jersey: Ablex Publishing Corporation.

Mortimer, J.T. and Sorensen, G. 1984. "Men, Women, Work and Family." Pp.139-167 in Borman, K.M., Quarm, D. and Gideonse, S. (eds.), Women in the Workplace: Effects on Families. Norwood, N.J.: Ablex Publishing Corporation.

Voydanoff, P. (ed.) 1984. Work and Family: Changing Roles of Men and Women. Palo Alto: Mayfield Publishing Company.

About the Contributors

Kathryn M. Borman is Professor of Education in the
Department of Educational Foundations at the University
of Cincinnati. She has studied and written in depth on
the subjects of childhood interaction and socialization,
competence and the development of the self-concept, work
roles, family dynamics, and the internalization of
culture. She has received various research grants and
consulting assignments to analyze and report on these
issues, and she has organized conferences on children,
families, and work. Borman received a B.A. in English at
Miami University in Oxford, Ohio, an M.A. in English at
Mills College in Oakland, California, and a Ph.D. in
Sociology and Education at the University of Minnesota.

Shirley Merritt Clark is Professor of Education,
Sociology, and Higher Education and Chair of the
Department of Educational Policy and Administration at
the University of Minnesota. She previously served as
Assistant Vice-President for Academic Affairs. Her field
of special interest is the sociology of education, and
recent research has involved investigation of faculty
careers and teacher vitality and productivity as well as
the sociology of youth in modern society. She is active
in a multitude of roles in professional associations,
academic committees, and community service groups. She
has presented and published numerous papers on family
structure, sex role implications of delinquency, and
changing social roles for women and for youth. Clark
received a B.A. Magna cum laude in Sociology and Social
Psychology and a M.A. in Sociology from Bowling Green
State University, and she was awarded a Ph.D. in
Sociology from Ohio State University. She is a member of
several honorary societies.

Michael D. Finch is Assistant Professor at the University
of Minnesota's Division of Health Services Research and
Policy. He is currently studying employer-based health
insurance plans and the effect of capitation on medicaid
expenditures. Finch has published articles on the
effects of employment on self-esteem in adolescence and
early adulthood; persistence and change in human

development; and processes of achievement in the transition to adulthood. He earned a B.A. in Sociology and Anthropology and was named Outstanding Graduate in Sociology at Western Washington University. He received M.A. and Ph.D. degrees in Sociology from the University of Minnesota.

Viktor Gecas is Professor of Sociology and Rural Sociology at Washington State University. He is currently involved in research on social psychological and family implications of work-related injury, particularly as related to self-concept, and on the development of competencies in adolescents. He is active on a number of academic and association committees, and he served as a consultant on the Injured Workers Project for the Department of Labor and Industry of Washington State. He has organized and participated in many professional conferences, and he has published extensively on the topics of family socialization, the adolescent, and self-esteem; the effect of work on family roles and interaction; and the development of the self-concept. Gecas earned his B.A. at Beloit College, and he received M.A. and Ph.D. degrees in Sociology from the University of Minnesota.

Jeylan T. Mortimer is Professor of Sociology and Director of the Life Course Center at the University of Minnesota. She has received numerous research grants and has served on the National Science Foundation Review Panel for Sociology as well as on other review panels of federal agencies. She has conducted extensive study of the relationships among work experience, family life, self-image, and attitudes through the work career. She is currently initiating a longitudinal study of adolescent workers, including the factors which draw them into the workforce, the features of their occupational experiences, and the psychological impacts of their work. Mortimer earned a B.A. Summa cum laude at Tufts University, and she received M.A. and Ph.D. degrees in Sociology at the University of Michigan. Academic honors include membership in the Sociological Research Association and election as Fellow of the American Association for the Advancement of Science.

Mary Corcoran is Professor of Educational Psychology and
Higher Education at the University of Minnesota. She is
also a Licensed Consulting Psychologist for the State of
Minnesota. Previously, she served in various capacities
in educational planning and research at the university
and was involved in educational testing and research at
several institutions. Recent research has focused on
individual and organizational conditions contributing to
faculty vitality. She has published and presented many
papers dealing with higher education, faculty vitality,
and professsional socialization. Corcoran received a B.A.
Cum laude in Mathematics from Hunter College, a M.A. in
Psychology from Stanford University, and a Ph.D. in
Educational Psychology from the University of Minnesota.
She has been honored with several professional
association awards.

Ellen Greenberger is Professor in, and former Director
of, the Program in Social Ecology at the University of
California at Irvine. She has received a number of
agency and institutional grants and contracts to study
the relationship of early work experience to adolescent
socialization, learning, family and peer relations, and
psychosocial development. She has also published and
lectured extensively on these subjects. Greenberger
earned her A.B. at Vassar College, and she received M.A.
and Ph.D. degrees in Clinical Psychology at Harvard
University.

Melvin L. Kohn is Professor of Sociology at the Johns
Hopkins University. He previously served as Chief of the
Laboratory of Socio-environmental Studies at the National
Institute of Mental Health from 1960 to 1985. He has
been active in various professional societies, including
holding the office of President of the American
Sociological Association. He has published numerous
books and articles on the interrelationships of social
stratifications, work, and personality. Kohn received a
B.A. with distinction in Psychology and General Studies
and a Ph.D. in Sociology, with minors in Social
Psychology and Industrial Relations, from Cornell
University. He has been awarded several honors and
fellowships for outstanding research and service.

Geoffrey Maruyama is Professor in the Department of
Educational Psychology at the University of Minnesota.
Current research interests include school achievement
processes; school desegregation; social influence
processes; applications of structural equation
techniques; and cooperative learning techniques. He has
published articles and presented conference papers on
physical attractiveness, popularity, self-image, and
academic achievement; training teachers to deal with
diversity; social influence processes; cooperative
learning strategies; and theory and applications of
attitude formation. Maruyama earned a B.A. with honors
in Psychology from Macalester College, St. Paul,
Minnesota, and he received M.A. and Ph.D. degrees in
Social Psychology from the University of Southern
California in Los Angeles. He has been awarded several
academic and research honors and grants.

Joanne Miller is Associate Professor of Sociology at
Queens College and a member of the doctoral faculty at
the Graduate School of the City University of New York
where she also serves as Associate Director of the Center
for Social Research. Her research career began as a
Post-Doctoral Fellow in the Intramural Research Program
of the National Institute of Mental Health. She later
became a Research Scientist in the Laboratory of
Socio-environmental Studies at NIMH. Between 1982 and
1985, she served as the Program Director for Sociology at
the National Science Foundation. Her research focuses on
the micro level processes and institutional factors which
influence the social organization of work activity and
the effects of job experiences on the worker. She is
currently studying the structure and legitimation of
authority relationships in the firm. Her previous
research includes cross-national studies of work outcomes
and comparative analyses of gender in the workplace and
in the home. Dr. Miller received her Ph.D. from the
University of Wisconsin-Madison in 1975.

Michael L. Schwalbe was a lecturer in sociology at the
University of California-Riverside while co-writing the
chapter on the social psychology of job-related
disability. He is now Assistant Professor of Sociology
at North Carolina State Unversity. His teaching
interests include the sociology of work, social

psychology, and social problems. His research focuses on
the psychological effects of work experience,
social-structural factors in the etiology of mental
illness, and the political economy of cognitive
development. Schwalbe has published a number of articles
on social class, work conditions, health, and
self-esteem. He earned a B.S. in Sociology at the
University of Wisconsin-Stevens Point, and M.A. and Ph.D.
degrees in Sociology at Washington State University.

Kazimierz M. Slomczynski is Associate Professor of
Sociology at the University of Warsaw's Institute of
Sociology, Warsaw, Poland. He is also Principal
Investigator of the research program on social structure
at the Institute of Philosophy and Sociology of the
Polish Academy of Sciences. Previously, he was a
Visiting Scientist at the Laboratory of
Socio-environmental Studies at the National Institute of
Mental Health and a Visiting foreign Scholar at Osaka
University, Japan. He has conducted research at major
Polish scientific institutions, and he has taught at
universities in Poland, Scotland, China, and the United
States. He has participated in many conferences and on
the committees of a number of professional associations,
and he has published numerous books and articles.
Slomczynski has been awarded various honors for
outstanding research and teaching. He received a M.A. in
Sociology from the University of Lodz, and Ph.D. and Dr.
hab. degrees in Sociology were conferred by the
University of Warsaw.

Glorian Sorensen is Assistant Professor of Medicine in
the Division of Preventive and Behavioral Medicine at the
University of Massachusetts Medical School, and Research
Associate at the Harvard University Institute for the
Study of Smoking Behavior and Policy, where she conducts
research on worksite nonsmoking policies. Dr. Sorensen
is Principal Investigator on a study funded by the
National Cancer Institute on "Dietary Prevention of
Cancer in the Worksite" and on a study of "Job Factors,
Family Responsibilities, and Risk Factors for Coronary
Heart Disease in Men and Women." She is also Project
Director at the University of Massachusetts for the
multicenter study, the "Community Intervention Trial for
Smoking Cessation." Previously, as a postdoctoral fellow

at the Division of Epidemiology at the University of Minnesota School of Public Health, she directed a worksite-based intervention study of smoking cessation. She has also conducted research and consulted on public health, health care for the elderly, and sex differences in the relationship between work and health. She has published articles and presented papers on a variety of related topics. She received a Masters Degree in Public Health and Ph.D. in Sociology from the University of Minnesota.

Author Index

Subject Index

Achievement in school, 8, 274

Adolescent work, 5-7
and adult employment, 24, 39-41
and cognitive skills, 35
and educational attainment, 41-42
features of 6, 7, 23, 30, 54, 56-57, 71
meaningfulness of, 29
and practical knowledge, 26, 35
and schooling, 36-39
and self-reliance, 25
and social maturity, 36
and social participation, 29-30
use of earnings, 23-24
and work habits, 26
See also Age-segregated youth employment

Adult work role
transition to, 51-52: and mentoring, 65, 68-72

Age differences
in determinants of job satisfaction, 110-112, 127
in educational attainment, 124(table), 125, 144(n4)
in effects of education on earnings, 128, 129-132(figures)
in effects of substantive complexity on job satisfaction, 141
in effects of work autonomy on job involvement, 141
in effects of work autonomy on job satisfaction, 118, 129-132(figures), 136
in effects of work overload on job satisfaction, 118-119
in income, 123, 124(table), 125, 144(n4)
in job satisfaction, 115-116, 123, 124(table), 144(n4)
in stability of work conditions, 129-132(figures), 133, 134 (table), 135
in work autonomy, 124(table), 125, 144(n4)
in work experiences, 116
in work overload, 124(table), 125, 144(n4)

Age-segregated youth employment, 6, 24, 30, 33-34, 273-274

Age strata, 115, 140

Aging
and disability. See Disability (job-related)
of higher education faculty, 201-202, 215-216, 276. See also Aging, and productivity; Work career, mid-career blockage
and productivity, 203-205, 212-216
of the work force, 201

303